COUGAR ANNIE'S GARDEN

July 2000

To Joe, In appreciation of our
friendship and the good times
we spent together over the
years in British Columbia

Best Wishes Dr Bob.

COUGAR ANNIE'S
GARDEN

Margaret Horsfield

SALAL BOOKS

Published by:
Salal Books
P.O. Box 1021, Station A
Nanaimo, B.C., V9R 5Z2
Toll Free Number: 1-888-858-5455
Fax: 250 753 9468

Designed by Vic Marks
Typeset by The Typeworks

Editor Elizabeth McLean
Maps by Briony Penn

Printed and bound in Hong Kong by C&C Offset Printing Co., Ltd.

CANADIAN CATALOGUING IN PUBLICATION DATA

Horsfield, Margaret
   Cougar Annie's Garden

   Includes bibliographical references.
   ISBN 0-9697008-1-4

   1. Rae-Arthur, Ada Annie, d. 1985.   2. Rae-Arthur family.
3. Gardens—British Columbia—Boat Basin.   4. Boat Basin
(B.C.)—History.   5. Hesquiat Harbour Region (B.C.)—History.
6. Women pioneers—British Columbia—Biography.   I. Title.

SB466.C33C68 1999   971.1'203'092   C99-900557-X

Contents

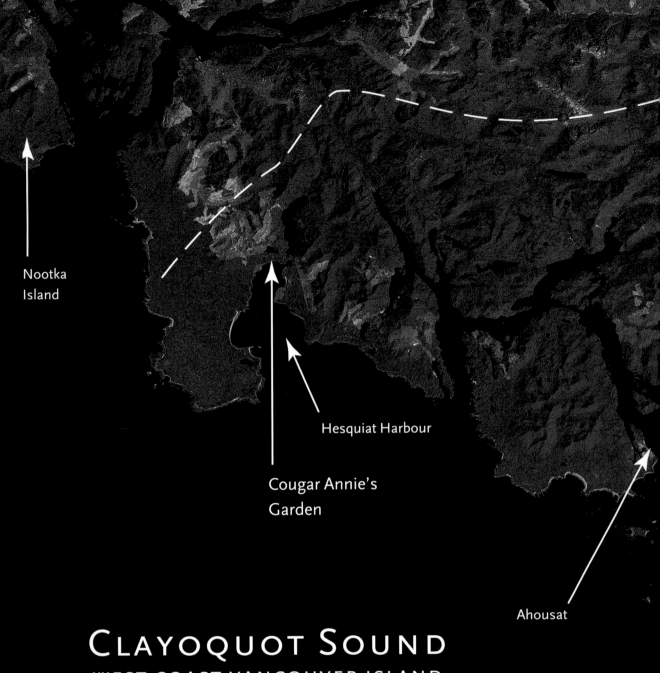

Nootka
Island

Hesquiat Harbour

Cougar Annie's
Garden

Ahousat

Clayoquot Sound
WEST COAST VANCOUVER ISLAND

N

O   25 km

— — — Clayoquot Sound watershed

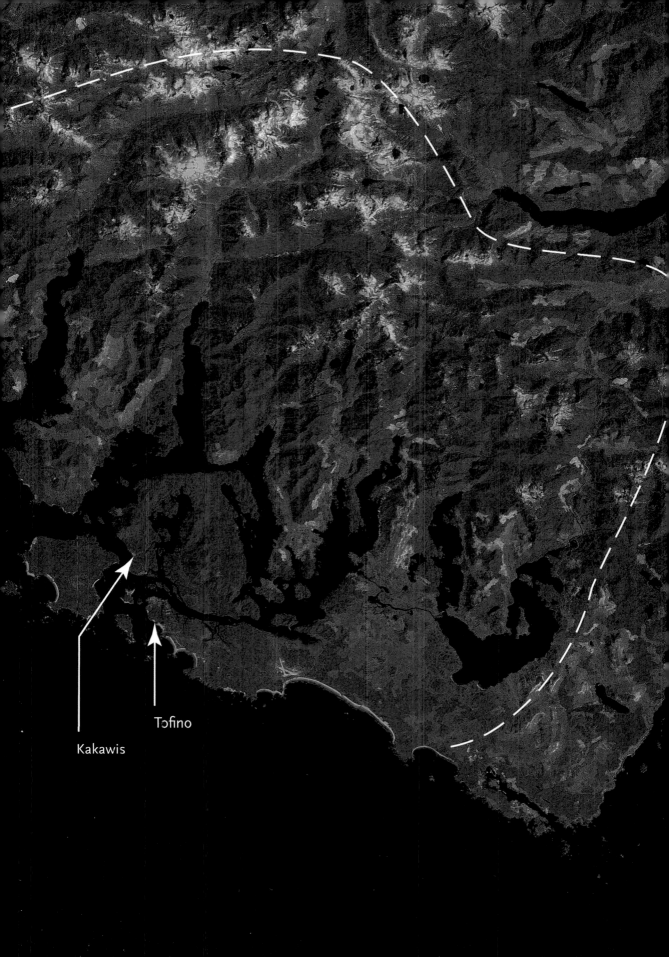

Kakawis

Tɔfino

This book is in memory of Ada Annie Rae-Arthur, 1888–1985

Foreword

IF SURVIVAL HAS been Canada's most noteworthy achievement, as Margaret Atwood and other savants have claimed, few epics of surviving against impossible odds can equal the story set out in this book. This is the saga of Cougar Annie's garden, situated, literally, in the middle of nowhere, on the west coast of Vancouver Island. Cougar Annie was the ultimate survivor.

Born Ada Annie Jordan in Sacramento, California, in 1888, she married and as Ada Annie Rae-Arthur came to a tract of west coast wilderness at the head of Hesquiat Harbour with her husband and three children in 1915. Here she made her garden. "From its beginnings as a rough stump farm hacked out of the bush," writes Margaret Horsfield, "through the years of dogged productivity in order to feed and sustain her family, this garden was Cougar Annie's recreation as well as her job. Over the years, a pleasure garden began to take shape in the wilderness, a rambling acreage of shrubs and trees and perennials, a half-lost garden walled in by tall trees and taller tales."

Ada Annie finally left her garden in 1983, nearly seventy years after she arrived, having survived every imaginable inhospitable act of God, the presence of a Japanese submarine during World War II, not to mention four husbands and the birth of eleven children. She died two years later, at the age of ninety-six.

Until recently, the garden has been a window to the past, but now it looks ahead. New life has come to this magic bush garden. The Boat Basin Foundation has been established to care for and maintain the garden for future generations, and the foundation will also encourage botanical education in the area. The preservation of this garden is one of those essential projects which, because of its obscure location, too easily lacks the priority of other, more accessible causes.

Read Margaret Horsfield's moving text and leaf through the photographs in the pages that follow. Only then will you understand why the quest to keep Cougar Annie's dream alive is so important. It must not be allowed to die.

Peter C. Newman
Hopkins Landing, B.C.

Hesquiat Harbour from Mount Seghers, looking south.

COUGAR ANNIE'S GARDEN

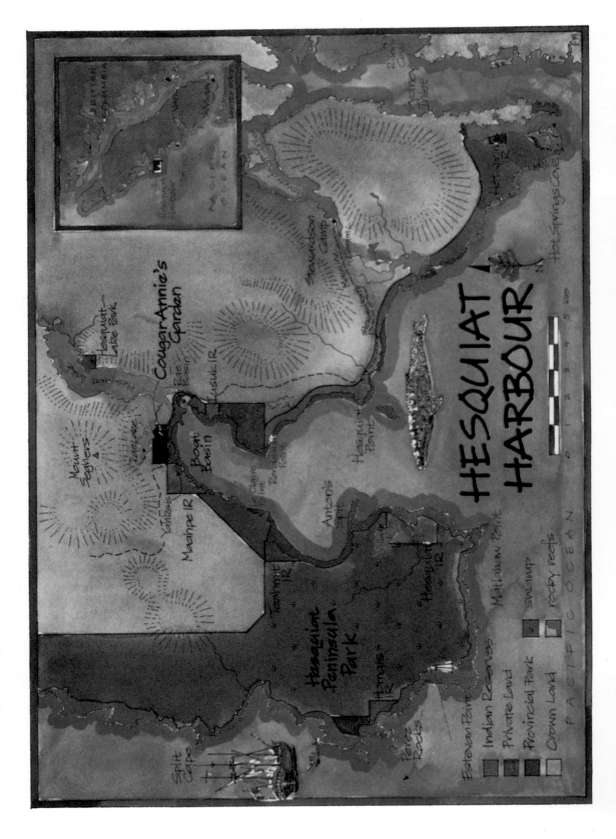

Introduction

IN THE MIDDLE OF nowhere, hidden on the west coast of Vancouver Island, Cougar Annie's garden has endured for over eighty years. Surrounded by rainforest and mountains, this is a place remote and charmed. Strange with beauty, powerful with story, the garden casts a strong spell.

Many tall tales are alive here, many haunting rumours, many reminders of human courage and folly. This garden has sheltered—and continues to shelter—dreams and schemes without number. It has thrived—and continues to thrive—against great odds.

In 1915 Ada Annie Rae-Arthur came to this tract of west coast wilderness at the head of Hesquiat Harbour with her husband and three children. Here they cleared the land and made their garden. Still blooming, still flourishing, it has witnessed much change. This garden has become a valuable link within the local scene; it has seen much coming and going; it has played an intriguing role. It is a garden hard to reach, and harder still to comprehend.

History here is elusive, obscured in a fog of coastal mythologies. Stories grow on this coast like the forest, they grow tangled and dense and they quickly spread—some people say by means of a mysterious kelp telegraph. Penetrating these tales, groping through them to find grains of truth, trying to squeeze facts from them is challenging, often futile. The tale-tellers cling to their stories, immune to evidence, obstinately convinced that they and only they are right.

It's all clear-cut up there now. All around Hesquiat Harbour. And the old lady's garden has been levelled. Every flower has disappeared. A friend told me that.

Cougar Annie had six husbands, you know. She killed two of them for sure. She drilled one with a shotgun as he was crawling up the front steps.

When her last son was born she cut the umbilical cord with her teeth. She told me that herself.

There's a guy from back east who's bought up most of the land around the harbour, including the garden. And he's punched through a private road, right to the east coast of the Island, just for his own use.

Exaggerations, half-truths, prejudices, distortions and gossip all feed into the tangle of stories surrounding Cougar Annie and her garden. The last laugh is hers, though, for Ada Annie Rae-Arthur died with her mysteries intact. Much will never be known about her. Her life was largely undocumented.

Yet she did leave behind her garden, a garden of grave and lasting beauty. From its beginnings as a rough stump farm hacked out of the bush, through the years of dogged productivity, this garden was Cougar Annie's recreation as well as her job. She loved to garden, to experiment with planting as many different species as she could obtain. Over the years, a pleasure garden began to take shape in the wilderness, a rambling acreage of shrubs and trees and perennials, a mesmerising, half-lost garden walled in by tall trees and taller tales.

Nearly fifteen years after her death, Cougar Annie's garden flourishes in its clearing, a place unfrequented and mysterious, surrounded by the rampant growth of the temperate west coast rainforest. Time has played many strange tricks here, but still in this garden past lives can be decoded, past endeavours traced. The flowers, shrubs and trees of the garden; its design, style and oddities; the very fact of its improbable survival in the bush: all combine to reveal countless details, countless stories.

Not only the garden, but the collapsing buildings and sheds scattered throughout the clearing also breathe forth stories. Messy artifacts left in place are strangely powerful, strangely telling. Damp piles of books thick with mildew, old tools, a rusty stub of a knife, handwritten labels from old flower beds, scraps of paper, a clutch of sticky photographs—all yield hints of the lives lived here, lives unrecorded and only patchily recalled. From these hints and relics, images begin to radiate, at first dim, but gradually coming into focus. Slowly, a fragile web of information takes shape, and the place is peopled once again. Unlikely businesses took root here: a general store, a post office, a nursery garden. A large family grew up here, and a small strong woman grew old here, very old indeed.

Ada Annie Rae-Arthur lived out her own particular dreams and schemes. Never systematically recorded, perhaps never even articulated, these can be deciphered from what she left behind in her garden and house, and in sifting through and investigating the many tales told of her. How she lived her life can be understood in many different ways: as part of the romantic Canadian myth of roughing it in the bush, as heroic and wayward ambition, as pure cussedness. More helpfully, perhaps, Cougar Annie's garden and all it reveals can be understood within the context of an evolving interest in this coast and its history, an interest that tries to integrate the many disparate and sometimes jarring elements making up the whole picture.

For while we may be tempted to think of Cougar Annie and her garden in terms of splendid, stubborn isolation, both are part of a much greater whole and can best be understood in the context of this whole. They fit into a pattern of land settlement and blind hope, of grim courage and broken dreams, of disenfranchisement and bitter loss, all of which have helped shape history on this coast. Because this part of the coast is far more isolated now than it was eighty years ago, Cougar Annie's garden seems a complete anomaly, but it was a venture entirely in keeping with the spirit of its time.

The area surrounding Hesquiat Harbour has known many conflicting aspirations and ambitions over the years: those of First Nations' people, those of missionaries, settlers, sealers, traders, fishermen, surveyors, loggers, lightkeepers, prospectors, environmentalists, and of the visitors who come and go. Some of the aims and ideas of this assortment of people may seem strange and incomprehensible, but they have not been inconsequential. Most have left their mark either on the surrounding landscape or within Cougar Annie's garden itself.

Hiking along the beach or through the forest, traces of past endeavours become immediately evident: blazes on trees, claim posts, ancient marks on giant cedars, wire from a disused telegraph line, rotted remains of old buildings, vestiges of shipwrecks, signs of former habitation half-visible along the shore. And in Cougar Annie's house and garden, the haunting remains of store and post office, the stacks of old letters, the rusted traps, the collapsing goat sheds, the withered pelts, the glow of rhododendrons overhead, the wrenching beauty of blossom on lichen-covered fruit trees, the still heap of mossy stones covering a grave—all evoke past lives, past hopes, past dreams beyond number.

Significantly, Cougar Annie's garden offers not only a window into the past, but a vantage point looking to the future in this area. All around here fresh plans and ideas are emerging with the new millennium. The future development and preservation of the region will be discussed and disputed and, hopefully, revealed through these plans and ideas: through First Nations' land claims, through land use decisions, through studies of the fisheries and forests, and through various schemes to revitalize and rediscover this area.

Here in the coastal rainforest of Vancouver Island, much of this remote garden has, improbably, survived and flourished. Much also has been lost, both in the garden and in its immediate surroundings. The garden offers many ways of understanding how history has unfolded and continues to unfold in the vicinity. Having evolved over many decades to become a dauntless survivor on the coast, Cougar Annie's garden now stands sentinel, a symbol of hope and continuity in an ever-changing landscape.

#
In the Garden Now

NO ONE LIVES in the garden now. A scattering of old buildings, damp and crooked, appears along the narrow boardwalks and winding pathways—an old cabin or two, small collapsing sheds with salmonberry bushes bursting through the broken shingles and, in the centre of the garden, an elderly house falling gently to one side, slowly rejoining the native earth on which it stands.

The front door of Cougar Annie's house leans drunkenly open, hanging by one rusted hinge; its white paint, flaking away, is still bright, gleaming through the rain at the end of the long walkway leading into the garden. The front porch, behind the white door, is impassable, its floorboards broken and the inside door jammed shut by the weight of the settling house. Around the other side of the house, a rickety wooden chair teeters on the back step, barring entry to the dark, dank interior.

The roof dips and sags, its cedar shakes, worn paper-thin by decades of heavy rain, barely held in place by corroding nails. The walls are crumpling like an old accordion, the floor is buckled and rotten. Month by month, the angle of the house increases, listing uncomfortably to one side like a tired old lady in a wheelchair. Built in 1923, the house has reached the end of its days: almost nothing remains within its dying shell. Nothing, on first glance, but mildew and sour old wood. Just an abandoned and rotting house, one of many on this coast. A house that was the centre of a lifetime of endeavour, now blurred and lost; a house that sheltered a handful of people, now dead or scattered. Here stands a scene of apparently irredeemable loss.

But cup your hands around your eyes, stand close, and peer through the cob-webbed windows. In the corner of what was once a kitchen, a bed stands crooked on the tilting floor. Like a child's cot, this wooden, high-sided bed, painted blue, belonged to the diminutive, tough woman whose presence haunts both house and garden: Ada Annie Rae-Arthur, known also as Cougar Annie.

This was her garden, her home, her bed. On a tiny shelf beside the bed, in the now crumbling kitchen, still sits her Bible, reduced to a sodden mass of pulp, perhaps the very Bible her first husband, Willie Rae-Arthur, occasionally borrowed. He would use its thin pages to roll cigarettes, much to the horror of visiting missionaries. A lonely old cardigan of shrunken brown wool still hangs on the wall next to a faded picture, perhaps torn from a calendar, showing an incongruously jolly vase full of hothouse flowers. And a straw hat, soft with damp and mould, is still on its hook. Cougar Annie loved hats. She owned several, and always wore one when she was out in the garden, to complete her usual ensemble of long dress and gumboots.

A long disused string swings from the ceiling, a rusted can at the end. This was her light, hanging in a tin can low over the table. Back against the wall on deep sagging shelves, dozens of large sealers full of preserves lurch sideways; many have already fallen and smashed. Thick with dust, their tops nearly rusted

through, the contents of these jars are not remotely appetizing now, or edible. Yet they are stern reminders of the dauntless industry and energy that once kept this place going. Big two-quart jars, most of them, filled with faded berries in syrup, cloudy marbled meats of doubtful origin—this one could be cougar, that one bear. Who knows? Cougar Annie was famed for wasting nothing. Many jars of chicken stand like old laboratory specimens, the pale plucked skins and bones shining through the dusty jars, an occasional feather floating in the amber liquid. And salmon, its orange-pink flesh fading to grey, hung with shreds of shining scales.

No one can enter the house now; the danger is too great as season by season the house leans further to one side, the floor collapses, bits of the roof tumble down. But imagine what it was like, until recently, to enter this house, to pick gingerly over broken floorboards, to squeeze through doors jammed almost completely shut, to go cautiously up the ladder to the attic. Here the sense of ruin has been complete for many years.

In the attic, curtained with thick cobwebs, the dank smell is even more powerful than downstairs. Yellowed heaps of papers and magazines are stacked all higgledy-piggledy. Old *Western Producers* and *Vancouver Suns* crumble the moment they are touched and the overpowering smell of mildew rises from the pages. Here also are messy heaps of disused fishnets, innumerable boxes of dirty bottles under the dripping and collapsing roof, old shivery piles of worthless junk. Hang-

ing from the rafters are weird and decayed pelts, mostly small ones, marten and mink, curling at the edges and covered with mould. At the very back of the attic, way over in the corner, lurks something large and dark, perhaps a cougar pelt, but because the floor of the attic is impassable, no one dares crawl across and the strange shape remains a mystery. Perhaps there are two cougar pelts, perhaps more, perhaps nothing but shadows and old smells.

From the tiny window of the attic, through the white veil of cobwebs, a heart-lifting view stretches down to the garden entrance. Past the laburnum tree heavy with flowers and hung with lichens; past the gnarled fruit trees; down the long board-walk; past the old rose arch; past the vegetable garden and beyond to the deep growth of trees standing between the garden and the beach. Everyone coming from the beach enters the garden this way. They always have, making their way along the raised walkway through the forest, in through the gate and up to the house; coming to visit, to buy stamps at the post office, to buy eggs or chocolate bars at Cougar Annie's little store, to deliver supplies, to bring news of the outside world, perhaps just to see the garden.

No post office now, no store, no Cougar Annie. Just the stories and the garden. The stories, like all great stories, live on, and grow. So does the garden, although at certain times, in certain lights, it seems timeless, unchanged by passing years.

꽃

Enter this garden by moonlight if you can, by the full bright moon of a clear west coast night. Then the shadows are strange and sharp, the spirit of the garden uncanny. Then relics of past lives leap to the eye. Time evaporates. An enchanted old garden is young again, transfixed in the bright night.

By moonlight the faded grey cedar structures of the garden are luminous, shining in the night. Old cedar boardwalks radiate, fresh and new in the moon-light as they wind through the many paths and openings in the clearing, past

Walkway leading from the beach to the garden, 1973.

curving lines of salal and rhododendron. Collapsing outbuildings and sheds take on an eerie shine; sharp shadows of their half-broken, half-open doors strike across the grass. Through gaps in the walls, the moonlight angles into these crumpled sheds, clear slashes of light showing a jumble of old tools and piles of wooden boxes.

Cougar Annie's dim and vacant house seems alert in the moonlight. Its broken and cobwebby windows reflect the light, ghostly eyes looking out from the shingled walls. People who lived here seem to live again: a small determined

woman could yet be there tenaciously working into the night, paring her dahlia tubers in the kitchen by kerosene lamp, filling her next grocery order, doing her post office accounts, scheming up a way to sell more eggs, planning when to bring in new goats, all the while her children asleep in the dark rooms behind her. In this moonlight, even the long-gone livestock seems only to be sleeping: chickens perched in the outbuildings, goats in their sheds, rabbits in their hutches, geese on the alert, while perhaps, around the clearing, a cougar stalks, scenting easy prey.

All the artifacts of industry and activity lie mute, their outlines etched sharp in this light: a rusted trap hanging on a tree, old clouded jars of preserves in a broken shed, a handmade wooden wheelbarrow half-buried in grass. The remains of an old pot-bellied stove gleam oddly in a thicket of salmonberries, and antique chickenwire clings to an awkwardly tilting fencepost, the rust and the rot invisible by moonlight. Scraps of oilcans in which smudge fires used to burn, overgrown by bushes in daylight, emerge clearly on the ground near one of the old apple trees.

These antique fruit trees seem younger in the night. The sweeping patches of lilies, some of them chest-high, seem more graceful, the mossy paths more flowing. Lichens and liverworts and old man's beard glow white on the trees. Beds of hostas brush your ankles as you walk through the night garden, their shadows sharp-edged on the grass beneath. Planted perhaps seventy years ago when they were a newly fashionable plant, these hostas are one of countless imports to the garden, brought in by Cougar Annie over many decades. Even in her last years, when her sight was failing, she could not resist new plants, new cuttings, always adding to her nursery beds, always curious to know what would grow and thrive in her garden.

Around the large clearing that contains the garden, the forest stands silent; large cedars loom dark against the sky, the grey spike-tops of the trees bleached white by the moonlight. The larger and older of these trees bear traces of human activity from hundreds of years ago. Canoes were cut from these trees, long lines of bark were stripped, planks were cut. And the forest thrived. Now only small patches of this old strong forest remain, hung heavy with moonlit moss, eerie in the night.

Behind the garden the mountains rise, silent and changed. Their scars are stark in this light, their sides no longer soft with trees but bald and bright with clearcut and the sharp swathe of landslides. The crosshatching of logging roads shines like strands of ribbon winding up the mountains; the few remaining trees stand sentinel, reaching towards the moon. And the sound of streams running down these slopes carries far in the night air, a gentle sound in the moonlight—although perhaps, on reflection, not so gentle. If Cougar Annie had wandered in her garden at night, even thirty years ago, she would not have heard this water running down the slopes. Now that so many trees have gone, water can run unchecked down the steep clearcuts, water dangerously free of the once strong roots of the trees that held firmly to the slopes, water sweeping away much of the fragile earth and rendering unstable entire mountainsides.

⁂

In the garden, walk carefully, watch where you put your feet. Many small bridges, just a board or two each, span the network of drainage ditches that criss-cross this clearing, ditches still lined with the original cedar boards put in place by the

Rae-Arthurs, crumbling now with age, but still draining this boggy piece of land, making the garden possible, a garden that is, against all odds, so alive, all year round.

Come the pelting rains of winter, and the garden changes. Then the tissues and strands of stem and leaf from summer flowers lie plastered, transparent, to the ground; the graceful fronds of ladyfern darken and wilt; the cedar posts and cedar shakes of the buildings appear almost black with damp; rust seems to grow visibly on metal; mildew thrives. The garden birds are dishevelled in the winter rains, their feathers spiky with wet, the crest of the Stellar's jay flattened.

In this garden in the pour of rain, wet takes on a wetter meaning. The thick mosses underfoot are flooded sponges, the pathways around the garden become splashways inches deep in water. Trees and shrubs drip unceasingly above the cedar boardwalks; some of the boards come adrift from their assigned places and float gently above the paths.

Yet even in the rain the place vibrates with colour. The holly bushes in Cougar Annie's garden, planted probably eighty years ago and now over thirty feet tall, are scarlet with berries and the many varieties of cotoneaster have gone mad. Great fans of branch and berry stand fifteen feet high and more, sometimes appearing above the young hemlock and cedar trees now ringing the homestead.

In this gentle, wet climate, where the annual rainfall averages 165 inches, sap starts to rise in the twigs as early as November. Almost as soon as the leaves fall from trees and bushes, the branches show new signs of life. Red twigs glow, and buds form hopefully all through the dark days of winter when the rains are perpetual and the atmosphere dull. The place is bursting with energy and vitality, even though it is largely forsaken in winter. Only the strong of heart stay around here, or even visit, in the rain.

This garden simply never stops growing, nor do the surviving stretches of forest nearby. Even in the darkest months, buds are brightening not only in the garden, but on shrubs in the forest. Stems of huckleberry are pink, incongruously bright against the dark trees; salmonberry branches seem, all winter long, on the verge of bursting into leaf and flower. The mosses radiate all shades of impossible green in the damp filtered light on the forest floor, and back in the garden the wet leaves of rhododendron, salal, hebe, berberis are often suddenly ablaze, gleaming winter-green in the unexpected bursts of low and lovely light, when the sun shines in fits and starts through a veiled sky.

Winter and spring merge into the longest season of the year. Daffodils appear above the moss, stubborn grey-green shoots, sometimes weeks before Christmas, though it will be March before they bloom. Hard bright buds appear on the azaleas by December or January, just as the snowdrops and aconites come into bloom. Rogue salmonberries, those great garden invaders, are early with their flowers; by late February the delicate dark pink blooms appear. By March, the beds of lilies and irises are well on their way, tough pale leaves knifing upwards, slow and sharp, through the moss and grass.

Occasional snowfalls blanket this early growth in winter, and ground frosts persist well into March, biting the tips of new leaves, flattening young foxglove plants, leaving a fretwork of lacy ice on the pathways. But only for a short while. Frost rarely lasts for more than a few days, and the garden throws off this indignity quickly.

The first blossom on the elderly fruit trees signals the slow pleasure of true spring. Plum blossom appears early, a faint scattering in the branches of the grey lichened trees. In the sifted, silvery light of a March mist, the flowers are difficult to see, difficult to distinguish from the other lacy growth in the trees. Old man's beard is prolific here, thriving in the gnarled grey twigs of the old orchard, hanging from the crooked trees like a drooping, graceful blossom. It forms an airy, lightweight canopy, glowing in the half-light of every season, particularly strange in the spring when it intermingles with the fresh blossom.

These fruit trees, plum and pear, crabapple and quince, apple and cherry, seem at first glance far too old, too grey and gnarled, to bear blossom or fruit any longer. Yet every spring, blossoms appear on every fruit tree; every spring life reasserts itself in these branches and then fruit starts to form.

Later, in the mesmerising days of full summer, the garden drones with

mosquitoes and the grass is quick with garter snakes and the air thick with damp heat. Then also, come the bears. Some are always here, planting large footprints on flowerbeds and pathways from early spring until late in the year, leaving large heaps of droppings to mark their passage. In late spring they come regularly for the salmonberries, stripping the bushes of this early fruit, orange-red and succulent. But the summer attractions are even greater. The bears shuffle through Cougar Annie's garden in search of the fat red huckleberries that are so prolific here; they come for the salal berries and eat such quantities that their droppings are purple for weeks on end; they come also for the fruit that year after year appears in the old orchard. Shambling along the pathways and boardwalks, the bears bend down the berry bushes for a snack, and then, large and lumbering, they take to the trees.

Climbing can be hazardous here for the bears; old brittle branches sometimes crack under their weight. They swipe awkwardly at the fruit with large paws, every year bringing a few more limbs crashing to the ground. Some trees yield their fruit readily—a tired plum tree beside Cougar Annie's house laid itself down on the ground years ago and is now horizontal. Still producing fruit, it is a ready-made feeding platform for any bear wanting to walk along the trunk towards the ground-hugging branches. The fruit these trees yield would win no prizes, for it is small and often scabby. The bears seem not to care: all of the fruit here is part of their messy and marvellous summer food circuit, and has been so ever since the fences around the garden began to collapse. In Cougar Annie's day, no bear could approach the fruit trees without risking life and limb, for her gun was always ready to blast any animal encroaching on her garden.

The fruit trees are many decades old, some planted before 1920. Ada Annie Rae-Arthur brought them into her garden as tiny saplings, and sold them as part of her nursery stock when she first started her nursery garden business. These were all valued trees, either as stock or as producers. Their fruit was bottled every year and greatly treasured. Among the ghostly collection of preserves that remains in the collapsing house are a number of two-quart sealers of plums; dim and pale now, these plums have been floating in syrup undisturbed for forty or fifty years.

⁂

In the garden now an enchantment reigns. Yet having the leisure to enjoy this enchantment is a latter-day luxury, experienced mostly by visitors who have the freedom to come and go. This place has been created and maintained not by magic, not by imagination, but by unremitting hard work, by bloody-minded perseverance, at times by a desperation to survive.

Coming out to this distant coast back in 1915 required stubborn, even blind, optimism. Ada Annie Rae-Arthur and her family cannot have known what they were getting into; few settlers on this coast did. They headed into the unknown, hoping for the best: for more settlers with more children, for roads, for development, for a compliant and productive piece of land, for a brave new world to expand before them. Usually such hopes were ill-founded. Hoping for the best, most settlers on this coast found that the best did not come their way. Instead they faced the exhausting muddy turmoil of clearing land, building cabins, surviving in the hard lonely winter rain; they faced the blankness of isolation; they faced the harsh realities of being strangers in a strange and unwelcoming land.

Most did not stay long, but the Rae-Arthurs were fated to be different. They arrived complete with household goods, tools and a cow which was lowered, legs tied together, onto its back into the canoe which was to carry them and their

goods to the shores of Boat Basin from the coastal steamship the *Princess Maquinna*. The Rae-Arthur family was then made up of three young children, George, Frank and Margaret, all under the age of seven; their father, William Francis John Rae-Arthur, a Scot possessed of ineffable charm and vaguely convinced that a true gentleman should not have to do manual work; and their mother, Ada Annie Rae-Arthur, small and strong and grittily determined. Her fierce energy was to carry them all, come what may, into a new life.

CHAPTER 2

Ada Annie

S HE WAS ON THE STEP *with a gun, watching us, when we arrived. We saw her from the end of that long boardwalk, and we made our way up, shutting the gates behind us, and when we reached the house she had disappeared. Just like that.*

It was dark and raining, and I was all alone in the middle of nowhere with a little old lady who looked like a witch and killed mice and chickens with a flick of the wrist. And she claimed she'd killed seventy-two cougars in her lifetime.

She was very refined, a real lady. She told me she came from an aristocratic family in England and they had a title that her father—or maybe it was her grandfather—renounced. And her first husband's family had a title, too—but he was a ne'er do well—he was an alcoholic and an opium addict.

She's haunted me for years. A huge amount of mystique surrounded that place—it's the centre of a lot of energy, both good and bad. And strange things happened there, all the time. Granny had special powers, I'm convinced of that.

After all I'd heard about her, I expected to meet a giant of a woman. But this tiny, birdlike old lady with bright blue eyes met me at the door wearing gumboots and a long dress and she was totally charming. I helped chop some wood and she talked me into buying three dozen eggs that I didn't even want. A lot of them were bad.

Colourful and varied were the impressions Cougar Annie made on people who met her. Great and tall are the stories they now tell. Her reputation on the West Coast had plenty of time to develop for she lived at Boat Basin from 1915 until 1983, and rarely left. Her mystique increased year by year and by the time she was in her eighties and nineties she had become a living legend. Small wonder, for the bare outline of her life at Boat Basin is extraordinary. Her garden flourished on an isolated tract of land on the far west coast of Vancouver Island, an area with no roads and no settlements. She lived there sometimes all alone, even though she married and outlived four husbands. She bore eleven children, eight of them at Boat Basin. Renowned as a cougar hunter, she was an outstanding markswoman. She operated a general store, a post office and a nursery garden business that shipped plants all over Canada. She was a stubborn, wily, feisty, difficult woman. She was a survivor.

When asked about her life and her background, Cougar Annie was a highly selective storyteller, sometimes a highly inventive one. Different people have heard different stories from her, and while the broad outlines sometimes agree, the details often do not. But left behind amongst the objects in her house are tantalizing scraps of paper, a few photographs, and a number of books, all of which help to provide information about her early life and in turn lead to other sources of information. From all these sources, tentatively and slowly, the early life of this woman comes together.

Although she was born Ada Annie Jordan in Sacramento, California on June 19, 1888, Ada Annie was to be a person of many names. Through marriage she would take four more surnames: in turn, Rae-Arthur, Campbell, Arnold and Lawson. Her signature always bore her initials: *Mrs. A A Rae-Arthur, Mrs. A A Arnold, Mrs. A A Campbell, Mrs. A A Lawson*. Her father, her first husband Willie Rae-Arthur and her great friend Robert Culver simply called her Ada. Towards the end of her years she was famed as the Cougar Lady, and sometimes called "Cougar Ada." but more often "Cougar Annie." And as she aged, "Call me Granny," she would say to visitors and friends.

Ada Annie was the second child of George Jordan and Margaret Elizabeth Coleman, both of whom came from Hastings in England. Hers was a restless childhood: her family often shifted and moved according to her father's whims and ever-changing ambitions. She and her mother followed George Jordan from California to England, to South Africa, to Lloydminster in Alberta, to Winnipeg and finally, by the time Ada Annie was in her late teens, to Vancouver, where her father had settled and was working as a veterinarian.

By the time Ada Annie was born, George Jordan and his wife Margaret were living in the foothills of the Sierra Nevada Mountains, a long way from their origins. Their way to the west had not been easy: their first child, Margaret, had died of cholera in Brooklyn, probably in the mid-1880s. Before their marriage George had already travelled widely in North America and had lived both in Florida and the Midwest. According to Ada Annie, he had returned to England in order to marry and then to emigrate.

George Jordan and Margaret Coleman had married at the Wesleyan Chapel in Hastings on May 4, 1883, she at twenty-four years of age, and he ten years older.

Their marriage certificate shows the same address for both of them, 86 High Street, a detail requiring no explanation given that Margaret's occupation is listed as "Lodging House Keeper." The marriage certificate shows George's occupation as "carpenter," a designation he changed as often as he was able throughout his life.

Of the two, Margaret is the more elusive figure; little is known of her between the time of her marriage to George Jordan and her death in Vancouver in 1909, shortly after her daughter Ada Annie had married Willie Rae-Arthur. Margaret's parents were Mary Ann Coleman and William Coleman; the 1881 census lists him as "Builder." Earlier, when the family lived at St. Mary in the Castle, Margaret's birth certificate describes him as "French Polisher." Margaret was one of two daughters; the other was Ada Alice who, along with her father, was one of the official witnesses at Margaret's wedding to George Jordan.

Margaret Coleman

In her later years Cougar Annie recalled that her mother played the organ at a church in Rye, near Hastings. She also alluded to her grandfather, William Coleman, as the vicar of a parish church in Rye, but William Coleman's affiliations with any church are difficult to trace. His name appears in no official directories as an ordained minister, though he could well have been a lay preacher at the Wesleyan Church, in either Rye or Hastings.

William Coleman's name does appear, unexpectedly and only once, in a tattered heap of books recovered from the kitchen of Cougar Annie's collapsing house at Boat Basin. His signature "Wm Coleman," precise and faded, appears on the flyleaf of a obscure, mouse-eaten leaflet of hymns, followed by his neat inscription of the year "1881." This *Sunday Scholars' Service of Sacred Song*, published in London by the Sunday School Union (Price Fourpence) must have come from England with Margaret Coleman and eventually fell into her daughter's possession, ending up at Boat Basin to linger for years in oblivion. Perhaps the Rae-Arthurs occasionally opened this leaflet and mustered the energy to sing such hymns as "O, Not by Strength" and "Sweet is the Calm," but chances are that the leaflet lay disregarded, decade after decade, in this isolated cabin in the bush, a far cry from the strait-laced respectability of a Wesleyan congregation in the south of England.

A sepia photograph, faded almost to extinction, shows Ada Annie Jordan at the age of seven or eight years, together with her parents, all of them staring boldly at the camera, heads held high. The name of the photographer appears underneath, and the place: Watsonville, California. As an old lady, Ada Annie spoke of a large fruit farm her father owned, a farm with two thousand fruit trees near Watsonville, not far from Oakland. This farm, she said, had been damaged or destroyed in an earthquake in the 1890s. George Jordan's agricultural pursuits in California also found him raising goats, at one time owning more than five hundred, according to his daughter. But California and all its prospects could not hold George Jordan. Not long after the family portrait was taken, the Jordans' sojourn there ended.

George was on the move by 1897, taking his family from California to England, via New Zealand and Australia. From Britain, the family headed to South Africa where, according to Cougar Annie, her father served in the Boer War with the Royal Engineers. He might have served as an enlisted man; no records exist of his holding a commission, and the Royal Engineers have no record of his name.

Before leaving for South Africa the family spent some time in England, presumably in or near Hastings. Cougar Annie recalled having lots of money in England, with maids and servants in the house, and receiving lavish gifts from distant relatives. These relatives were, she claimed, highly placed in society, connected even to the Royal Family. She insisted that both her mother's and her father's families had distinguished connections, mentioning the Ashburnham and the Elphinstone families, titled gentry with long lineages. She also maintained that George Jordan's family were influential and wealthy landowners, and that his father was titled. Official records do not bear out any of these claims. Census information about the families of both George Jordan and Margaret Coleman indicates that they were working people, not leisured aristocracy. Their distant relatives could, of course, have been almost anything, but the immediate families, according to birth, baptismal and marriage certificates, were labourers.

After the end of the Boer War, the Jordan family settled in Johannesburg and

Portrait of the Jordan family in California, about 1896.

there Ada Annie's interest in gardening really began. Donna Sharpe, who stayed with Cougar Annie for several months in the early 1980s, clearly recalls the old lady showing her, with great pride, a tattered clipping from a South African newspaper featuring a photograph and an article about the young Ada Jordan winning a competition in horticulture in Johannesburg. George and his family remained there for a few years, where George worked importing and selling furniture. Perhaps the venture failed, or perhaps George was terminally restless, but he was soon on the move again, across the world once more, this time to Lloydminster, Alberta.

George Jordan.

In the first decade of the twentieth century, Lloydminster did not have much to offer, just a couple of log houses and an immigration office, according to Cougar Annie. George acquired land and started a cattle ranch, an ill-fated enterprise. A disastrous prairie fire wiped it out and George was unable to feed his stock. He was forced to sell up and shortly afterwards he moved to Winnipeg with his wife and daughter, who was by then in her late teens and increasingly able to take care of herself and her mother, no matter what venture her father was pursuing.

Stories of George Jordan are not attractive. He was a domineering man, not always kind. As an old lady, Cougar Annie recalled that to punish her for some misdeed her father tied her pet dog to the back leg of a horse, which kicked the dog to death. He took pets away from her if she became too attached to them and did not allow her to associate much with other children. Hers was a lonely childhood, always apart from others, never integrated, repeatedly on the move across continents, rarely feeling at home.

George started to teach his daughter to shoot when she was only seven years old, and during the years in South Africa she became a deadly accurate shot. In Lloydminster, George taught her how to trap, though not allowing her to keep and sell the pelts herself. He raised her like a boy, not permitting her to wear girl's clothes until she was seven or eight years old, giving her the most difficult chores to do, and demanding that she prove herself to be as good as a boy. However else it may have marked her, this upbringing unquestionably provided her with valuable skills. Robert Culver, who spent several years at Boat Basin in the late 1960s and early 1970s, recorded a story in his memoirs in which Ada Annie pays a veiled tribute to one of the skills she learned from her father:

Ada Annie in South Africa, about 1902.

*Ada said one time in Vancouver before she was married she was working in
a law office over a mile from her home . . . and was going home after dark
on a long bridge in Vancouver, when she noticed a man not far behind,
walking fast and catching up to her. She started to run, but he ran too, and
caught up to her. He grabbed hold of her and told her he was going to take
her to his place and that it would be useless for her to try to resist. She told
me her father had once told her how to handle such a situation if it ever
came up. So she said to the man, "All right, but I have to tie my shoe." So he
stood close beside her while she knelt down to tie her shoe. Quick as a flash,
she grabbed his leg and pulled him off balance. He fell heavily, she jumped
up and ran for home as fast as she could go, and had no more trouble with
the man. She was like that . . . she seemed to always know the right thing to
do if any sudden emergency came up.*

For her cool self-sufficiency, Ada Annie had reason to thank her strong and rest-less father who would not tolerate his daughter showing any weakness or fearing any man. No doubt this attitude stood her in good stead when she found herself roughing it in the bush, for there she was as good if not better than any of the men she met. There, she was able to show her real strengths and never feared domina-tion by anyone.

George Jordan was in his mid-fifties when he moved his family to Winnipeg and decided to train as a veterinary surgeon. The training had to be completed in Chicago, so leaving Ada Annie and his wife in Winnipeg, off he went. While he was away, Ada Annie lived with her mother in boarding houses and worked at T. Eaton and Co. The 1906 Henderson's Directory for Winnipeg lists neither George nor Margaret Jordan, but lists the eighteen-year-old girl as "Jordan, Annie, Saleslady, T. Eaton Co. Ltd. boards 562 Victor." The following year, Henderson's Directory shows "Miss Annie Jordan, 262 Nora Street," and in 1908 she has moved once more, to 324 Edmonton Street and appears in the directory as "Jordan, Ada, steno T. Eaton Co."

In the course of her travels, Ada Annie had managed to pick up some useful qualifications. Her handwriting and letters bespeak a woman at ease with the written word, one confident and fluent in expressing herself. In her early teens in Johannesburg she had taken business courses in shorthand and typewriting, an ambitious and modern kind of training for a young woman. A mildewed pam-phlet entitled *Pitman's Shorthand Primer* (Price 6d), still at Boat Basin, attests to this training. The exercises are neatly checked off, with the dates of completion, such as "16.2.01" "20.2.01," pencilled in the page margins. These entries continue

Ada Annie, about 1907.

throughout 1901, the year Ada Annie was thirteen years old. Another book remaining at Boat Basin, another faint echo of Ada Annie's education and aptitude is a tiny Webster's Pocket Dictionary "containing 10,000 more words than Walker's Dictionary," in which the words "To Miss A.A. Jordan, Winnipeg, Canada" are carefully written in faded ink.

Having completed his veterinary training, George Jordan uprooted his family for the last time and headed to Vancouver, where he started a veterinary hospital at 995 Seymour Street. Ada Annie continued to work as a stenographer and she also helped her father to run the veterinary business. Then one day, as she told the story, who should walk in but Willie Rae-Arthur with his dog, a dog he had brought from the Isle of Mull where, before coming to Canada, he had been living at a discreet distance from his family in Glasgow. In more ways than one, Ada and Willie each met their match, then and there.

William Francis John Rae-Arthur came from a highly respectable family. His father, also William Rae-Arthur, had died many years before Willie met Ada Annie, and had been an eminent civic politician. For a brief period he had held the highest office in the city of Glasgow, the office of Lord Provost, an elected position roughly equivalent to that of mayor. Willie's sister Isabella had married a prominent industrialist, Charles Dube, the owner of the British North-West Locomotive Company. She was widowed at a fairly young age and was left extremely wealthy.

What George Jordan made of the match between his daughter and Willie Rae-Arthur goes unrecorded. But the impressive family background of the Rae-Arthurs must have influenced him, for he made no obvious objections, as he had to an earlier liaison of Ada Annie's, which he had forced her to break off. Some sources claim that George Jordan introduced the couple, that he courted the Rae-Arthur connection believing he might obtain a veterinary position through the family in Scotland. Whatever the truth of this, George Jordan would certainly have had a say about his daughter's future plans: he had controlled her, or tried to, since she was born and he was not a man to relinquish control lightly.

William Francis John Rae-Arthur and Ada Annie Jordan were married on September 4, 1909. He was thirty-six years old, she was twenty-one. Some days later the *Daily Province* announced the event on the Social and Personal page: "In the First Presbyterian Church, Vancouver, on Saturday last, 4th inst., the pastor, Rev. Dr. Fraser, united in marriage Mr. W.F.J. Rae-Arthur of Glasgow and Miss Ada Annie, daughter of Dr. and Mrs. G. Jordan, 995 Seymour Street."

Just over two months later, on November 20, 1909, another announcement appeared in the *Daily Province:* "At the Vancouver General Hospital this morning

Wedding Portrait, 1909.

there passed away Mrs. Margaret Elizabeth Jordon [sic], the wife of Dr. Jordon, Seymour Street. Mrs. Jordon was in her fifty-first year. She leaves a large circle of friends to mourn her loss. The funeral took place this afternoon from Harron and Co's chapel to Mountain View cemetery, where Rev. Mr. Elliott, pastor of Grace Church, officiated."

Now George Jordan was left a widower, and his house empty. The young couple took up residence at 2285 West Broadway where Ada Annie kept chickens and started to breed Pomeranian dogs. She began buying and selling animals as pets, purchasing them at the back door and selling them through the front at considerably higher prices. Over the next few years she gradually developed a profitable business which she recalled in an interview for an article printed in the *Vancouver Sun* in 1974: "People were always coming to me for pets for their children . . . and while I may have been a bit of a wheeler dealer, I did have three children to raise."

The first baby was born in 1910, on September 23rd. George William Rae-Arthur was graced with the names of both of his grandfathers. Sixteen months later, on February 9, 1912, along came Frank Stephen Rae-Arthur, and in a further nineteen months Margaret Ada appeared on October 7, 1913. As the family grew in size, the Rae-Arthurs' fortunes seemed to be growing with them. By 1914, as Cougar Annie recalled with some pride, the pet business attracted up to eleven dollars a day, and she had two Finnish girls to help. The family also had Chinese servants, and was sufficiently well-off to buy one of those marvellous new inventions, a motor car. And in 1912 their social calendar positively glittered, for in September of that year the Duke and Duchess of Connaught, the Governor-General of Canada and his wife, were visiting Vancouver, and the Rae-Arthurs were, according to Cougar Annie, among the guests invited to a banquet and reception at the Hotel Vancouver to honour the viceregal couple. This invitation apparently arose from a connection Willie Rae-Arthur had with the Connaughts during his days at university in Scotland.

During those early years in Vancouver, Willie Rae-Arthur worked. When he and Ada Annie first met he was a hospital orderly in Vancouver, a post obtained for him through the Salvation Army, which had, according to Cougar Annie, been retained by William's sister in Scotland to keep an eye on Willie and to keep him out of trouble. This arrangement cannot have lasted long: the Vancouver Directories of 1910 and 1911 list Willie as a clerk for Canadian Pacific Railway. Cougar Annie described Willie as a dispatcher earning $65 per month, a salary she had expected would increase to $125. But Willie apparently spoiled his chances by throwing an inkwell through the plate glass window of a door, perhaps not caring for such mundane work. Indeed he may not have cared much for any work. Willie's mind was on other matters.

Trouble was brewing for the Rae-Arthurs. Willie was attracted to drink, and the opium dens of Vancouver's Chinatown began to exert an equal attraction. Ada Annie blamed the Chinese servants for introducing him to such places. He must have been a good customer in Chinatown, and the effect on the family was worrying. The house saw a lot of unwelcome comings and goings of people deemed to be a bad influence on Willie, and as his addiction worsened money began to disappear and Willie sold off the family valuables. The Jordan and Rae-Arthur families were not amused as they watched Willie's health being damaged and the family's money disappear. After a troubling illness, Willie's doctor told Ada Annie that the drink and the drugs were endangering her husband's life and he must remove himself from all temptation.

As things went from bad to worse, George Jordan became involved. His exact role is unclear, but he was certainly instrumental in moving Willie and Ada Annie out of harm's way and up to Boat Basin. Together with Willie's sister Isabella in Scotland, Jordan is reputed to have provided the means and the impetus for the troubled family to leave Vancouver and to set up house on the distant west coast of Vancouver Island. His generosity was limited, though: when Ada Annie and Willie needed to buy lumber to build a new house, he loaned them money and charged interest. In her later years, Cougar Annie spoke of how difficult it had been, paying off to her father what she called the "mortgage."

The Rae-Arthur family set out for Boat Basin with the assurance that Willie's sister Isabella would, through a solicitor, pay ten sovereigns a month to her sister-in-law. Ada Annie was to take Willie away from the fleshpots of the city to a farm in the country, and there take care of him. The arrangement held firm for many years. Ada Annie did keep Willie out of trouble, she did take care of him and raise his family, she did put her heart and soul into making their home at Boat Basin a workable property. In turn, Isabella regularly paid the ten sovereigns a month, but whether she or any of the Rae-Arthur family back in Scotland gave more than a passing thought to Willie's family, growing up in extremely difficult conditions out in the Canadian bush, is questionable. Perhaps the Scottish Rae-Arthurs were grateful to Ada Annie, perhaps they felt—and quickly suppressed—an occasional twinge of Calvinist guilt about the needs of all those children, perhaps they were simply relieved beyond words to have Willie out of their hair.

CHAPTER 3

Willie

T HE TALES TOLD of Willie Rae-Arthur are engaging, the scraps of information tantalizing. Willie was the black sheep of the Rae-Arthur family in Scotland: a drinker, a ne'er-do-well, a gentleman who cared not for hard labour. Yet Willie Rae-Arthur had an irrepressible spirit and a carefree sense of humour that keep surfacing, all these years later, in many different ways.

No doubt about it, Willie was a charmer. He drew amusing sketches of himself and his wife, he sang and played and wrote poetry and told stories to the children while his wife laboured in the garden. He rowed to Tofino—a full day of hard travelling each way—for social gatherings with his buddies, he relied on his rich sister to send money, and he poked gentle fun at the well-meaning parcels sent to his children from his earnest family in Scotland. Responsibility sat lightly on his shoulders: Willie was not a man to take life too seriously.

"Oh, my dad was kind to us kids," his daughter Rose recalls. "He never hit us or shouted at us. He liked to have fun." The disciplinarian in the family was Ada Annie. She was the one who wielded the long strap. "When I got older I used to get hold of the strap and cut bits off it when Mother wasn't looking." Rose says with a chuckle. "But Dad, he never used it."

Willie's humour and sense of fun are revealed in his own writing, time and again. He wrote funny comments in official correspondence, jokes in the family genealogy. His flowing copperplate handwriting comes to light in the most unlikely places, for he had the habit of writing on the flyleafs of books, and on any blank pages he could find within any book. As a result, the odd collection of books remaining in Cougar Annie's house tells more of Willie than of any other member of the family. Many of these books fall open to reveal a bit of Willie's writing.

"Please roll over and leave me more room in bed," he writes at the bottom of his list of "Progenies" which appears on the blank pages at the back of a book entitled *Family Prayers*. This sentence appears after he has listed nine of his children, and numbered them, leaving several numbered blanks at the bottom of the page for future "progeny." And when he writes to his sister in Scotland to thank her for a box of clothes, after pointing out that she must be "ever so much larger" than Ada because the used coat was far too big, he adds with a nonchalant dash of the pen, making it clear that he really does not give a damn, "there was nothing of my line in the boxes—I assuredly cannot be in my oldest sister's good graces."

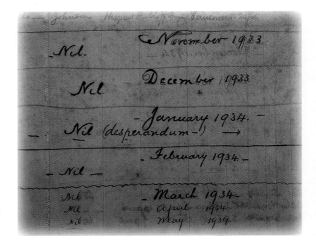

His signature is an attractive flourish inside many of the books. "W.F. Rae-Arthur, Boat Basin, Hesquiat, B.C." appears time and again, followed by the date, and sometimes prefaced with the words "Stolen From." Willie was always prepared to add a jaunty touch to whatever he was writing or recording. In the large ledger entitled *Dominion Government Telegraph Office*, he and Ada Annie recorded all the telegrams sent or calls made on their telephone, and the amount of money they paid for each call or received from Hesquiat people and visitors using the phone. Willie often had to record the dismal word "Nil": no calls made, no money received, month after month. In January of 1934, to break the tedium of making the same entry yet again, he writes "Nil desperandum."

Willie was born in 1873 in Glasgow and educated at Kelvinside Academy, one of the city's best schools. There he learned both Latin and Greek, and developed his confident way with words. A handsome book entitled *Heroes of African Discovery*, imprinted with the school's crest and motto, somehow has found its way to Boat Basin—a book plate inside the front cover announces that this was awarded to Willie in 1883 as first prize for arithmetic. According to Cougar Annie, after completing school Willie attended university in Glasgow and there met and consorted with many titled and aristocratic young men. Certainly Willie's social status in Glasgow was good enough that this could be true.

His father was a prominent citizen of mid-Victorian Glasgow, well known in the business community and renowned in civic politics, a self-made man who had done very well indeed. Born in 1817 of middle-class parents in the area of Glasgow called Gallowgate, William Rae-Arthur Senior received a good education, attending the well-known "High School," at that time one of the best schools in the city. At a young age he entered the textile trade, eventually joining a successful calico printing and dyeing business in the city, and later becoming a partner in another dyeing business, Messrs. Muir, Brown and Co.

By 1855 he was head partner at Muir and Brown, and shortly thereafter his career in civic politics began. In 1857 he became a member of the Town Council, and over the following twelve years he served as a council member, holding a variety of increasingly important positions, including Deputy River Bailie, River Bailie and Treasurer of the Corporation. He was also elected Burgh Magistrate, a position he held for three years, and, in a manner befitting an ambitious civic politician, he served on every important committee possible.

In 1869 William Rae-Arthur was awarded the highest civic office in Glasgow. He was elected Lord Provost of the city, having already stood for this office once before and failed. This successful election was without doubt one of the greatest moments of his life. In his lengthy acceptance speech, Lord Provost Rae-Arthur stressed his understanding of the honour bestowed upon him: "The honour," he said, "is one that might well be coveted by any man, and is a reasonable and just object of ambition." He continued, expanding on his understanding that the office of Lord Provost "has claims upon the person holding it . . . very much heavier and different from those which fall to the lot of any other man in the Town Council." He gives the general impression in his speech of a man well satisfied with his eminent position and confident of an unequalled ability to fulfil his duties.

In the annal *The Lord Provosts of Glasgow from 1833 - 1902* Lord Provost Rae-Arthur receives fulsome praise for the way in which he discharged his duties in this "honourable and onerous position." In his two years in this office, Lord Provost Rae-Arthur knew some thrilling moments and made many grand speeches, several of which, in ringing Victorian style, aimed to "raise the moral or better the physical condition of the masses."

Records of the Town Council show that William Rae-Arthur never drew back from a good political skirmish. He had no qualms about making enemies and, indeed, about calling names. One of his opponents, James Moir, was inflamed by an insult levelled at him by Mr. Rae-Arthur, an insult concerning Mr. Moir's well-worn coat, and by inference, his poverty. These comments, according to Mr. Moir, gave rise to "a great deal of bitterness and ill-feeling, and I am sorry to say that the explanation made by him is not accepted as sufficient." Mr. Rae-Arthur dealt with this in a long and flowery speech, a masterpiece of circumlocution, waving aside Mr. Moir's objections with evident charm and sang-froid, throwing in quotations from the Bible and Shakespeare, avoiding direct apology altogether, and ending with a vague generality about how every man has the right to utter sentiments of his own, and concluding "on that broad and liberal ground I desire to be acquitted. . . ." Mr. Moir retired in confusion.

The Lord Provost Rae-Arthur lived very much in the public eye. He and his wife, Margaret Boyd, had the honour of attending "the Queen's Birthday Drawing Room at Buckingham Palace" on May 6, 1871. He officiated at countless grand and sumptuous banquets in the presence of the great and the good of the expanding city of Glasgow; he took the chair at worthy meetings trying to raise funds for the wounded in the Franco-Prussian war; in honour of the marriage of Princess Louise he officiated at "a full dress conversazione and promenade in the Corporation Halls." In 1870 he had the solemn duty of presiding, jointly with the Earl of Dalhousie, over a large procession and elaborate ceremony marking the laying of the foundation stone of the Albert Bridge in Glasgow.

William Rae-Arthur, Lord Provost of Glasgow.

This event was undoubtedly the most important civic event of the Lord Provost's career, widely reported—with illustrations—in the newspapers. The procession was huge, the ceremony lavish. According to the *Illustrated London News,* "The Lord Provost, municipality, magistrates, the bridge trustees, the grand lodge of Scottish Freemasons, and other persons of dignity met Lord Dalhousie at the cathedral." George MacGregor's *The History of Glasgow* picks up the story with relish: "Outside the Cathedral, a procession, including about three thousand masons, was formed and marched, amid a drenching rain, down High Street . . ." and after following a long and detailed route this procession "passed through a triumphal arch" where the foundation stone was laid "in the presence of an immense multitude." According to the *Illustrated London News*, at the

Albert Bridge Ceremony, from the Illustrated London News, *June 19, 1870.*

bridge, "A platform with galleries and stands for the spectators was set up . . . with various decorative devices. When the procession arrived, the Queen's Anthem was played by a band of music and the Lord Provost Arthur . . . requested the Grand Master of the Grand Lodge of Scotland to lay the stone." The Grand Master was the Earl of Dalhousie.

A complex set of Masonic prayers and rituals ensued, all of which would have been new to Lord Provost Rae-Arthur. In order to participate in the ceremony he had been hastily initiated only the day before as a Freemason in the Lodge of Glasgow St. Mungo's No. 27. This unusually speedy initiation shows, according to a history of this particular Lodge, "how important it really was in those days to be a Member of the Craft." At the end of the speeches and ceremonies, Lord Provost Rae-Arthur presented the Earl of Dalhousie with a silver trowel, and all the dignitaries retreated to enjoy a lavish banquet in the Corporation Galleries.

Lord Provost Rae-Arthur was not fated to continue for long in the limelight of civic affairs in Glasgow. As the records tactfully state, "the ill fortune which overtook him during his Lord Provostship" was grievous, for "the year 1871 was one of commercial gloom" and "business exigencies compelled him to resign before he had been more than two years occupant of the civic chair." His resignation and his subsequent dedicated efforts to try to save his troubled business "commanded the respect and sympathetic admiration of all." But however gently the official records deal with William Rae-Arthur, to resign his high-ranking civic position must have been a terrible blow to him, a loss of face and of status to a man so ambitious and productive. He never held public office again.

Willie Rae-Arthur Junior was born two years after his father had withdrawn from politics. The former Lord Provost was then fifty-six years old. Willie never knew him during his heyday as a successful businessman and civic leader. Instead Willie knew an ageing father fighting to save his business and disapproving of his young and reckless and charming son who was so fond of strong drink. Family lore tells of Willie being sent away in disgrace to the Isle of Mull, where the Rae- Arthurs had some influence, and of having escaped this unwelcome incarceration to travel the world on cargo ships before eventually arriving in Vancouver. He certainly never returned to Scotland. But like so many other emigrants from Scotland, all his life he defined himself as "Scotch," and continued to receive newspapers from home, sent perhaps by his family. A copy of the *Glasgow Weekly Herald* from December 1936, folded, wrapped in brown paper, stamped, and addressed to W.F. Rae-Arthur Esq., Hesquiat, Vancouver Island, British Columbia has lain unopened in Cougar Annie's house at Boat Basin for decades.

In *Bull of the Woods,* his swashbuckling autobiography, Gordon Gibson tells a story about the Rae-Arthurs, father and son, a story that rings true, although details of dates and names are unreliable. Gibson's father, William F. Gibson, visited Britain in the early days of his connection with the west coast of Vancouver Island, and tried to interest British investors in the timber business in British Columbia:

> By lucky chance, [Dad] was invited to meet the Lord Provost of Glasgow, and when Dad was showing him pictures and maps of the timber stands, the Lord Provost asked if there was any place in that wilderness for his son, who was an alcoholic. Evidently, the Provost had hired a tutor to keep an eye on his son but the tutor had become an alcoholic too! So the Provost was looking for a place where liquor was not available. As a result of this conversation, Dad brought the Provost's son back to Vancouver, and helped

marry him off to the daughter of Dr. Sleeth, a veterinarian [this should read Dr. Jordan]. *After the wedding Dad arranged for them to file a pre-emption of 160 acres in Hesquiat Harbour on the west coast of Vancouver Island. The couple raised a large family up there, and the young bride became known as the "cougar woman" in later years, for shooting these animals.*

Gibson did not, in fact, talk to the Lord Provost of Glasgow, but to a former Lord Provost, a man probably near the end of his days. This version of events implies that Willie Rae-Arthur was sent over to Canada in the late 1890s when he was in his mid-twenties and when his father was still alive. Long-time West Coast fisherman Ian Macleod heard much the same story about Willie when Ian and his father were fishing on the coast in the 1930s: "Willie was a rich good-for-nothing alcoholic. His dad said 'Take him away' to Mr. Gibson, and he paid Willie to stay away."

Willie's father could well have sent him to Canada and paid him to stay away. This was certainly a common enough practice. Many a settler came out to Canada as the black sheep of the family and received a regular remittance payment from home to ensure their continued absence. Stories of these "remittance men," who were usually educated ne'er-do-wells—often younger sons—from good British families, add many a lively twist to the history of colonial settlement. They rarely became upstanding citizens or model settlers, but their idiosyncracies and talents provided a ready source of gossip, entertainment and fun in many communities. Willie certainly fits the pattern.

Although the story seems likely, no available records prove that Willie came to Canada in the late 1890s with William Gibson. The first solid proof of Willie's presence in Canada is a listing for him in a Vancouver directory for 1909, just before the time of his marriage to Ada Annie Jordan. By that time, if anyone was paying Willie a remittance, it was his sister Isabella. His father was long dead.

When William Rae-Arthur died in Glasgow 1897 at the age of eighty, he was not a prosperous man. His reputation as a civic leader remains intact in the annals; official documents speak highly of him following his death, and his funeral was attended by the current Lord Provost of Glasgow and other dignitaries of the city. But no documents, civic or personal, explain what misfortunes really befell this once prominent citizen of Glasgow, or his family. It is clear, though, that William Rae-Arthur's declining years did not match his earlier glowing prospects. His estate was valued at two hundred and thirty-seven pounds, nine shillings and tenpence, an estate by no means negligible, but not that of a highly

Cloncaird Castle.

successful businessman. And in his will, only one daughter, Margaret, is named. His son Willie is not mentioned at all, nor are his other children, Isabella, Agnes and Thomas. Perhaps by the time the will was written, Willie Rae-Arthur had proven himself, in the eyes of his conservative and disapproving father, to be beyond redemption and therefore not deserving of even the smallest inheritance. Or perhaps his father knew his daughter Isabella would look after Willie, come what may.

Isabella had done extremely well for herself. Having inherited a considerable fortune, several millions of pounds, from her first husband Charles Dube, Isabella put her money to good use. In 1904 she bought Cloncaird Castle, near the village of Kirkmichael, in Ayrshire. Described in local literature as "a notable mansion," the tower of Cloncaird dates back to 1496, although most of the existing structure was built during the nineteenth century. Isabella devoted herself to renovating the castle and its grounds, and she dedicated herself to local charities. For many years her portrait hung in the county hospital in the nearby city of Ayr, in honour of her role as benefactress. Now it hangs at Cloncaird Castle, where Isabella is far from forgotten.

Stories of Isabella are many and marvellous. She was a notable personality, a talented pianist and a dedicated gardener. Her distinctive taste and sense of style still dominate Cloncaird: the billiard room was transformed by the Art Deco themes she introduced; she installed remarkably lovely ceilings and wooden panelling throughout the castle; she imported great amounts of Italian marble for the foyer, along with Italian workmen to install the marble. She also renovated the stables and turned them into a cottage, redesigned the gardens and introduced a variety of rare plant species. The current owners of the castle speak appreciatively of her work on the place, conscious of her important role in bringing

Mrs. Isabella Wallace of Cloncaird Castle.

the castle into the twentieth century, and conscious also of the important place she fills in local mythology. Many people in the area claim to have encountered Isabella's ghost, and the owners have little doubt that her presence haunts Cloncaird to this day. Mysterious footsteps pace the hallways and ghostly piano music is rumoured to drift from the music room, gate latches open mysteriously and flowers rustle strangely in the garden that Isabella so loved.

Having renovated the castle to her liking, in 1908 Isabella married the former owner, Colonel Hugh Wallace. By the time Willie and Ada Annie were married in Vancouver in 1909, Isabella Wallace was the doyenne of Cloncaird, a patroness of the arts in Ayr, a woman of powerful dignity. To the end of her days, even after her second husband's death when she lived alone at the castle, she dressed formally for dinner and, attended by the butler and the maid, dined in solitary splendour in the large dining room. When she died in 1947 the castle passed into the hands of the local hospital board; apparently she did not consider the family of her distant brother when making her will. The Rae-Arthurs in Canada were a long way away and she had never had much to do with them, certainly not directly. Her contact with them had generally been at arm's length, carried out through lawyers.

This woman was not one to tolerate an underachieving brother lightly, nor would she wish him to disturb her own world. Yet she could disregard neither him nor his family if their need was acute. For many years she did her duty. She may have been paying a remittance to Willie for many years before his marriage; she certainly provided money to Ada Annie during the early Boat Basin years. A faded letter from a firm of solicitors in Glasgow, still in Cougar Annie's house at Boat Basin, indicates that payments from "Mrs. Wallace of Cloncaird" continued until 1930.

Someone in the family also provided books. Not a vast number, but a significant few, and these provide peculiar insights into the attitudes and expectations that bedevilled Willie and Ada Annie. A small clutch of them, mostly novels, survives at Boat Basin. Many are predictable period pieces: Charles G.D. Roberts's *The Heart of the Ancient Wood,* inscribed "Ada from Dad," Ralph Connor's *The Patrol of the Sundance Trail* and Ernest Tompson Seton's *Two Little Savages.*

More significant than these are the stickily romantic novels preaching pious lessons about men who fall into bad ways only to be rescued by the love of good women, novels of breast-heaving sentiment and overwhelming moral sensibility. Quite a few of these have surfaced in Cougar Annie's house. Take Charles Frederic Goss's novel, published in 1900, *The Redemption of David Corson.* Handsomely bound in green and gold, the book's message is unmistakable. Its very chapter headings tell the tragic tale of the hero's fall from grace. In the first chapter, "This Other Eden," all is well, but the ensuing chapters "And Satan Came Also" and "The Flesh and the Devil" follow as David Corson falls into bad ways, until his eventual salvation in a chapter entitled "Out of the Jaws of Death." The once virtuous David discovers the fearsome joys of hard liquor, rejects the teachings of the Bible, goes forth to gratify his appetites and desires, and finally redeems himself through exile to a wilderness home, through the love of a good woman and through his worship of nature.

The heroine of the piece is David's long-suffering wife who "acted from a single, undivided impulse; it was to do him good and bring to him the final beatitude of life." She manages to rescue him, weans him off the drink and brings him back to their farm where the "charms of this pastoral existence gradually came to his support in his heroic resolution." David then exiles himself to a distant tract of "Timber land" to expiate his sins, "determined to make a clearing there and establish a home." Later, flushed with success, he thinks his "clearing was a kingdom, his cabin a palace." Through this place, the novel attests, David is truly saved.

It was his own! He had carved it out of a wilderness! Here was ground which had never been opened to the daylight. Here was ground which perhaps for a thousand, and not unlikely for ten thousand years, should bring forth seed to the sower; and he had cleared it with his own hands. . . .

Another remarkable pair of novels at Boat Basin, both written by William Black, is a set of small, insignificant books in faded red covers. Their tattered pages positively gush romantic sentiment. The first, *White Wings*, features a young laird in Scotland who, in a state of dazed admiration, falls in love with a young Englishwoman who has the "courage and nerve of a dozen men." The second, *White Heather*, tells of the downfall and salvation of Ronald, a Scottish gamekeeper, who falls desperately in love with the doctor's daughter. Convinced his suit is hopeless, Ronald leaves the pure air of the Highlands for the fleshpots of Glasgow, and there falls into wicked ways, "drinking himself to death and in the lowest of company." The heroine, secretly in love with Ronald, is stricken with horror when she hears this news:

> *Ronald - Ronald that was ever the smartest and handsomest of them all,*
> *the gayest and most audacious . . . had in so short a time become a bleared*
> *and besotted drunkard, shunning the public ways, hiding in ignoble haunts,*
> *with the basest of creatures for his only friends? . . . And was this the end?*
> *Was he never coming back? The proud young life that promised so fair*
> [was] *sucked under and whirled away in a black current. . . .*

When this young lady stops lamenting her lost love, she proves most resourceful. Having sent Ronald a piece of white heather to signal her concern for him, she goes to Glasgow and discovers that Ronald is not beyond redemption. She asks him to give up the drink. "Well," he replies, "it's easily promised and easily done, *now,* indeed, I've scarcely touched a drop since ever I got the bit of heather you sent me." So the demon drink is vanquished, Ronald and his lady love marry, he secures a good position as a forester, and they return to the highlands.

A slightly different message, just as pointedly aimed at the Rae-Arthurs, radiates from the pages of another cheap romance entitled *What Can She Do*, by E.P. Roe. Here, when her wealthy family falls on hard times, society girl Edith courageously takes her mother and sisters into the country and creates a market garden in the grounds of a humble cottage. Love comes her way in the person of Arden, an impractical and unsuccessful local farmer. "She so woke her dreamy lover up, that he . . . at once commenced the culture of small fruits; she giving him a good start from her own place."

Edith's control of their finances is closely related to her control of their love life. This novel leaves no doubt about who is in charge. She says to Arden " . . . here is your way out of trouble, as well as mine. We are near good markets. Give up your poor, slipshod farming . . . and raise fruit. I will supply you with vines. We will go into partnership. You show what a man can do, and I will show what a girl can do." Arden, a sensible man, seizes this opportunity. "Ah, Edie, Edie, woman once got man out of a garden, but you, I perceive, are destined to lead me into one; and any garden where you are will be Eden to me." Edith then shocks everyone by having the marriage performed in her own beloved garden. "Why not? she asked. "God married a couple there once."

From the virtues of market gardening to the evils of drink to the redeeming qualities of hard work, the messages emanating from this strange little collection of novels are unmistakable, the sermons implicit and clearly directed at Willie Rae-Arthur. Did he laugh as he read these books or could he possibly have taken them seriously, and felt ashamed? Did Ada Annie ever bother looking at them and feel a swelling sense of her own worth and redemptive powers? Perhaps Willie and Ada Annie simply ignored these books. After all, they had far more pressing concerns than reading romantic fiction. Establishing the garden, for instance. And that was to become Ada Annie's chief occupation and her chief love; for nearly seventy years she would not, could not, stop working in her garden.

During their years together at Boat Basin, Willie is the one who often found time to stop. The place never took possession of him the way it did of Ada Annie. His mind was elsewhere; his attention was not fully engaged by this expanding bush garden. "He couldn't do much of anything," Ian Macleod remembers. "Mr. Rae-Arthur wasn't practical, couldn't do anything with his hands. But he was sure interesting to talk to." As a teenager, Ian Macleod knew the Rae-Arthurs, encountering them on fishing trips up the coast. He describes Willie Rae-Arthur as a short, slight man with a Scottish accent and unruly grey hair. Once every two months, sometimes more often, Willie would paddle for many hours in a dugout canoe or in a rowboat to go to Tofino. There he would stay overnight, and the next day he would get a haircut and join the usual collection of expatriate British men who gathered regularly in the general store, sitting around the pot-bellied stove, talking about the old country. This group discussed the Oxford and Cambridge boat races, argued about British politics, recited Shakespeare and Burns to each other. Willie did not see the British newspapers as often as the other men, so he always enjoyed the political discussions. "He was an educated man, all right," said Ian Macleod. "They all were, those Brits."

In spare moments, Willie Rae-Arthur wrote poetry and sketched in a leatherbound book, at the back of which he did a sketch of himself reclining under an apple tree and smoking opium from a large and bulbous pipe. Above him at the top of the picture he drew the fierce figure of a small woman shouting at him to go to work. Willie probably did go to work when asked, or at least he would affably assure everyone that he intended to work. His correspondence with the Lands Department shows this technique beautifully. When applying to pre-empt a second parcel of land some years after the family arrived at Boat Basin, Willie was clearly not in a hurry to do the required work, and in letter after letter the lands commissioner tells him to get on with it. On January 13, 1929, this official wrote that "Although Mr. Arthur is very keen to retain this pre-emption he is making no effort to get the necessary improvements done." Willie's replies are untroubled, like this one of August 17, 1929.

Many thanks indeed for your registered letter of the 6th inst (which I at first thought was my pay cheque) re: P.R. No 1868. In reply to same the reasons why so very little has been done so far on this land is that I have been away at work during the summer months of each year. I am just finished on a job now and am going home and will get extra busy on this land and hope to fully satisfy your requirements.

After having given Willie the benefit of the doubt and several extensions, the lands commissioner gravely concludes in a letter of September 7, 1929 that "Mr. Rae-Arthur is not endeavouring to live up to the terms of the 'Land Act'" and that "I am not satisfied that he is making an honest endeavour to comply with the Act and it seems to me this pre-emption should be cancelled." And indeed, this second attempt at pre-empting land came to nothing. Willie had by then successfully laid claim to one tract of land in this god-forsaken coastal wilderness, he had made a gallant effort to pre-empt a second—at least on paper—and surely that was enough.

Willie Rae-Arthur leaves no record of his own feelings about going out to Boat Basin, but for a high-living man-about-town this place must have seemed dire exile. He was definitely in disgrace in the eyes of his family. In her old age Cougar Annie occasionally spoke with some bitterness about having to leave Vancouver penniless and with her head down. For each of them the reality must have been galling. Willie had gambled away the family's money in the opium dens. Bound to him, his wife had to take care of her husband and start a new life for the family. She was a survivor; at all costs she would make good, but the costs were going to be high, and the family would be running on her strength alone. Willie's wayward behaviour ensured that they found themselves at Boat Basin; only his wife's tenacity could ensure that they stayed there.

CHAPTER 4

A Parcel of Land

Inside the front and back covers of the romantic novel *What Can She Do?*, Willie Rae-Arthur's handwriting extends across the blank pages. The writing is less elegant than usual, in pencil rather than in his usual flourishes of black ink; it looks hasty, with words scratched out and occasionally barely legible. "Declaration to be sent in duplicate with a fee of $2 to the Commissioner of the . . ." one phrase reads, tailing off into unreadability.

On one page the words "20 chains" are crossed out, followed by scribbled notations "name in full" and "date," and then an unpunctuated sentence: "I intend to apply for a pre-emption of 160 acres of land bounded as follows commencing at this post thence north 20 chains thence west 60 chains thence south 40 chains more or less to north Boundary of Indian Reserve." Inside the back cover, two closely written pages continue in a similar vein, this time punctuated and in numbered point form, and Willie's final point reads:

> *My application to record is not made in trust for, or on behalf of, or in collusion with, any other person or persons but honestly on my own behalf for settlement and occupation, for agricultural purposes, and I also declare that I am duly qualified under the said act to record the said land. And I make this solemn declaration conscientiously believing it to be true and knowing that it is of the same force and effect as if made under oath and by virtue of the Canada Evidence Act.*

This unexpected find within the pages of a cheap romance is the rough draft of a legal document. Willie Rae-Arthur is drawing up his application to pre-empt land at Boat Basin, using whatever paper came to hand. He was evidently there when he wrote this draft, scouting out the lay of the land and preparing to launch his legal application for pre-emption following all the rules and procedures. For some reason he had this novel with him, and he used it as notepaper. Perhaps by the time he was jotting down all this information and making these notes, he had moved, complete with family and books and all possessions, to Boat Basin. Perhaps they had simply forgotten to bring any paper. Willie was probably making these notes in early April of 1915.

He was clearly keeping busy. Pre-empting land had to be done according to the rules, or at least had to be seen to be done according to the rules. The parcel of land in question must be properly staked and demarcated, for a start. Willie describes the process.

> *I did locate the said land by placing at the SE corner thereof a post of at least four inches square and standing not less than four feet above the surface of the ground. The said post is about 40 chains distant* [he writes "East" above this] *from the NW corner of lot 1479. I on the same day did affix to the said post a notice with the following words thereon* [a long blank follows] *and did also inscribe on the said post the name WRA and the letters at SE corner.*

Willie Rae-Arthur may well have had company as he beat his way through the bush establishing corner posts and affixing notices and measuring out the chains of the parcel of land he hoped would be his. He may have been taking advice from someone with more experience as he scribbled legal jargon in his hastily improvised notebook. After all, he had no previous knowledge of this kind of rough bushwhacking, nor had he any experience of this type of land measurement or of this carefully worded application to pre-empt land. The procedures were daunting and Willie no doubt needed some guidance. The man rumoured to be a guiding influence in bringing the Rae-Arthurs to the coast did have the necessary experience, did know this area of land, and could well have helped Willie carry out these challenging tasks. Known by many as Old Man Gibson, William Gibson was the father of the legendary Gibson brothers who made a powerful impact on the coast with their colourful logging ventures and their shingle mill at Ahousat.

Many stories connect Gibson to the early days at Boat Basin. He did some of the first selective logging here, taking out choice trees near the beach, and he built a small cabin for himself and his men. The clearing is still faintly visible where this cabin stood, a clearing Tommy Rae-Arthur called "Gibson's Lawn." And Gibson apparently built another cabin back from the beach on the property that was to become the Rae-Arthurs' pre-emption. According to Gordon Gibson's autobiography *Bull of the Woods*, the Rae-Arthurs bought this cabin from his father for a hundred and twenty-five dollars. The Gibson connection is also affirmed in other sources.

> *It was in the year 1915 that Mr. W. Gibson of Vancouver, father of the well-known Gibson brothers of West Coast fame, sought to encourage settlement by pre-emption of a somewhat desirable portion of land situated at the head of Hesquiat Harbour. Two families arrived and established themselves in that area, one by the name of Rae-Arthur and the other a Mr. Wheeler and his wife. The Rae-Arthurs had a young family, the Wheelers had none.*

So writes Mike Hamilton in his unpublished memoirs. Hamilton was a regular traveller up and down the coast, and he worked on the telegraph line between Ahousat and Nootka. He knew both the Rae-Arthurs and the Wheelers.

Allan Wheeler and Willie Rae-Arthur were possibly acquainted even before arriving at Boat Basin; they could well have helped each other in that spring of 1915, tramping through the bush, hammering in stakes, measuring out the edges of their respective properties, and filling out pre-emption documents. Certainly their names are filed side by side in many legal documents connected with the land, for they applied to pre-empt land at Boat Basin at almost exactly the same time. Allan Wheeler's formal application to pre-empt is word for word the same as Willie's draft on the blank pages of *What Can She Do?*, except for the legal description of the land, but it is signed and dated at Hesquiat, April 13, 1915, and witnessed by W.F. Gibson. Willie's official application is dated a month later, on May 24, 1915, again signed at Hesquiat, this time before a Justice of the Peace, Mr. E. Gillam, who was also Captain Gillam of the *Princess Maquinna*, the much-loved coastal steamer that for forty years travelled up and down the West Coast.

Both the Wheeler and the Rae-Arthur applications to pre-empt land at Boat Basin were officially recorded in Victoria, on June 2, 1915. One after the other, their names and the legal descriptions of their respective parcels of land appear in an imposing ledger, now kept in the Provincial Archives, listing pre-emptions for the Port Alberni district. Their names are buried deep in this book, difficult to find amongst the host of like-minded pre-emptors.

This large ledger is a roll-call of would-be settlers seeking land on the West Coast. Page after creamy, lined page, year after year, the copperplate hand of some long-dead bureaucrat lists all the hopeful pre-emptors on the coast. This list bears witness to many broken dreams and long-lost schemes. Countless self-proclaimed settlers tried to pre-empt unlikely tracts of land all over British Columbia. Some of them were greedy opportunists, pre-empting one tract of land after another, perhaps doing a bit of logging but never truly intending to farm the land or to settle. Some were genuine, earnest settlers who came and who stayed. In this particular ledger, one of so many for the province, well-known West Coast names appear amongst the pre-emptors: names such as Arnet, Clarke, Gibson, Grice, Jensen, all of whom have descendants on the coast to this day.

This method of acquiring land was complex, though it sounded marvellous. Pre-emptions were free, large tracts of potentially productive land available to aspiring settlers who wished to "improve" the land and reside upon it. According to an early twentieth-century publicity pamphlet entitled *How to Pre-Empt Land in British Columbia*, "Any of the vacant unreserved surveyed lands of the crown in the right of the Province, not being part of an Indian settlement, may be pre-empted." The maximum area for a pre-emption was 160 acres, and the land had to be used for agricultural purposes.

After taking up residence, the settlers could apply for the land to be crown-granted, but their work on the land, their so-called "improvements," was subject to scrutiny. Travelling throughout the province in the course of their work, a bevy of lands inspectors from the provincial government kept a close eye on pre-emptors. Only after a government inspector had visited and had made at least one report, and often several reports on successive years, could a settler apply for a "Certificate of Improvement." Once this was granted, the Lands Department would then decide whether or not the land should be granted to the settler. Only after this decision could the land become the settler's freehold.

Because the system of pre-empting land was chiefly designed to increase the amount of agricultural land under cultivation in British Columbia, the very notion of pre-empting on the west coast of Vancouver Island was slightly mad. This was unlikely land for agriculture, by any estimation. As Father Augustin Brabant, the founder of the Roman Catholic mission at Hesquiat gloomily observed:

The coast is rugged and rocky, presenting in its entire extent the appearance of desolation and barrenness. The hills and mountains run down to the beach; the valleys are lakes, and a few patches of low land, to be encountered here and there, are covered with worthless timber. No clear land is to

be seen anywhere, and no hopes can be entertained that the west coast of
Vancouver Island will ever be available for agricultural settlements.

This unguarded comment about agricultural settlements is one of Brabant's more trustworthy observations. He is quite right: the land near Hesquiat, like most land on Vancouver Island's west coast is a poor bet for agriculture. The odds against farming in this setting were, and are, daunting if not overpowering, as the Rae-Arthurs found as they struggled to clear the land and establish their garden. The settlers at Cape Scott at the turn of the twentieth century also found this, far more bitterly and at far greater cost, when they attempted to establish their doomed dream of a communal market garden on the exposed northwest corner of Vancouver Island. Settlers on Vargas Island, farther south, were to find much the same when they arrived. Many of them, like Dorothy Abrahams, came from England, and were completely unprepared for the landscape they faced. Mrs. Abraham's arrival on Vargas in 1911 was a total shock to her: "There were no fields, no grass, no people, no anything! ... I thought, 'What desolation!'"

This impossible dream of creating English fields and meadows in the deep forest took possession of countless settlers all over Vancouver Island. Eustace Smith, whose family arrived in the Black Creek area around the turn of the twentieth century spoke for many when he said:

> *I wanted a farm as I remembered farms to be in England ... I guess we all*
> *had that idea, "gentleman" farmers. In the Old Country a big farm would*
> *make you landed gentry, land was associated with wealth. Here it meant*
> *toil. You became a serf to your own land. The wilderness gripped it, held on*
> *to the farmer's dream of wide green pastures with the massive dark roots of*
> *the great forest. It seemed then that we could never break that grip, could*
> *never make it loosen and give up the land to us.*

And yet agricultural endeavours persisted, even in the hostile west coast terrain. Most have left scant traces. On Vargas Island, for instance, the outlines of clearings made by settlers early in the twentieth century are faintly visible from the air, along with lines left by old fences and ditches, and barely discernible pathways to the coast. Yet, however harsh the work and however bitter the defeats, many settlers clung to the familiar ideas of agriculture and farming, partly because these were understood to be *civilised* undertakings, in a landscape that seemed overwhelmingly *uncivilised* to newcomers. Coming as they did from entirely different landscapes, they had arrived planning to change the land, to tame it, to make

49

it produce in a way they understood. And they often persisted against their own better judgement.

Certainly the mission at Hesquiat, despite Father Brabant's clear dismissal of the agricultural potential of the area, insisted on trying to instill agricultural values into Hesquiat people who had never tilled the land or imposed their will on it in any way. The very charter of the mission at Hesquiat, entitled *Instructions pro Missione in Hesquiat*, specifies, entirely in Latin, that one of the duties of the priest in charge of the mission is to "inspire the love of agriculture." To this end, perhaps, Brabant arrived at Hesquiat with a little herd of cattle, cattle which were to become legendary in the area as they broke free of their enclosures and roamed wild in the forest.

Father Charles Moser, a Swiss priest, was Brabant's successor in the mission at Hesquiat, and he, even more than Brabant, longed to teach Hesquiat people about the joys of farming and raising cattle. He did not have much success but he enjoyed trying; judging from his memoirs he was never happier than when he was in the garden he established at Hesquiat Village and when tending to the cattle. In August of 1914, when the eyes of the world were turned to the brooding calamity in the Balkans, Moser radiates delight about one single apple: "As I went along my orchard I discovered to my great joy the first apple since the trees had been planted in the spring of 1911. I was so glad to see it. It weighed nine and a half ounces." The same year he records with pleasure that his potato patch yielded 332 pounds.

Mercifully for posterity, Father Moser had other interests as well. He occasionally took time off from instilling the love of agriculture and spreading the Roman Catholic faith to pursue a favourite hobby. He was a keen amateur photographer whose pictures provide a unique record of a period of coastal history. He photographed almost everything: land clearance, church painting, Hesquiat families, scenery, visitors to the area.

Father Moser even took his camera with him when he went visiting. On one of his trips across the harbour to Boat Basin in his dugout canoe, he stashed the camera in a waterproof leather bag under the prow and went ashore to visit the recently arrived settlers, Willie Rae-Arthur and Allan Wheeler. He photographed the two men in front of their new, raw cabins at Boat Basin, probably some time in 1917. Allan Wheeler looks straight at the camera, stocky and bareheaded, tensed to return to work. Willie Rae-Arthur stands nonchalantly at ease on his porch, propped up against a post with his legs elegantly crossed, looking aside, hat tilted rakishly over his forehead.

The Rae-Arthur and Wheeler properties were adjacent. Their cabins were probably no more than a couple of hundred metres apart, although admittedly through deep forest. In the parlance of the Lands Registry, Rae-Arthur was on Lot 1599, Wheeler on Lot 1600, both in the Clayoquot District. Their simultaneous arrival and settlement at Boat Basin was entirely typical of land pre-emptions up and down the West Coast at this time, indeed, all across Canada. Records show time and again that pre-emptions were made in pairs, or even in bunches, as men set out together for remote areas—perhaps on the recommendation of someone familiar with the area or of someone trying to develop the area—to pre-empt parcels of land that they thought desirable, parcels of land surveyed some years earlier and distinguishable on a map only as straight-edged, numbered blocks. Apart from pre-emption there were other means of acquiring land, including outright purchase and was under the Soldiers' Homestead Act, a favourable deal offered to returning soldiers during and after the First World War. Again, such acquisitions were often made by two or more people in any given area at one time.

Inside Hesquiat Harbour in the early years of the twentieth century there were not many surveyed lots, fewer than a dozen in all, representing only a small proportion of the land in the area. One of the first of these to attract any interest was Lot 1477 on the east side of the harbour. This was pre-empted in June 1898 by Captain George Heater, the master of a sealing schooner and a regular visitor to Hesquiat Village. This property appears to have remained in Heater's possession until 1922, though there is virtually no evidence that he visited it during those years. Nearby are three other lots, numbered 1478, 1480 and 1481, purchased by three different men on the same day, men no doubt acting together: William George Underdown purchased Lot 1478; Frank Gandon,1480; Harold Trenchard, 1481. They did not pay much for their land; Trenchard, for instance, paid one hundred dollars for 247 acres. All these properties reverted to the Crown within a couple of decades, usually because of non-payment of taxes.

Tracing the history of land pre-emptions leads into a maze of perplexing questions about details of tenure. Directly in front of the Rae-Arthur property, Lot 1479 was pre-empted in 1897 by Anton Luckovich and the land crown-granted to Luckovich the same year that the Rae-Arthurs arrived, 1915. Later it reverted to the Crown for non-payment of taxes. Luckovich may have lived on this property, he may have tried to develop it and "improve" it, but this seems highly unlikely because there is ample proof that Luckovich lived across the harbour near Hesquiat Village where he ran a store. The store was to the north of the village near the point of land reaching out into the harbour, a feature known to this day as Anton's Spit.

Originally from Austria, Anton Luckovich was a familiar figure in Hesquiat for many years. He was amongst the first white settlers in the harbour, perhaps *the* first after Father Brabant established the mission at Hesquiat in 1875. Luckovich appears to have been well-established at Hesquiat by 1891; according to the census he was living there with his wife and two young children and working as a "General Trader." Writing in 1893, Father Brabant mentions Luckovich in a letter to a fellow priest: "This is an answer to your question about settlers. . . . I must acknowledge the presence here—about two miles from the mission—of a Slavonian married to a half-breed woman, with a family of three little children. He keeps a small store for the Indians, and has been a resident of this section about four years." In 1894 Luckovich and his family are also named in an article about Hesquiat appearing in *The Province.*

In the census of 1901, Luckovich is still listed as a resident of Hesquiat, still described as "General Trader" and by then the father of seven children. He stays put, and is quick to make himself useful during the building of the lighthouse at Estevan Point. His name surfaces in the earliest correspondence about the lighthouse, and by 1906 he is closely involved in the preliminary work before construction begins. His name features on a lordly telegram from the decision-makers in Ottawa to the Marine Agent in Victoria, dated November 7, 1906: "Let Lukovitch proceed with clearing and tramway Estevan by day's labour." He was clearly a handy person to have on site and is referred to by the Marine Agent as a "highly reliable man," invaluable in providing essential local details to the distant bureaucrats about such matters as where to land boats bringing construction supplies to the exposed setting of the lighthouse. Luckovich was stationed at Estevan for several years both during and after the construction.

Father Moser refers to Luckovich frequently, calling him the lightkeeper, although Anton never officially held that position. The two men saw each other fairly often; in 1913, just after Christmas, they shared an unfortunate dinner, of which Moser writes: "We prepared a canned pudding which he had previously sent me. After he had gone I felt quite ill with pains in my stomach, I wondered if it was the pudding and how Anton was faring." Everyone in the vicinity seems to have known Anton, and shopped occasionally at his store. In their own language, Hesquiat people called Anton Luckovich "Sour": he sold sourdough bread at his store, and the name stuck for years. His children were sometimes called "Sour's daughter" or "Sour's son."

Why Luckovich decided to pre-empt land in the inner harbour at Boat Basin back in 1897 is a mystery, given the evidence of his rooted existence at Hesquiat

Willie Rae-Arthur at Boat Basin, about 1917.

and Estevan. Perhaps William Gibson encouraged Luckovich to make the pre-emption and then set up a deal with him in order to buy a few of the better trees on the property. Certainly some early selective logging has been done here, as evidenced by the occasional massive stump nearly engulfed in the forest along the shore. Yet this cannot explain why the land was crown-granted to Luckovich in 1915; officially he should have been living there and making agricultural improvements in order to receive the "Certificate of Improvement" required for a crown grant. The land was not long in Anton's clear possession; five years later the Crown had resumed control for non-payment of taxes.

Of all the parcels of land in Hesquiat Harbour once registered as pre-emptions or purchases, only two have remained privately owned. And only one of these, the Rae-Arthur property, has been continuously occupied since it was first pre-empted. The other, Lot 1146, originally purchased by Benjamin Hale in 1911, passed eventually into the hands of Pacific Forest Products and was partially logged in the late 1970s.

Would-be settlers in this harbour simply did not stay. Some may never have tried to live on the tracts of land briefly registered in their names, but were making land grabs on impulse, and, soon losing heart, gave up any idea of holding onto the land. Perhaps they erected small cabins on their properties and attempted a bit of prospecting, perhaps they sold a few choice logs, but they have left almost no evidence of their tenure. This brief flurry of land acquisition did not last long, it came to a halt after the early purchasers and pre-emptors faded from the scene. From the mid-1920s onwards, very little buying or selling or claiming of land is recorded inside Hesquiat Harbour.

To understand the Rae-Arthurs in the context of their time, the *idea* of the ready availability of land must be taken into account, along with the ideas of expanding settlement and agricultural ambition. Though seeming a complete anomaly in the silent isolation of Hesquiat Harbour today, the Rae-Arthurs fitted in perfectly with the West Coast activity of 1915. They wanted to establish a profitable garden, they wanted to stay, and they were prepared to risk a bit of isolation until more people arrived and the area developed. And at first, everything looked fairly promising. Certainly there were periods of having no one else to talk to, but out in the harbour and all up and down the coast there was a lot of action, and a confident sense that more action would soon be coming.

Father Moser lived in Hesquiat Village on and off throughout the 1910s and 1920s. And while he complains occasionally of personal loneliness, he also makes abundantly clear in his memoirs that a continuous bustle of coming and going was the norm. At times the native people in the village numbered up to 150. They came and went in canoes and on sealing schooners, they travelled ceaselessly to various jobs up and down the coast at canneries and whaling stations and hop fields, and they moved with the seasons to their traditional fishing and hunting grounds.

Steamers regularly called at the village during these years, usually about twice a month, including the *Tees,* the *Queen City,* and after 1912 the famous *Princess Maquinna* took over the West Coast route. The newly established lighthouse at Estevan Point was operating from 1908, with lightkeepers coming and going, as well as builders and maintenance men and wireless radio crews. Hesquiat Village itself had a store and a post office, as well as its own wireless radio. In 1914 a telephone line arrived in the village and a phone was installed in Father Moser's house, allowing him instant access to news of the outside world. He pays scant

Allan Wheeler in front of his cabin.

attention to the war raging in Europe, but in his memoirs he notes the day in early 1915 when "we heard over the phone that King George had been thrown from his horse."

The priest's house was headquarters not only for the village telephone but also for the post office. This large house boasted a guest bedroom as well. At times almost too many visitors arrived. An entry from Father Moser's memoirs indicates the ceaseless activity of the summer of 1913:

> *I went by canoe to Kakawis, it took over nine hours by outside passage. I returned on the* Princess Maquinna, *a fine CPR ship specially built for the West Coast run which was making her maiden trip. She was a great improvement on the* Tees. *On board were two wireless men and their wives*

en route to Estevan. These days it seemed as though my house was full all the time, Prospectors, Lighthouse keepers and their wives and children; Indian Agent, Policemen, men looking for land, miners looking for claims. All and sundry partook of my hospitality, there being no other place to stay, I was always glad to have them though sometimes I had to stretch the house somewhat.

"Men looking for land" were a constant presence. Several times in his memoirs Father Moser casually mentions men who arrive looking for land on which to settle. One of the more interesting showed up in 1913: "Next time the steamer came in it brought . . . a Russian Pole who had come to look over the land with the idea of establishing a Russian Polish Colony, a Mr. Wrotnowsky." What became of Mr. Wrotnowsky's dream goes unrecorded, but it did not unfold here. No Russian Polish colony ever appeared at Hesquiat. A couple of years later, in July of 1915, Moser records that a Mr. Goellner, of Detroit, arrived to "take up land in the Inlet," presumably Sydney Inlet. Only a few weeks later, in September 1915, Mr. Goellner reappears at Hesquiat, awaiting the "down steamer." "He was very disappointed and said he was going to Vancouver to look for work." This was a land-rush and, just like a gold-rush, that dream—as attested by the number of would-be settlers whose pre-emptions are marked "cancelled" and the numbers of land purchases that ended up reverting to the Crown—was much more enticing than the reality.

In the early decades of the twentieth century the west coast of Vancouver Island seemed to promise infinite possibilities, infinite scope for development. Far more traffic went up and down the coast then than now; far more people lived there. Slowly and surely the coast has been depopulated since the late 1930s. Many ventures were tried and abandoned, many communities established and deserted, many enterprises flared into brief life and then faded. Many faded because the resources they were exploiting—pilchards, dogfish, whales, seals, huge fir and spruce trees near the shore—were no longer so readily available. But back in 1915 no one remotely anticipated this kind of loss or depopulation. However difficult the Rae-Arthurs' circumstances were, they never imagined their isolation would increase over the years. They had come to stay and to make a go of it, to start anew. Others would soon follow. And in the beginning, for a while, they had near neighbours. The Wheelers were almost within hallooing distance through the bush. Unfortunately the Wheelers did not last long.

Catastrophe struck Allan Wheeler and his wife less than two years after their arrival. Two different sets of memoirs document the events, one by Mike

Anton Luckovich's house and store.

Hamilton and the other by Father Moser. Mike Hamilton was a close witness, for he was with Allan Wheeler at the time. Hamilton was in charge of maintaining the telegraph line that ran between Ahousat and Nootka, and in the autumn of 1917 he employed Allan Wheeler to help him for a brief period following the temporary closure of the pilchard reduction plant in Riley's Cove where Wheeler had been working. When their work on the line had finished Hamilton offered to take Wheeler back to Boat Basin, a journey Hamilton did not relish in his "old, slow tub of a boat." He writes of what happened then:

To make matters worse it was early winter, November. Snow had fallen and the sky was lowering and ominous looking. . . . Heavy seas greeted us as the boat nosed its way into open water . . . after almost three hours of slow travel in a most unfriendly sea, we arrived at our destination to our great relief. It was getting dark and we proceeded to a sheltered cove . . . and anchored the launch safely as we thought and took our tender, being a small dugout canoe, and paddled to the beach where we made a landing close to Wheeler's home. It had been windy the previous night and about a foot of snow had fallen. As we entered the short trail from the beach I could see the house through the trees. Something about the scene, and I couldn't explain exactly what, suggested a lack of welcome. The stove pipe through the roof did not indicate any sign of life. . . . It was definitely cold and there was no one to greet us. Wheeler called out to his wife in his usual way, but there was no response. "Must have gone over to the Rae-Arthurs," he muttered. . . .

But Helen Wheeler was lying dead in the bedroom. Wheeler and Hamilton immediately went over to tell the Rae-Arthurs who, according to Hamilton, "had no suspicion that there was anything wrong, as sometimes days would elapse without the two neighbours contacting each other."

Father Moser's memoirs pick up the story, although telling it rather differently. Moser recalls receiving a call from "Rae-Arthur" on January 30, 1917, saying that one of his daughters had burnt her arm badly and asking Moser to call for a doctor. No doctor could come, the weather being bad, and the following day Rae-Arthur called again to say the child was better, but that "he had found the dead body of Mrs. Wheeler." The discrepancy in dates between Moser and Hamilton is not surprising, for both were writing their memoirs many years after the events. In this case, Moser's dates are more reliable as they are based on his diaries, and they agree with the official certificate of death. The discrepancy in the accounts of how the body was discovered, and by whom, is harder to explain. Quite possibly Willie discovered the body, called Moser, and either they sent for Allan Wheeler to come home without explaining to him or to Mike Hamilton what had happened, or Wheeler was already on the way and arrived home unaware of what awaited him when he entered the cabin.

Father Moser went over to Boat Basin on January 31st, the day after the call from Willie. "Three Indians took me over to Boat Basin. Mrs. Wheeler must have been dead some time as her body was quite stiff, her husband was working at a fish plant." Moser also notes that "Mike Hamilton and Captain George Heater brought Mr. Wheeler home, later in the evening Mike's launch was found on Yaksis beach all broken up. By working in the surf he and some Indians were able to save the fittings and engine though they were soaked to the skin. Afterwards Mike and Capt. Heater came to me for dry clothing and food and shelter for the night." Mike Hamilton's memoirs recall the loss of his launch with great anguish and he credits Moser with sending out a search party to find him after he had been frantically paddling around Hesquiat Harbour in search of his wrecked boat.

The death of Helen Wheeler was a big event. Whether or not the neighbours saw much of each other or even liked each other, losing their immediate and only neighbour so soon after arriving at Boat Basin must have been a tremendous shock for the Rae-Arthurs. "Mrs. Rae-Arthur was kindness itself," recalls Mike Hamilton in his memoirs, "and provided us with some warm food, doing everything she could to help in the sad and unhappy circumstances."

The ever-busy Father Moser, back at Hesquiat, had to ensure that Mrs. Wheeler was properly buried, and that certain legal formalities were observed. "Mrs. Wheeler could not be buried," he writes, "until the Doctor arrived, but when the steamer came on Sunday there was no Doctor, so a lively conversation took place between the Doctor, the Clayoquot Policeman, and myself, over the telephone, but in the end my statement of death was taken and the burial took place." Helen Wheeler was buried, according to the death certificate, at Hesquiat, on February 5, 1917, six days after her supposed date of death.

Wheeler Creek.

Such use of "Hesquiat" in official documents often means Boat Basin. Marriage, birth and death certificates often refer to Hesquiat for events that clearly occurred at the Rae-Arthurs' home in the inner harbour. As for Helen Wheeler's place of burial, she was probably laid to rest somewhere in Cougar Annie's garden.

When Barry Lorton stayed at Boat Basin in the early 1980s to help look after Cougar Annie, Helen Wheeler's name came up in conversation soon after he arrived. "The old lady told me right away that Helen Wheeler was buried in the garden, near one of the apple trees where the chicken coops were. Maybe she was trying to scare me. It was spooky—dark and rainy and the flashlight didn't work and I had to make my way out to my cabin through the mud, past this bit of the garden every night. She told me also about all the other graves out there in the garden, further from the house."

Helen Wheeler was thirty-four years old when she died, and the scribbled cause of death on the death certificate says only "heart disease." Following her death, Allan Wheeler left Boat Basin, and his land eventually reverted to the Crown. The only mark the Wheelers left behind is in the name "Wheeler Creek," a little creek running along the edge of Cougar Annie's garden. Here, for decades, Cougar Annie and her family would go for water in the summertime when the rain barrels ran dry. A tin cup was always there, at the edge of Wheeler Creek, and still the dim outline of a path leads back to the Rae-Arthur garden. The creek itself flows through the forest, past the site of the Wheeler's cabin, and widens to a dark tea-coloured stream as it approaches the beach, deep and cool and fine for drinking. The forest has reclaimed whatever clearing Allan Wheeler hewed out of the woods; the cabin where Helen Wheeler died has disappeared without a trace.

Even without the sadness of his wife's death at Boat Basin, Allan Wheeler did not do well in pre-empting his chosen parcel of land. It measured only 89 acres, much smaller than most pre-emptions on the coast, and although it may have looked attractive, bordering as it did on both Rae Lake and Hesquiat Lake, it was difficult to clear and almost impossible to consider for agricultural use. The lands inspector's report for 1921 is curtly dismissive: "Small patches could be tilled but area as a whole is not suited to agriculture. . . . Rough topography, dense underbrush, poor soil, poor timber, remote situation and infrequent transportation are factors that would prevent any sound-minded agriculturist from settling on the area." But by then, Allan Wheeler had already been long gone, not bothering to inform the Lands Department that he had abandoned his pre-emption.

The "Land Classification Reports" of the inspectors often contain pithy assessments and unromantic truths about pre-empted parcels of land, assessments no doubt coloured by the irritated exhaustion of the inspectors who had to cover great distances in rough circumstances to view the properties. Going to Boat Basin meant travelling several days from Victoria, viewing many inaccessible tracts of land where settlers' dreams were either flourishing or, more likely, foundering. Judging from several of the early reports about both the Wheeler and Rae-Arthur properties, the inspectors had slim hope for the success of either family.

Yet by 1920, grudging approval was granted to the Rae-Arthur property in the Land Classification report: "Area is comparatively level Pine and Cedar Swampland. Most of area suitable for tillage when cleared and drained. . . . Area is suitable for raising mixed farm crops. Remote location and lack of market other than that offered by local Indians fishermen and others may eventually discourage the pre-emptor." But the inspector underestimated these particular pre-emptors. By then they had been in place for five years and they had outfaced many discouragements. They were not about to leave.

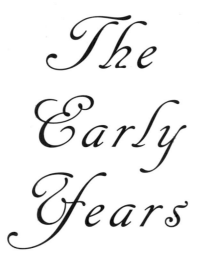

CHAPTER 5

The Early Years

ALONG THE BEACH at Boat Basin the trees loom, dense and imposing, their branches sweeping down to the beach to form a wall of impenetrable forest just above high tide mark. When the Rae-Arthur family arrived here in April 1915, they faced this tangle of green with little if any idea of what lay in wait for them once they went up the beach through the thickets of salal and into the forest. Somewhere through there, a couple of hundred yards back from the beach, was the land they had laid claim to. Somewhere was the rough log cabin, built for them and sold to them by the Gibsons.

Skunk cabbages were probably flowering then, bright yellow on the damp forest floor, as the family made its way for the first time through the dense undergrowth. As they looked up at the massive cedars, at the light filtering through layer after layer of rainforest growth, at the brilliant mosses high in the branches, at trees growing out of trees growing out of crumbling deadfalls, as they scrambled over fallen logs and pushed their way through low branches, as they wondered, perhaps, about the unknown creatures watching them, just out of sight in the forest, the Rae-Arthurs were stepping into an entirely new world. They had reached what would prove to be a point of no return.

Here they were. They had done it. They had left Vancouver forever. For Willie Rae-Arthur it signalled an end to a city life that had been going from bad to worse. For Ada Annie, it signalled a new existence more demanding than any she could have imagined. For the children, the rigours and joys of this new landscape would now dominate their lives.

No record exists of the thoughts going through Ada Annie's mind but, determined and courageous as she was, that moment of arrival, clambering into a canoe from the steamer which had brought them up the coast, and paddling for shore complete with luggage, cow tethered upside down, three small children and husband, must have been daunting. But no doubt she entered the silence of the forest with her head up as they tramped the short distance to their new home, her gun probably close to hand.

Many years later, when her reputation on the coast had spread far, when she was famed as a cougar hunter and known by some as Cougar Annie, when her family had grown and her various enterprises were established, the pioneer achievements of Ada Annie Rae-Arthur were occasionally discussed in books and newspapers. Invariably, much is glossed over, as in Dorothy Abraham's autobiography *Lone Cone*: "At Hesquiat there lived an interesting family who had carved their home out of the bush, and had a wonderful garden, many children and a goat farm. The woman was one of the best shots on the coast, and the fame of her cougar bag has gone abroad. Theirs was a rough life and very isolated, but they loved it and seemed to thrive on it." Such a cheerful, heightened description typically masks a life that was, certainly at first, dreadfully difficult.

Cougar Annie did not talk much of the early years. In 1974, when quoted in an article in the *Vancouver Sun*, her comments seem guarded. "It wasn't the easiest thing for a born-and-bred city girl to cope with, but it was something that had to be done. I had to find a way to support my family because my first husband,

The beach at Boat Basin

Raised walkway through the forest, built in the Rae-Arthurs' early years.

willing as he was to work, knew as little as I did about living in the bush." In an earlier article in the *Sun*, published in 1957, reporter Alex MacGillivray drew blunt conclusions about the early days and the problems she and Willie faced: "Her husband was in ill health. While he looked after the children, [she] took a mattock and axe and cleared her land. What she couldn't cut or rip with the mattock she burned."

Piecing together the fragments of information about the Rae-Arthurs at Boat Basin from 1915 through the 1920s can provide only limited insight into their lives, but a number of points are abundantly clear. One is that Willie Rae-Arthur was completely unsuited to being a pioneer, hacking and hewing an existence out of the forest. Secondly, clearing the land here, as everywhere on this coast, was a punishing undertaking. Thirdly, the Rae-Arthurs had a terrible struggle to keep the family fed and clothed. And finally, during their early years at Boat Basin, Ada Annie Rae-Arthur was repeatedly pregnant. Between 1915 and 1931, she bore eight more children, all of them at Boat Basin.

In the tattered little book with a faded green cover bearing the title *Family Prayers*, nothing at first seems particularly remarkable. One of several books of prayers and scripture quotations at Boat Basin, this book lay unregarded for years in Cougar Annie's house. The inside back cover, though, contains a Rae-Arthur family tree in Willie's handwriting. "Progenies," as he calls them, are listed, one after the other, complete with dates and place of birth.

The first child born at Boat Basin was Isobel Agnes, at 12:10 AM on August 31, 1915; her mother had evidently been pregnant when they arrived in April. Then, according to Willie's list, came Rosina Boyd at 8:15 PM on November 16, 1917, followed by Helen Buchanan at 12:30 PM on June 20, 1920. Thomas Jordan arrived on August 12, 1923, Lawrence Robert on September 18, 1927, and Willie's last entry is for Marjorie Elizabeth, born on June 3, 1930. The birthplace for every child is inscribed as Hesquiat B.C., except the three eldest children, George William, Frank Stephen and Margaret Ada, all of whom were born at 2285 West Broadway in Vancouver, the former family home.

Willie's list of "progenies," impressive though it may look, is guilty of omission. Death certificates show at least two others were born at Boat Basin: Agnes, on May 16, 1926 and another, described on her death certificate only as "Unnamed Female Child", on July 28, 1931. Agnes lived only three-quarters of an hour; the unnamed child lived only five minutes. The place of burial for each is given as "Hesquiat," the same burial place given for Marjorie Elizabeth, who also died as an infant, her brief life lasting only two days. Three infant deaths within five years, and Lawrence Robert, who survived, was also born in that period.

By the time the last of these infants died, Ada Annie was forty-three years old and had borne at least eleven children since the age of twenty-two. Willie's list indicates that for several of the Boat Basin births a nurse, from either Vancouver or Victoria, attended; for Thomas Jordan a Mrs. Whitman was there to help; for Marjorie Elizabeth Dr. Dixson from Tofino was there, although the death certificate indicates he attended only on the second day of Marjorie's short life, presumably having been called because the baby was dying. Dr. Dixson must have become familiar with the Rae-Arthurs' circumstances; he signed all three of the infants' death certificates. He is the same doctor appearing often in the memoirs of Father Charles Moser, having been called repeatedly to attend to the sick and dying in Hesquiat Village following outbreaks of smallpox or tuberculosis among the native people there.

A note above Willie's entry for the birth of Isobel Agnes Rae-Arthur in 1915 uniquely states "No doctor or nurse." But Ada Annie was not entirely on her own even for this one, the first at their new home. In his memoirs Father Moser describes what happened when Mrs. Rae-Arthur's time was upon her. In the middle of a period of hard work when he was painting the church at Hesquiat Village, Moser recalls, "I received an SOS to go to the confinement of a white woman. I took my Doctor book, and my Ergot and went along with an Indian midwife. There was nothing to do, the woman was alright, but needed patience. I spent part of the night with the Indian in a shack on the beach, and the baby was born at midnight, another little Rae-Arthur."

Imagining the scene brings vivid pictures to mind, the priest and the midwife paddling across the harbour as the summer evening darkened, arriving on the beach at Boat Basin to follow a new, rough trail through the forest up to the house, there finding Ada Annie in labour for the first time in this forsaken place, probably with a nervous Willie in attendance and three young children somewhere in the small cabin, sleeping or hiding. The priest, prepared to assist with the birth if necessary or to administer prayers to the dying, finds himself not really needed and retreats to the beach. The midwife assists as much as she is able or as much as she is allowed to assist and eventually goes down to the shack on the beach for some sleep. And the next morning, after visiting the mother and new baby, out go priest and midwife again, pushing the dugout canoe over rock and sand, into the water, and back across the vast harbour to the village. Father Moser's diary rarely mentions the Rae-Arthurs, even though they were just across the harbour from the village. He never again refers to a birth at their home, so his brief reference to Isobel's birth provides the only outside information about the children born at Boat Basin.

Father Moser was not alone in having a "Doctor book." Cougar Annie had one herself, or perhaps it was Willie's, because his flourishing handwriting on the title page declares "Stolen from W.F. Rae-Arthur, Boat Basin, Hesquiat, B.C.," and on the next page follows a note in pencil in the same handwriting "Baby Born 12:30, June 20 1920, Helen." Entitled *The Doctor at Home and Nurse's Guide-Book*, this early twentieth-century volume of over 600 pages devotes only a page and a half to childbirth. The entry begins solemnly: "As it sometimes happens, especially in the case of those who reside in the country, and at some distance from medical assistance, that the child is born before the doctor has time to be sent for, it will be well for those who are in attendance to know how to act in the meanwhile. It is desirable, therefore, to lay down a few plain rules for the guidance of those who may at any time be thus awkwardly situated." No plain rules follow at all; nothing whatever is said concerning how to assist a woman in labour or how to deal with complications in childbirth. Most of the entry is devoted to ensuring the survival of the child.

In the early 1980s, when the frail and elderly Cougar Annie needed help in order to remain in her house at Boat Basin, Chris Marshall and her husband were employed to help care for her. During their stay, Chris became pregnant with her second child and she decided to have the baby at Boat Basin rather than going to the hospital in Tofino. As the time of the birth drew near, Chris asked Cougar Annie for advice, but "She didn't seem to want to talk about childbirth.," Chris recalls. "She just said that if I had problems to come and get her, and that I should stay in bed for three days afterwards. That's what she always did, I guess." No doubt Cougar Annie could have helped if problems had arisen; over her many years at Boat Basin she repeatedly went to Hesquiat Village to assist women in childbirth.

With the ever-increasing tribe of children to care for, with land to clear and a garden to grow, the work was unending. Chris Marshall once asked Cougar Annie how she managed to do anything at all with all those young children underfoot, only to be told that when there was no choice you just did what you must. If her husband was not around, or was unable to help, Cougar Annie would bank down the fire in the stove, tie the baby—there was always a baby— in the highchair, put the young ones in the big playpen in the corner, lock them all in the house to keep them from wandering and then go outside to work. The children old enough to be any help were probably only too glad to be out of the house and working alongside their mother, even in the endless rain of winter. "We worked all the time out in the garden or getting wood or looking after the animals," recalls Rose. "We all had jobs, and Mother made sure we did them, too."

The most pitiless job of all during the early years was clearing the land. Think of clearing that heavily treed area without any machinery whatsoever—a ghastly notion to anyone accustomed to chain saws. Cutting one large tree with a six-foot crosscut saw could easily take two people a whole day or even two, depending on the difficulties of the terrain. Then came the toil of removing the branches and cutting the trunk for firewood. And then came that greatest curse of all—getting rid of the stumps.

66

Land clearing at Hesquiat Village around 1920.

Stump removal became an obsessive industry amongst settlers on the coast. Some, like Father Moser, could call on others for help and had access to explosives. He recalls the activity in 1913: "During August I employed some Indians to shoot stumps, but they didn't seem much good at it, after having used up a couple of boxes of stumping powder they still hadn't got one stump out."

Stumps were blasted and hacked and levered out of the ground with agonizing slowness, and then hauled away by sweating horses. In Cougar Annie's garden stumps were just burned, slowly smouldering in the ground for weeks and even months. "Stumps were burning all the time I was a child," Isobel remembers. "All the time." But this was a slow and unsatisfactory method, especially given the enticing rumours of the high-tech gadgets becoming available. In 1915, as Father Moser recalls with satisfaction in his memoirs: "I now had a stump puller which had been sent up on a recent steamer, land clearing was made much easier. The stump puller was worked by a cable and pulled the stumps out in no time. . . . The Indians were very intrigued with the stump puller and were all quite keen to work with it. One day pulling out a very large stump it snapped a three quarter inch cable, fortunately no one was hurt."

In one of Willie Rae-Arthur's letters to the Lands Department about the management of his land and his proposed developments, he requests to be allowed to pre-empt the adjacent Lot 1598. His original pre-emption has proven to be not 160 acres as he believed, but a mere 117 acres because, as he explains in an injured fashion, "the Government Surveyors cut off the best piece of land which I expected to be on my crown granted lot." He needs more land for his goats to graze, he explains, for the flock now numbers over fifty. And should Willie be allowed to pre-empt this extra piece of land, he has a marvellous proposal for clearing the land properly. He writes, "The proposition below [is] to have the brush all cleared off by a flock of goats, later putting a gasoline stump-pulling outfit to work to get the land cleared up for agricultural purpose." He then adds that once the land is so easily cleared, he could set sheep and cattle on the meadow he has created.

Cedar alongside the original trail to the Rae-Arthurs' cabin.

None of this happened. Rose has no recollection of a "gasoline stump-pulling outfit" ever being used in her parents' garden. She laughs at the thought. "The only stump-pulling machine was me," she says. "I'd hang onto the end of the long bar levering stumps out of the ground, and my brothers would push down on it."

Settlers on this coast often seem entirely mad, entirely obsessed about clearing the land. People like Fred Tibbs have become legendary for their madcap ventures. Tibbs took it upon himself to clearcut a small island near Tofino because he wanted to build a castle, with a bicycle track around the island for good measure. In an interview quoted in *Settling Clayoquot*, Bill Sharp recalls Tibbs at work: "I'd row over and we'd talk about, oh gosh, clearing land. That's about all you did in those days is talk about what you're going to clear and how you're going to do it and how you're going to take this stump out or that...." By 1920 Tibbs' island was bare, though he did leave one tree, a tall spar over a hundred feet high with a long ladder going up to a platform he built at the top. Tibbs would ascend to this perch every morning at eight to play his trumpet, and the tune of "Come to the Cookhouse Door Boys" would resound over the top of his wooden "castle" painted white with red and blue trim. He wrote to a niece in England, saying that one day she should come to see her "uncle's desperate efforts, turning a wild, rugged bit of forest into a little patch of England."

Compared to some people on this coast that attracted so many mad dreamers, the Rae-Arthurs were the epitome of good sense and sanity. At least they did not attempt the impossible or the ridiculous. They cleared, in the end, about seven acres and never seriously pursued Willie's more grandiose ideas of clearing parts of the adjacent property. They had more than enough to handle on their original pre-emption.

Cougar Annie slowly expanded her garden as the land was cleared. Once the first earth could be turned, she lost no time in establishing a large potato patch and a vegetable garden. She discovered—perhaps she had suspected as much—that the soil was rich and deep, and she quickly realized that once the land was ditched and drained, an excellent garden would be possible.

From the very outset at Boat Basin, Cougar Annie indulged herself in her garden. Her recreation was to experiment with as many plants as she could obtain, and she could argue the necessity because she intended to run the garden as a nursery business. So she brought in rhododendrons and azaleas and heathers and dozens of flowering shrubs, and not only fruit trees and filberts and walnuts, but many decorative trees and exotic species from Asia. She planted whatever she could get her hands on: broom, weigela, cotoneaster, berberis, forsythia, laburnum, hebe, deutzia, stephanandra, escallonia, spirea, hollies, gorse, viburnum, pernettya, hydrangeas, climbing roses, honeysuckle—not to mention quince, grapes, currants, raspberries, gooseberries and strawberries. From nurseries and seed houses all over Canada, and even from overseas, she purchased many varieties of tulips, daffodils, narcissus, lilies, irises, hostas, gladioli, peonies, daisies, montbretia and dahlias.

Cultivated patches of earth and garden beds, at first established only near the house, began to be placed farther away. A patchwork of small fenced areas within the rough clearing set out several specific zones—for the animals, for the vegetable beds, for the nursery beds, for the fruit trees, for delicate shrubs. Meandering pathways wound around smoking stumps and young fruit trees and potato patches and freshly turned beds of earth, perhaps following the ways originally taken by the Rae-Arthurs' goats as they wandered through the bush, grazing on undergrowth. The number of narrow ditches dug to drain the wet soil increased year by year into a complex network criss-crossing the whole clearing, all of them lined and bridged by hand-split cedar boards.

As the garden expanded, so did the livestock. Dozens of chickens and rabbits as well as ducks and geese roamed the garden or, if the fences were in place, stayed safe within their enclosures. The goat population went up and down, sometimes as many as fifty, sometimes a dozen or so, and four black pigs, well remembered by Rose, because they chased her father into the raspberry patch. The lands inspector who visited in 1921, Mr. R. Gritten, reported: "Crops raised include 10 fruit trees (3 bearing) small fruits, 1 acre potatoes, 1 acre mixed agricultural produce, 2 ½ acres sown in grass. Stock owned includes 19 goats and 100 chickens. The pre-emptor is a bona fide settler and has made an excellent showing." On the same visit Gritten tallied the assets on the property. His list is thorough and detailed: log house 14' × 20', value $200; hen house 10' × 12', $60; shake house 10' × 12', $25; log store house 10' × 14', $60; lumber goat house 10' × 10', $60; 1000 ft. wire fence, $175; 5 acres cleared (not all stumped), $1000; ½ mile foot trail, $100.

INSPECTION BRANCH—DEPARTMENT OF LANDS.

Victoria, File No. _____
District File No. _____

Name of Inspector _____ G.L.Davies.   Date of Inspection _____ Oct 25th
Land District _____ Clayoquot   Lot No. _____   Forest District _____ Vancouver
Land Recording District _____ Alberni   P.R. No. 1652   Date of P.R. June 2nd 1915
Atlas Ref. or Location : At the head of Hesquiat Harbour West Coast V.I.

Name of Pre-emptor :   Mr Rae Arthur

Particulars as to Occupation :   Continuous residence since date of filing. In residence at the time of Inspection.

Nature and Value of Improvements :   Log house 200   Log hen house 60.
Shake shed 35   Log cabin 75
Lumber shed 75   Pig pen 25
1200 feet woven wire fence 100   Shake shack 15
5 acres cleared , most of patch in garden and root crops, some few stumps remaining. 1,500
10 Fruit trees and quantity of small fruits
Stock at present 40 goats 150 chickens

Only a year later, another inspector's report was submitted to the Lands Department by Mr. G.L. Davies, valuing the five acres of cleared land with "some stumps remaining" at $1500, adding that a pig pen had been built, and that the wire fence now measured a total of twelve hundred feet. Pleasing these lands inspectors was essential if settlers like the Rae-Arthurs were to receive their "Certificate of Improvement." Once the inspectors could see, year by year, some genuine proof of industry and productivity, the certificate would be forthcoming, and then the land could be crown-granted. After that, when it was safely in their possession, settlers would never again be subjected to the scrutiny of an inspector.

The inspector's report of 1922, submitted by Mr. G. L. Davies, strongly supports the Rae-Arthurs. Lands inspection reports like these rarely show a human face of either the inspector or the settlers, but this report is different. "Pre-emptor should be given his Certificate of Improvement," writes Davies firmly. "I have rarely come across an example such as these people, who had made such a good showing under such extreme handicaps. There are four small children of school age that are being deprived of any schooling. The obtaining of the Crown Grant has become a thing to be striven for with these people, and it is probable that pre-emptor can obtain financial assistance from his relatives when he has obtained the C.G. This will enable him to do the proper thing with his children, who are at the present time growing up under conditions far worse than the very worst of the native Indians." This report proved to be a sadly mixed blessing for the Rae-Arthurs.

A year later, on August 31, 1923, William Rae-Arthur's crown grant certificate was filed on his behalf in the records office in Victoria. After eight years of living in the bush, the land he had pre-empted was his, freehold and clear title. It would remain in his name until his death in 1936, when it became the property of Ada Annie Rae-Arthur. Even though, according to common report, most of the hard labour in the garden and even in clearing the land was done by Cougar Annie, she could not be named as a pre-emptor of land. The husband, the head of the family, had to make the pre-emption application; wives could not apply, although widows, and what are engagingly referred to as "femmes soles," were permitted to apply to pre-empt land.

Being able to call the land their own should have been, and probably was, a relief to the Rae- Arthurs. The year 1923 should have been a great year for them; not only did the land grant come through, but that was the year they started to build the long-awaited new house, from milled lumber, with the help of men from Hesquiat Village, and with the assistance also of the older Rae-Arthur boys. But 1923 brought fresh trouble to Boat Basin, perhaps as a result of Mr. Davies' strongly worded report.

Davies may have done the Rae-Arthurs a good deed in hastening the crown grant, but he may also have done them a disservice in speaking in such negative terms of the conditions at Boat Basin, and in indicating that the children were "growing up under conditions far worse than the very worst of the native Indians." Certainly rumours about the Rae-Arthur family had flitted up and down the coast, rumours that the children were as wild as little animals, that they were not properly clothed or fed, that some of the fishermen avoided going in to Boat Basin because they were all so "weird." But to be faced with an official report like this was far more serious than coastal gossip could ever be.

When Davies wrote his report in 1922 there were six Rae-Arthur children. The four eldest, George, Frank, Margaret and Isobel were of school age but had never attended school. Their mother had attempted to teach both George and Frank by obtaining correspondence courses for them, but her efforts went awry. Stories about what happened vary, both within the family and amongst people who knew Cougar Annie, but the outcome was that the following year, in April 1923, the three eldest children were removed, against their parents' wishes, and taken away to school in Vancouver.

Father Charles Moser was at Christie's School at Kakawis, a few hours down the coast from Hesquiat, when the ship called in, bearing the Rae-Arthur children away from Boat Basin. He writes in his memoirs: "Several visitors arrived . . . including the Principal of the Reform school of Vancouver, also Constable Woods from Alberni and Constable Anderson from Clayoquot. They had been up to Hesquiat and brought with them three of the Rae-Arthur children to be put to school." Why the Reform School should have been involved is anyone's guess, and the principal's presence on the boat may have had nothing to do with the Rae-Arthurs. A separate account of the children's departure states that a "School Inspector" came to take the children away; another says the Children's Aid Society acted on instruction from Ada Annie's father in Vancouver, who wanted the children to go to school. No account but Moser's mentions the presence of the two constables who may or may not have had a role to play in the removal of the children, although, typically, when native children ran away from school or refused to attend, police constables were sent to fetch them. The constables' role could have been to make sure the Rae-Arthur children were collected, or simply to act as escorts.

The children stayed in Vancouver for several years and shortly after their departure the fourth school-age child, Isobel, was sent to join them. For a substantial portion of time they were unhappily housed at the Children's Aid Home in Vancouver, in the charge of the Superintendent of Neglected Children, and for at least three years—some accounts indicate as long as five years—they did not see their parents, despite repeated requests and protests from Willie and Ada Annie and despite requests from the children themselves.

The children must have felt entirely abandoned in Vancouver. Even their grandfather appears to have quit the scene by then, for while George Jordan may have put in his oar and insisted the children go to school, and while he may have played a role in removing them from Boat Basin, he was preoccupied with problems of his own by the time they arrived in Vancouver, if indeed he was still there.

George Jordan had remarried in 1910, only a year after his first wife's death. His new wife, Mary Alice Ross, was considerably younger and the marriage was troubled. By 1918 George and Mary Alice appear to have stopped living together, and in 1922 she initiated divorce proceedings. The legal documents dryly state that "The respondent failed to appear." Nothing is known of George Jordan following that date. He disappears from all Vancouver directories after 1922, leaving his wife in charge of the house they had shared on Cornwall Street, where she worked as a music teacher. Typically, George seems to have moved on, perhaps to embark on yet another enterprise. By the early 1920s he was, however, approaching seventy, and even he may have been running out of career changes by then. But he certainly moved away from Vancouver, and probably out of the province, for no death certificate exists for him in British Columbia. His estranged wife remained in Vancouver, where she died in 1948.

What Ada Annie thought of her father's actions cannot be guessed. They were certainly still in contact with each other during the Rae-Arthurs' difficult early years at Boat Basin. George Jordan visited at least twice, once in 1917 when his arrival on the *Princess Maquinna* was observed by Father Moser at Hesquiat: "May 9th. Dr. Jordan, Father of Mrs. Rae-Arthur, arrived for a few weeks' holiday bringing with him a wheel-barrow, which much to our amusement was still covered with barn manure. He also brought a lot of tools intending to do some work whilst visiting his family." During that visit, Ada Annie would have been pregnant with her daughter Rosina, born the following November. And Rose recalls another visit by her grandfather, several years later. "He threw one of the boys into the bushes for being rude—that's about all I can remember. But he was there right enough." Isobel, the sister next in age to Rose, also recalls this visit and her childish delight when her grandfather gave pennies to the children.

The four younger children, Rose, Helen, Thomas and Laurie were spared the fate of the elder ones. They grew up at Boat Basin and their schooling was entirely through correspondence courses. A number of old school textbooks still at Boat Basin powerfully evoke the Rae-Arthur children. Their presence here can be strongly sensed in these books: struggling with the correspondence courses, dawdling at their lessons, striving to spell correctly. Childish handwriting covers the flyleafs of the books, where signatures of almost all the children appear, some superimposed on top of others. Small piles of these textbooks have been ignored for decades, heaped in a damp shed in Cougar Annie's garden.

Covered with mould and mildew, the books fall open. Ttitle pages declare the names of the books' owners: "This book belongs to his honer George Rae-Arthur" says one *Canadian Reader,* while *Highroads to Reading* bears the faint, partly erased signature "Helen Rae-Arthur" on top of which, firmly printed and cheerfully misspelled, is the name "Tomas Rae-Arthur." The same firm hand, still unconcerned about spelling, lays claim to an arithmetic book: "Tom Rae-Arthur, Grade For." And a reader, dated 1927, is signed "Rosie Rae-Arthur, Hesquiat B.C." in grubby pencil on the front page, while on the back she declares this to be "Baby Peanut's book" and then carefully lists the names of every member of the family:

"George, Frank, Margaret, Isobel, Rosina, Helen, Tom, Lorance, Ada Annie, William Frank."

At the bottom of the heap of textbooks in the damp shed, another revealing document comes to light, one typical of the strange relics that still show up at Boat Basin. It is a frail and elderly map of Vancouver Island, printed in 1912, and on the blank side of the map some rough jottings appear in both ink and pencil. The paper is discoloured and tattered, the writing is faded, and the subject of the jottings, once decoded and pieced together, is financial.

Two hands are at work here: the elegant flourishes of Willie Rae-Arthur, and the quicker, more businesslike writing of Cougar Annie. They are recording columns of figures, with brief notes beside the figures. Here is an estimated annual household budget, including the cost of the new house: 3 Hay 75.00; 3 Oats 60.00; 45.00 Freight; 100.00 House; 120 + Living. This adds up to a required sum of $400+. Above are calculations of costs, including "Shingles 30, Nurse 40." And the sum of $93 is listed three times, apparently as income, with the months July, August and September following the notations. Perhaps this money was earned by Willie in the summer months of that year. After all, Willie does claim in one of his letters to the Lands Department, that he has been "working away" in the summer, possibly at one of the fish plants nearby, as did Allan Wheeler.

The finances enabling the Rae-Arthurs to remain at Boat Basin were both complex and meagre. Willie had informed the Lands Department that more money would come from his family once the pre-empted land was officially his. If this were true, the years following the crown grant in 1923 should have been less straitened than the initial years at Boat Basin. And compared with the severe hardships of their earliest years on the coast when the First World War made prices higher and goods more difficult to obtain, matters probably did improve after 1923. In a letter written in 1926, Ada Annie speaks defiantly of receiving a "substantial monthly allowance" from Willie's family and claims that she and her husband are able to provide for their children exceptionally well. But still, her elder children were kept away from her in Vancouver. Times were hard, and the authorities in charge of the children were unconvinced that the Rae-Arthur parents could care properly for all their offspring.

The family had grown rapidly, the garden was expanding, and the expenses of maintaining the place and the progeny were escalating. Staple foods such as flour and sugar and oats had to be purchased as well as feed for the animals, fencing, building supplies, and countless small necessities. Shoes for the children were not high on the list of necessities. They usually just went barefoot. "And sometimes there wasn't much food in the house," Rose recalls. "Especially if the ship was late coming in with an order. Sometimes we had porridge morning, noon and night. There was always porridge."

Rose also remembers receiving parcels of clothing from relatives in Britain. A torn and faded half-sheet of writing paper, found inside the book entitled *Family Prayers*, provides a glimpse of what these parcels were like. "Please tell Maggie," begins this note, perhaps a draft of a letter or a page forgotten and never enclosed in the envelope, "little Laurie is delighted with the springlegged monkey toy— that the auto rug makes a nice cover for Ada's bed—Helen is delighted with the Burberry coat and hat."

Another surviving letter, signed "Mrs. A. A. Rae-Arthur", is addressed to the young, newly married Amy Arnet in Tofino, who had been so kind as to send a box of clothes for the children. Dated October 5, 1929, the letter expresses courteous thanks for the "exceedingly useful box of clothing you sent, it was indeed more than kind of you to think of us," and goes on to offer Mrs. Arnet or any of her friends a "couple of dozen more or less large yellow pumpkins" that would "make excellent preserve and are always nice for pies."

Mrs. Arnet, along with many others living in Tofino, was aware of the Rae-Arthurs' needs because the fishermen going in and out of Hesquiat Harbour did keep a distant eye on events at Boat Basin. Her husband paid more attention than most. Carl Arnet fished at Hesquiat every autumn during the 1920s, and would often take the Rae-Arthurs a fish or two and buy some vegetables from their garden. Ed Arnet recalls his parents talking of the Rae-Arthurs.

> Hesquiat Harbour
> B.C. October 5th 1929.
>
> Dear Mrs Arnet,
> Many thanks indeed for the exceedingly useful box of clothing you sent, it was indeed more than kind of you to think of us— I wonder if any of your friends (or perhaps yourself) could use a couple of dozen more or less large yellow pumpkins weighing 5 to 20 pounds each? they make excellent preserve and are always nice for pies— the smaller pumpkins or Summer squash particularly will keep nice till Christmas time or after—
> Again with most sincere thanks
> Yours very sincerely
> Mrs A A Rae Arthur

My mother liked Mrs. Rae-Arthur, though I don't think they met more than a few times because Mrs. Rae-Arthur was always at Boat Basin, she never came out. Thinking about it now, it's kind of frightening to imagine her being up there with a husband who just wasn't capable of doing outdoor work, with all those children. That place must have been like a prison. I know my mother was concerned for her.

Keeping the family healthy and clothed and fed was a ceaseless worry in the early years. Mrs. Ann Hill, who was a nurse up the coast in Zeballos, recalls hearing how Mrs. Rae-Arthur carried a sick child on her back all the way around the rocky coast of Hesquiat Harbour and across to Estevan Point to get help, and how she had to spend a night in a cave en route. Les Hammer, former mayor of Port Alberni and postmaster for the area that included the Boat Basin Post Office, related a similar story of the sometimes almost desperate need of the Rae-Arthurs. During Cougar Annie's later years he came to know her well, and when she died he was interviewed by the *Alberni Times* for a newspaper article about her which appeared on April 30, 1985.

Hungry and starving she set out for Estevan Point Lighthouse with a baby on her hip and a toddler clinging to her skirt. Hammer said there was wild cattle in the area of the lighthouse that people used to hunt. Annie had the idea if she could get to the lighthouse she could hunt the cattle for some food. She had to leave in the middle of the night because of the tides, and all she had was a coal oil lantern to guide her. There were streams of water to cross on the rugged beach and it was tough going. Eventually she got to Hesquiat where she met a native Indian. The Indian took her back to the reserve where a call was radioed to the lighthouse for help.

Even given the tendency of West Coast stories to grow tall and fast, the hardships of the early years at Boat Basin were undoubtedly extreme. Ada Annie herself admitted that the children were neglected in order to get the land cleared and the garden established. She knew her situation was far from ideal, but she also knew the brutal realities of life there. Come what may and never mind the human cost, this garden had to grow. She, for one, was prepared to do whatever she had to do and nothing, not even the needs of her own children, could deter her.

CHAPTER 6

The Working Garden

COUGAR ANNIE JUGGLED many small-scale enterprises at Boat Basin. Some of these she carried on intermittently for many years: selling raw furs, for instance, and hunting cougars for bounty. Some lasted only a short while: briefly, she raised guinea pigs for a hospital in Vancouver, and she bred and sold pedigreed rabbits and mink. But three particularly important ventures carried on decade after decade: the nursery business, the general store and the post office. These were central to Cougar Annie's existence, essential in helping to transform her place from an ordinary stump farm out in the bush into a highly original working garden. The nursery business and the store came first, each venture evolving gradually during the 1920s.

The plant and bulb nursery and the general store suited Ada Annie Rae-Arthur perfectly. Each venture served a multitude of purposes, allowing her, in different ways, to carry on the small-scale, creative wheeling and dealing at which she had excelled in Vancouver when taking stray animals in at one door and selling them out the other as pets. These enterprises brought in only a small—often negligible—amount of money, but they enabled her to barter for various goods, they put her in touch with people who might be useful, and most importantly these enterprises encouraged her to carry on gardening.

❧

Right from the moment Cougar Annie arrived at Boat Basin, the idea of a plant and bulb nursery was already in her mind. No doubt the business started slowly, but by the mid-1920s her daughters can recall helping to fill orders; wrapping up parcels of bulbs, nestled in sphagnum moss, and packaging them neatly for shipment. These packages were then rowed over to Hesquiat to be shipped out on the coastal steamer, the *Princess Maquinna*.

Keeping this nursery business alive enabled Cougar Annie to do what she loved best: to garden to her heart's content and to make a bit of money on the side. Over the years she sold everything from roses and fruit trees to shrubs and bulbs, to ferns and mosses. She brought in stock constantly, as many plants and trees and shrubs and bulbs as she could afford, usually with a view to propagating them to sell as nursery stock. Sometimes no money would change hands at all, as she would exchange plants and produce from her own garden for stock from elsewhere. Stories tell of her receiving plants from as far away as Japan and Chile and New Zealand, sending bulbs overseas in return, and less exotically of doing the same kind of trade with growers in Vancouver and the Fraser Valley.

Correspondence with other growers, both requesting and selling nursery stock, still spills from shelves and drawers in Cougar Annie's house. Once tidily bundled and held with elastics, these papers are now completely mixed up. A letter from the Dominion Seed House in Georgetown, Ontario, dated 1935, requests information about "quantity offerings of dahlia bulbs," and the C.D. Morris Nursery in Ocean Park, B.C., in a letter dated 1968, offers six varieties of phlox and thirty-five "Azalea Mollis" at thirty cents each. Beatrice L. Palmer's 1951 catalogue of lilies, from her farm in Cobble Hill, emerges from a heap along with a letter dated November 7, 1939 from Edward Webb and Sons, suppliers of bulbs and seeds in Toronto. "We thank you for your kind order for bulbs," this letter begins, going on to provide a price list for tulip bulbs, available in bulk for $16.00 per thousand. Another letter from Edward Webb and Sons, a year later, provides information about seeds, and expresses thanks for a payment of $2.74, safely received. Envelopes printed with addresses of suppliers in Denmark and in Belgium have been kept in a special pile, their foreign stamps neatly cut out: one envelope addressed to Mr. A.A. Rae-Arthur, another to Messrs. E. and A. Arnold, still another to Mr. A.A. Campbell. Cougar Annie almost always signed only with her initials and many of her business correspondents assumed she was a man. Even formal documents, such as her business license to sell nursery stock, use only her initials.

In the early years at Boat Basin, Cougar Annie experimented continually, trying to establish different species, seeing what would grow and thrive here, seeing what she could profitably grow for sale. To this day, a striking variety of trees and shrubs appears in odd corners of the garden; they are no doubt survivors from early experiments, survivors that have lived long and done well. In common with all dedicated gardeners, Cougar Annie planted any number of attractive species just for her own pleasure and interest. The garden still boasts over a hundred different species of trees and shrubs alone, representing decades of planting and experimenting, and also representing what could be the earliest known introduction of some ornamental species on the coast. Amongst the trees she planted are a linden tree, a black locust, an English chestnut, a red-veined enkianthus, a huge liriodendron—now perhaps one of the oldest and largest of its kind in British Columbia—not to mention many varieties of ornamental cherry, crabapple and plum, and dozens of fruit trees. The Latin names of all her plants and trees were familiar to Cougar Annie, anyone who asked would hear a litany of favourites: *Berberis darwini, Escallonia organensis, Viburnum odoratissimum, Pieris japonica, Daphne mezereum, Philadelphus virginalis, Veronica traversi, Amelanchier alnifolia*—and on and on, including the Latin names of each of the many varieties of azalea and rhododendron and heather in the garden.

EXHIBITION DAHLIAS; FLOWERING shrubs; climbing roses, $1.00 doz. Perennial flowers; lilies; mixed dahlias; gooseberries; currants; blackberries, 50c doz. Gladioli, Montbretia, 25c doz. Peonies, 25c each. Strawberries, 40c—100. Mixed dahlias, $2.00 —100. Rae-Arthur, Hesquiat, Vancouver Island. 5-5-12-c

8 DAHLIAS OR ½ LB. GLADS., 25c. BOX 64, Leask, Sask. 2-4-21-p

A yellowed copy of the *Western Producer*, dated April 21, 1938, selected at random from a mucky heap of newspapers in one of the garden sheds, contains a page of small print advertisements for "Seed, Feed and Nursery Stock." In the middle of one column appears the following ad: "Exhibition Dahlias: Flowering shrubs; climbing roses, $1.00 doz. Perennial flowers; lilies; mixed dahlias; gooseberries; currants; blackberries, 50 cents doz. Gladioli, Montbretia, 25 cents doz. Peonies 25 cents each. Strawberries 40 cents per 100. Mixed dahlias $2.00 per 100. Rae-Arthur, Hesquiat, Vancouver Island."

The variety listed in this advertisement shows the impressive level of productivity in Cougar Annie's garden by the late 1930s. A marketable profusion of roses and berry bushes, shrubs and dahlias, lilies and gladioli and peonies was bursting from the garden. Never highly organised or disciplined, this garden always ran a bit wild, looked a bit ragged, but it was planted with a liberal hand, allowed to spread and grow as it wished, always expanding and developing, controlled just enough to produce what Cougar Annie needed and what the buyers wanted. The potential productivity of the place was probably evident to Cougar Annie from the very beginning; and its reputation had begun to spread even during the 1920s.

A timber cruise report from 1926 for the area around Hesquiat Harbour takes note of changes in the area. "Rocky outcrops are very common and make agricultural development absolutely impossible on areas that might otherwise be fit for cultivation. Some small areas, now under cultivation, with constant care, are being made to produce some of the finest vegetables and flowers in the country." Cougar Annie's garden by then had been under cultivation for nearly ten years; the price had been high, but the wilderness was at last bearing fruit.

Given the unpromising surroundings and the usual dire predictions about tilling the soil in this region, Cougar Annie's garden is blessed in its location, thanks to several highly localised features. In the clearing where the garden grows, deep sandy loam lies over an impervious subsurface of clay. The water always flowing down from the surrounding mountains wicks along the clay layer, and once the land is ditched, excess water drains from the soil and runs through the fringe of deep forest along the south edge of the garden and on to the sea. Protected by the forest from the storms and prevailing winds of winter, the garden holds heat and moisture in the summer, a warm flat bowl of land backed with mountains, a place of rampant and productive growth once the soil is enriched with compost and seaweed.

The location does have drawbacks. The chill of winter can be piercing here, for cold air flows down from the mountains at night, settles low and damp in the garden, trapped by the forest all around. Even on clear winter evenings, a bank of mist flowing over the mountains is a common sight, cold air streaming down to

Nursery bed.

hover low in the garden where ground frosts can be sharp and boardwalks icy, even in March.

Drainage also can be a problem. In the lower section of the garden the sub-surface of clay peters out and the soil does not drain well even when ditched. Sedges thrive in the boggy soil, and skunk cabbages flourish. Here are signs that an early garden was attempted and later abandoned. A collapsing trellis, overgrown ditches, long-forgotten bits of fencing and pathway show up if you peer through the salmonberries and young trees encroaching on this old part of the clearing, now disappearing from sight.

To this day, the shape of the garden reflects its time as a productive business. Near the house, a small raised bed, now a mass of buttercups, was the nursery bed. Here delicate young plants were nurtured until they could be planted out. In the open areas at the back of the garden, outlines of the original large flower beds still appear; here bloomed the carefully labelled dahlias and gladioli and lilies and irises and peonies that would later be dug up and divided, packaged and sold. Scattered in the sheds around the property, many of the old labels appear. On them are printed some of the varieties of dahlias that bloomed in these beds, a recitation of colourful names: Avalon, Jersey's Beauty, Jersey's Beacon, Jane Cowl, Crimson Beauty, Truly Fair, Black Narcissus, Salmon Queen, Pompeii, Landmark, Coral Seas, Friendship, Eighth Wonder, Tartar Prince, Climax, Croydon Robin, Beefeater, American Beauty, President Kennedy.

Dahlias always figured largely in Cougar Annie's production, and over the years at Boat Basin she became best known as a dahlia grower. Some of her stock originally came from Holland, some from Canadian growers. She grew nearly two hundred different varieties of dahlias in the heyday of the garden. Visitors recall with awe the teetering stacks of wooden boxes dimly visible in the dusty storage area at the back of the house. In these boxes the dahlias were layered in newspaper and stored away for winter, each box bearing a different label and containing a different variety of dahlia. Only Cougar Annie understood her way through this maze of dahlia boxes, and she would sit at her table for hours with a sharp steel knife in her hand, paring the tubers into small pieces and sorting them, sit surrounded by piles of dried sphagnum moss in which she wrapped the dahlias before packing them up for shipment. Meticulously packaged in cardboard shaped and formed into boxes, carefully tied with string, and franked with the Boat Basin postmark, hundreds of parcels of dahlias went off in the mail.

Tommy Rae-Arthur, in a letter to a friend in 1970, hints at the hours of labour involved: "Mother is keeping fairly well and working hard at the order packing its always a big job as she gets too many orders so it will take until springtime to get through with it all." At the time of this letter, Cougar Annie was eighty-two years old and not about to relinquish control of her dahlia business. Her dahlias travelled far and they are blooming still, most famously in her daughter Margaret's prize-winning garden in Campbell River, but also in Vancouver, in Victoria, in Terrace, in small towns across the Prairies and in Ontario.

Countless orders for dahlias and for other bulbs and plants remain in Cougar Annie's house. Neatly slit open, stacks of envelopes from all over Canada contain handwritten letters and orders from people who had seen the advertisements or

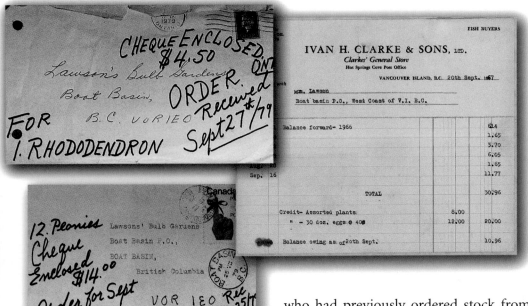

who had previously ordered stock from the garden. Once opened and read, the letters were carefully replaced in the envelopes which were then neatly labelled in large black printing: "12 Peonies, Cheque Enclosed"; "1 Rhododendron, cheque enclosed"; "1 Garden Surprise Package Special." A profusion of these tidily preserved orders have burst from the old, frayed elastic bands and now litter the floor, their dates all confused.

A three-cent stamp bearing the image of King George appears on the faded envelope of a letter from Port Alberni dated April 6, 1939: "Dear Sir: Have received your list of roses and ornamental shrubs, fruit trees etc. I would like you to send me a complete list of your stock prices and names of same and I would like to take up the agency for you if you care for me to do so . . . you could send me some order pads if you have them, hoping for a favourable reply." This hopeful soul also adds a P.S. "Could you tell me what the boat rate is from Port Alberni to your place?" Whether or not this would-be agent ever received a reply is doubtful. Cougar Annie wanted customers, not agents looking for a share of her minimal profits.

The correspondence from customers often contains a personal note of thanks for previous orders which arrived safely. A letter from Nova Scotia, dated 1979, is typical of many. "Your kind letter offering me the peonies at last year's price because you could not supply owing to the postal difficulties... is so generous and no doubt it has been extended to many customers; we hope very sincerely that you do not go bankrupt! It is my hope that this year the twelve different varieties of peonies will arrive in September and get safely bedded down. The daylilies I got from you years ago are a glory in the garden." Another note, dated 1976, comes from a happy customer in Devon, Alberta, and refers to an ad that appeared in the *Report on Farming*, asks for price lists, and concludes, "Hoping to hear from you as the begonias I had previous got were extra nice."

By the 1970s, Tommy Rae-Arthur was doing the lion's share of the correspondence for the nursery business. His mother was by then going blind. She could still pare dahlia tubers, her large rough hands —so strong and big everyone noticed them—feeling gently around the tubers for the eyes; she could even manage to parcel her wares in the accustomed manner; but she could not easily write letters. Tommy took infinite care to deal with customers fairly, often giving long and detailed explanations for any problems that arose. A customer in Rochester, Alberta, received the following epistle in 1978: "When we received your order in July, we had a long very dry and hot summer and found we had to pack so much water up from a creek for the garden so that sure kept us busy. Thanking you for your kind order and the money for it, so we'll not be sending your parcels till next spring. Very glad to hear the day lilies grew very nicely."

Some customers were not readily appeased, like this one in Vancouver dissatisfied with an order received in 1978 and asking for "*live fresh* sphagnum moss. That is if you can. I don't want that dead dry stuff.... I want the real live green sphagnum moss." Another disgruntled customer who did not receive her peonies with the rest of her order writes: "I'd sure appreciate some sort of settlement, after all I trusted your company for nearly a year.... Trusting to hear from you real soon.... P.S. How about sending me a small garden surprise package for my inconvenience, after all you've used my $11 plus for a year." But customers generally had little cause to complain; they often received more in their orders than they asked for, especially customers living in British Columbia. Believing it was unfair that B.C. customers should pay the same postage as customers in far-off parts of Canada for a similar order, Cougar Annie would often slip in a few extra bulbs as a bonus.

Advertisements for the nursery stock altered as the years passed. By the late 1960s she had long ceased to sell fruit trees and berry bushes; she sold more manageable stock—tubers and perennial roots and bulbs—items much easier to pack and ship, also lighter in weight, an important consideration for anything travelling by airmail. Demands for other products continued, for ferns and mosses and rhododendrons and azaleas and peonies and shasta daisies, but the demand for dahlias continued to dominate business. This advertisement, one of the latest ever issued, dates from 1980: "Choice Dahlias, 35 different $5.75, 50 different $7.50, 100 different $12.50." The ad goes on to list the prices of gladioli, peonies, daylilies—twelve different kinds for $5.50—lythrum, irises, azaleas, rhododendrons, heathers.

Toward the end of her days at Boat Basin, the dahlia trade was becoming a bit of a muddle; Cougar Annie had difficulty keeping the tubers all sorted into their proper boxes. The conclusion was simple: advertise and sell them as they were, all mixed up. The tone of the sales pitch changed accordingly: "At Boat Basin Farm," declared an advertisement in 1980, "the harvesting process, over fifty years, has resulted in mixed planting beds and thus the crop is sold on an assorted basis."

Even when she could scarcely see and rarely left the house, Cougar Annie continued to scheme up ways to keep selling nursery stock from her garden, and she continued to stay in touch with other growers. Visitors to Boat Basin frequently found themselves helping out: transplanting strawberries, digging up dahlias for the winter, answering letters. But by the early 1980s, after nearly sixty years, the nursery trade was grinding slowly to a halt.

Heaps of wooden boxes, handmade from split cedar shakes, remain in the back storage room of Cougar Annie's collapsing house; the dahlia paring knife, sharpened to a mere stub after cutting so many thousands of dahlias, lies rusty and disused beside the door. But no dahlias now grow at Boat Basin, nor peonies, nor gladioli. Other more robust species, grown also for the nursery trade, have survived healthily: many types of irises and daylilies and other perennials, while the rhododendrons and azaleas and countless flowering shrubs not only bloom, they go from strength to strength. The survivors in this garden are many.

In 1923 when Willie Rae-Arthur and Ada Annie built their new house in the centre of their garden, Willie proudly described it as a "substantial four room lumber house with attic and spacious front and back verandahs." But any extra space this new house afforded the family was soon claimed by various enterprises. The front porch filled with feed sacks and pelts and traps and grain bins, while plants and dahlias soon overtook any free space out the back. And one of the four rooms in the house soon became the Boat Basin Store, later incorporating the Boat Basin Post Office.

Decade after decade this odd little store lured people to the house, offering for sale bars of chocolate and tobacco and crackers and tinned food. Most of the customers were Hesquiat people: during the first twenty years or so there were probably some sixty people living around the harbour—sometimes more, sometimes less—and they occasionally dropped into the store to spend a bit of money. They did not have much to spend, so the revenue from the store was never great, but simply having the store gave Cougar Annie's place a certain status: it brought people to her house, it provided an outlet to sell her own garden produce, and it enabled her to purchase wholesale goods for the store and for her own use. Never one to resist a bargain, Cougar Annie was no doubt attracted to wholesale shopping.

Here at the store, Cougar Annie sold eggs from her multitude of chickens. Her egg-selling practices became famous, for she tended to keep the fresh eggs hidden behind the counter and selected much older ones—sometimes very old

The house, store and post office in 1979.

85

indeed—for her customers. She became renowned for selling bad eggs, not only to customers coming into the store, but up and down the coast. Whenever she could, she sent eggs on the *Princess Maquinna* to communities on the coast. Ann Hill in Zeballos remembers buying Mrs. Rae-Arthur's eggs when they arrived on the boat, but after a while she had to find another source; all too often the Boat Basin eggs were bad. Customers accepted this dubious egg trade good-naturedly; it was all part of the entertainment of visiting Cougar Annie. Bob Foster, who fished on the coast for many years and who knew the Rae-Arthur boys well,

Garden entrance, 1973, vegetable beds on the right.

remembers seeing eggs piled up everywhere in the store. He avoided buying them, but with no ill-will. "You just never knew if those eggs were five or twenty years old." Cougar Annie herself knew perfectly well how old the eggs were. Lined up in buckets behind the counter they were organised according to when they had been collected. Often a bit dirty, or with the occasional feather stuck to them, these eggs were unquestionably organic, and some customers rated them highly. "The best eggs in the world!" enthused a young woman who visited regularly from Tofino in the 1970s.

To keep the egg supply coming, Cougar Annie poured a succulent brew onto the laying mash she fed her chickens, a brew emerging from the large pot bubbling constantly on the back of the woodstove. Anything and everything went into the pot: dead birds, dead mice, skinned carcasses, any scraps or leftovers. All were popped into the pot and boiled. The stench was memorable, but the liquid poured onto the laying mash must have been potent because the chickens at Boat Basin were remarkably productive.

Also famously productive was the vegetable garden, and its steady supply of produce attracted customers to Cougar Annie's store. Many Hesquiat families living around the harbour relied on Cougar Annie for vegetables during the summer and autumn, sometimes bringing other goods in exchange, sometimes buying special treats at her store while there. Ruth Tom, who grew up at Hesquiat, recalls her father buying vegetables regularly, and eggs by the bucketful—once dropping a whole bucket, fifty cents' worth—on the rocky beach, and she

remembers the large vegetable garden that produced so much more than the Rae-Arthurs themselves could use.

Little enough now remains of the store in the wreckage of Cougar Annie's house, yet the small shabby room at the front of the house still manages to look like an eccentric rural store, even in its ruined state. The door, always bolted from the inside, is now jammed shut, and the old wooden fishnet float marked "Bell Pull" has fallen to the floor, no longer attached to the rope leading to a bell that would ring inside the house when customers wanted attention. Inside, tattered

posters, colourless with age, advertise gladioli bulbs and tulips. Yellowed notices, stuck with rusty thumbtacks, cover the walls and in one corner calendars are still pinned up, one on top of the other, six years deep. The most recent, from 1982, shows a basketful of puppies beaming cheerfully at the decayed disorder of the place. The counter stretching across the room guards the dark shelves lining the back wall, shelves still displaying a mess of unsold merchandise. Soggy bags of rice and flour that have long ago burst open, packages of salt, rusty tins of food with no labels, egg cartons, a few stacks of paper bags, a clutter of old damp papers. A door leads from the back of this room into Cougar Annie's living quarters; from here she would emerge to wait on her customers, sizing them up in her usual canny way, charging whatever price she fancied on that particular day.

The service in the store was always idiosyncratic, and prices tended to reflect Cougar Annie's whims and prejudices. Jim Haggarty recalls visiting the store to buy a few items and to get his mail when he was working on archaeological digs in Hesquiat Harbour in the 1970s. Once he showed up with the assistant lighthouse keeper from Estevan Point, and also with a native Hesquiat man. Eyeing them all suspiciously, Cougar Annie first allowed the lightkeeper to have his mail, then handed Jim Haggarty his, and finally served the man from Hesquiat. They then all made their purchases in the store and went on their way. Comparing notes later they discovered Cougar Annie had charged each of them different amounts of money for exactly the same items: she charged the man from Estevan least, the native Hesquiat most, and Jim Haggarty a price in the middle.

Cougar Annie was frequently suspicious of the native people of Hesquiat Harbour, even though she needed them, both as customers and as neighbours. She seemed to expect the worst—that fruit would be taken from the trees, that goods would be stolen from the store, that everyone was after her money. On more than one occasion she wrongly accused people of stealing. She also scorned, and probably feared, customers who drank too much and who would sometimes show up drunk at the store. Yet, paradoxically, she also catered to the drinkers, even while protesting their ways.

Both vanilla and lemon extract stood behind the counter. Each of these has a high alcohol content and can be consumed by people desperate for strong drink. Because they are considered foodstuffs they can be sold anywhere. By carrying these extracts, Cougar Annie must have known she was inviting trouble. Her daughter Rose recalls the sale of the extracts as a longstanding problem; once when only ten years old she was left in charge of the store and several would-be customers came in looking for vanilla and lemon extract. "They started roughing me up and I let out a big scream so they left me alone. It was a little scary."

Despite such incidents, Cougar Annie still sold the stuff, all the while protesting the bad ways of those who bought it. In his memoirs, Robert Culver recalls Cougar Annie saying "she had to be careful not to sell the Indians anything such as vanilla extract with alcohol in it, as they would buy that just to get drunk." His daughter Nairne Carter, who stayed at Boat Basin in 1955 as a young girl, recalls that "Mrs. Arnold didn't like it when they wanted to buy vanilla or lemon extract, because she knew they were going to drink it." But even though she voiced such sentiments, Cougar Annie continued to stock vanilla and lemon extract, sure of a ready sale, fully prepared to take money from people desperate for a drink, fully prepared also to blame them for the problem. Perhaps she considered her own role above reproach; many would not. Even in the 1970s, she kept the store stocked with these extracts. Visitors to Boat Basin recall seeing the wooden boxes with "Vanilla Extract" printed on the outside, and wondering why the store needed so much of it.

During her childhood days in the 1920s and early 1930s, Isobel remembers customers coming regularly into her mother's store. The traffic was limited but steady, including Hesquiat people, fishermen, and occasionally even the police and missionaries who regularly plied the coast in their boats. As time passed, trade slowed considerably. Don Culver recalls very few customers coming to the store during the months he spent there in 1955 when he was a boy. "Most days no one would come in—maybe just one or two a week," he says. "And we were sure pleased to see them." His sister Nairne concurs. Only nine years old during their months at Boat Basin she was always longing for company. "I was so happy when someone came to the store. Just the excitement of seeing somebody else was great."

Until the 1950s, goods came up the coast on the *Maquinna* from orders placed with wholesalers in Victoria. Amid the debris on the shelves at the back of the room are a number of carefully preserved order forms from the 1940s, orders Cougar Annie placed with Macdonald's Consolidated Wholesale Grocers in Victoria. Commonly included items on these orders are sardines, raisins, jam or marmalade, chocolate bars, cigarettes and tobacco, canned meat, matches, canned milk, ketchup, lard, peanut butter, tea, golden syrup, prunes, butter, yeast, sugar, cookies, hard tack biscuits, chewing gum. Occasionally suppliers substituted something new to be tried out at Boat Basin Store: one dozen cans of something called "Boiled Dinner" arrived on the ship in June 1946, along with an unusual order for six jars of sweet pickles. Pond's Vanishing Cream and Alka Seltzer occasionally appear on orders, along with Vaseline Hair Tonic, Eno's Fruit Salts and, as a rare treat, a limited order for toilet paper: "3 Rolls Only" sternly declares an order from 1945.

Cougar Annie used different suppliers from time to time, such as Scott and Peden in Victoria. Usually they only provided livestock feed, but sometimes groceries appear on their order forms—specifically bread, bologna and flour. All of the suppliers' order forms are carefully typed out, each cent accounted for, all substitutes or alterations duly noted in pencil, and the bill adjusted accordingly. Dealing with these regular suppliers must have been laborious, even rather dull for Cougar Annie. They played by the rules, requiring regular payment of bills, and during the war years they kept a strict eye on orders for butter and sugar, refusing to fill orders unless they received correct numbers of ration coupons and once returning nineteen butter coupons to Cougar Annie with a stiff note saying the dates were not valid. These suppliers could not be easily cajoled; they were not likely candidates for Cougar Annie's sometimes highly inventive methods of paying her bills.

Cougar Annie's store, her nursery business and later her post office all shared one obvious need. For these enterprises even to exist, let alone thrive, there had to be regular shipments of goods in and out of the harbour. Without the *Princess Maquinna,* Cougar Annie would have been at a complete loss. Between 1913 and 1952 the ship faithfully arrived every ten days in Hesquiat Harbour, bearing the mail, any goods she had ordered for her store or her nursery garden, and other necessities. The boat would anchor at Hesquiat Village and all the freight for Boat Basin would be unloaded into a canoe. A *Maquinna* manifest dated April 14, 1944 lists all the goods heading to Mrs. A.A. Campbell. Her order consisted of 16 sacks

No. 2 Wheat, 1 sack Oats, 1 Box Bread, 1 Box Groceries. Nothing special went to Boat Basin that day. But sometimes goats and chickens and geese and rabbits and hatching eggs arrived, not to mention young saplings and shrubs and large crates of bulbs and rolls of chicken wire and sacks of nails. The loading into canoes and rowboats, the unloading onto the beach, the endless packing of materials up to the house was merciless, backbreaking work, but at least everything arrived regularly and predictably, thanks to the *Maquinna*. The timing was sometimes awkward, especially if the ship arrived in the middle of the night. Many are the stories of having to paddle out to meet the boat in the pitch dark over rough, uncertain seas, of then loading goods into an unstable canoe or rowboat, always in fear of being swamped. Because there was no dock at Hesquiat, the loading and unloading was a risky operation, and if the seas were truly dreadful the ship sometimes could not anchor at all and simply continued up the coast.

Most who remember the *Princess Maquinna* speak of her fondly. She did the rounds between Victoria and Port Alice, carrying up to 150 passengers, some of them "round trippers," most of them heading for any one of countless small settlements, logging camps, Indian villages or canneries up the coast. She stopped at Port Renfrew and Bamfield, at canneries and logging camps on Barkley Sound, at Port Alberni, Ucluelet, Tofino, Clayoquot, Kakawis and Ahousat, then at Hot Springs Cove and an hour or so after that she would drop anchor at Hesquiat Village.

The Rae-Arthur children often rowed valiantly the six miles to Hesquiat from Boat Basin to pick up and to deliver the mail, to ship parcels, to sell flowers and fruit and eggs, just to see the life and action that the *Maquinna* brought into the harbour. On one memorable occasion, Cougar Annie somehow convinced the captain of the *Maquinna* to cross the shallow waters of Hesquiat bar and come the full length of the harbour, anchoring in Boat Basin. The Rae-Arthurs were invited on board for breakfast. "And wouldn't you know it," Rose remembers disgustedly, "they served porridge."

After visiting Hesquiat the *Maquinna* carried on up the coast, delivering freight and groceries and mail, delivering her passengers and picking up cargo at various bustling coastal settlements: Nootka Cannery, Friendly Cove, Tahsis, Ceepeecee, Esperanza and Zeballos. "And when the boat came into town," Ann Hill remembers, looking back to her days in Zeballos, "Everyone would go down to the store to get their mail, and sometimes we went on board for tea." The *Maquinna* carried a good deal more than mail and necessities to communities like Zeballos, for when the boat came in, the liquor also arrived, and the same was true of drugs. Hospitals relied on this supply line for their own requirements, and so did anyone receiving drugs illicitly. "Oh yes, the guys on drugs would be happy to see the boat," says Ann Hill. Had Willie Rae-Arthur wished, he could probably have smuggled opium up on the *Maquinna,* or strong drink. Perhaps he did, although his daughter Rose is adamant that no liquor or drugs appeared in their house, ever.

After leaving Zeballos, the *Maquinna* went up to Chamiss Bay to unload supplies for Kyoquot, then around Cape Cook into Quatsino Sound, and on to Winter Harbour and Quatsino Village. The final stop was at Port Alice, spending up to a day loading pulp at the mill, and then heading back down the coast, stopping at many of the same places again, loading gold bricks at Zeballos during the days of the productive gold mine, delivering the constantly roving missionaries to their missions, transporting the prospectors and miners and loggers and fish plant workers, taking the native children away from their homes to attend school.

On any given trip up or down the coast for over forty years, the *Maquinna* bore witness to countless coastal dramas: mothers left behind, crying as their children went off to school, sick people and pregnant women being taken out to hospital, policemen and school inspectors and Indian agents doing their often unwelcome work. Once on board the *Maquinna* many distractions were available. White cloths graced the dining room tables, and afternoon tea and midnight supper were served free to all passengers. Entertainments included music and cards and dancing, and out on the deck, weather permitting, passengers could play deck games. At every stop, depending on the docking facility and the

Princess Maquinna.

weather, a gangplank went down, and friends and visitors who came on board could stay until five minutes before sailing time, taking the opportunity to visit the concession stand to buy comics and candy. At Hesquiat, where no dock existed, passengers had to climb on board from canoes or small boats by means of a rope ladder, a most hazardous experience in rough weather.

After the *Maquinna* stopped her regular run up the coast in 1952, other ships delivered goods to Hesquiat, but none was ever as regular or reliable or well loved as the *Maquinna*. Cougar Annie continued to receive supplies from ships travelling up the coast, but as time passed she came to rely heavily on her son Frank, who would frequently bring his fishboat, the *Allendyne S.*, up to Boat Basin with supplies. Cougar Annie also began to place some of her grocery and feed orders through Ivan Clarke's general store at Hot Springs Cove. She had known Clarke for years and his whole family was familiar with her ways of wheeling and dealing. Ivan Clarke would fill her grocery orders and she would often pay, at least in part, with eggs or plants. She kept sacks of feed stored in a shed at Hot Springs Cove; the challenge was then to arrange delivery to Boat Basin. Art Clarke, one of Ivan's sons, recalls, "She'd sometimes talk some of the Indians into taking it up to her and she'd maybe give them ten dollars and some cougar meat and eggs."

All who remember doing business with Cougar Annie agree that she did not like parting with her money. Ivan Clarke's son Hughie recalls the merry chase she sometimes led him on the occasions when he arrived up at the garden with her order and wanted payment. "I'd go to the house to get paid and she just wouldn't be there. She knew I was there but she'd take off. Sometimes she'd even stay in the house and she just wouldn't come to the door, no way. She did that with lots of people—if anybody wanted to get paid for something she'd be hiding."

"She was a businesswoman," her daughter Isobel says. "She liked life on the farm, loved growing things, she was good at keeping the place going. And she sure kept a close eye on everything." Isobel recalls stealing a package of crackers and running off into the bush to eat them when she was very young. She was scared; she knew better than to be caught by her mother who, if she noticed the crackers were gone, would have probably taken the strap to her.

Being a good businesswoman and keeping the place going meant, for Cougar Annie, taking no nonsense from anyone, never giving an inch, always being alert to the smallest opportunity or advantage, and playing many a wily game. Being in charge of this working garden meant labouring every day, dawn till dusk, making her own chances, following her own rules and thinking first and foremost of herself and her garden. Indulging other peoples' whims was inconceivable, giving in to their demands or tolerating their weaknesses, unthinkable.

CHAPTER 7

Boat Basin Post Office

THE ROOM THAT housed the Boat Basin Post Office and store is small—no more than ten feet by twelve. A wooden counter stretches across it, with a hinged flap allowing those behind the counter access to the front door, to unbolt it for customers when they had rung the bell. Notice boards on each side of the door are papered with postal circulars and announcements, now grey and soggy with age.

To enter the post office, customers walked up the long boardwalk in front of the house, opened the screen door and crossed the porch, picking their way past grain bins and sacks of feed, a chair or two, a bench, a few hanging pelts and a jumble of tools and jars before reaching the blue door of the post office. Once inside there was more blue paint, on the counter, the walls, the shelves, paint now stained and dirty and damply flaking away.

The door is jammed shut now, the porch unnavigable, lurching at a strange angle; the windows inside are thick with dirt and cobwebs, the contents of drawers and shelves strewn, messy and thick with mildew, all over the floor. Yet despite this disintegration, a self-serving bustle of postal industry is still incongruously in evidence at Boat Basin. A quick glance over the sagging shelves inside reveals that keeping the post office business in order was a job Tommy Rae-Arthur took to heart. His neat, bold printing is on bundle after bundle of now useless envelopes containing sheaves of post office documents and held together with rotted elastic bands. Large and important-looking labels on these bundles declare in indelible black ink "Keep in Post Office"; "Christmas Circulars"; "Money Order Forms." The drawer behind the counter, swollen with damp and permanently open, contains a rubble of old pens, lead stamps, Registered Delivery forms, balls of string, labels for dahlias and discoloured labels declaring "Perishable"; "Insured"; and "Fragile." On the counter a book of Post Office Regulations for 1938 emerges from a scattered stack of publications.

A sense of almost comic unreality dominates the history of this little post office. Because of this mighty mouse of an operation, Boat Basin is on the map. Quite literally. Even the most sketchy road maps of British Columbia, certainly until the mid-1980s, all show Boat Basin because a post office was here and because places with post offices are, not unreasonably, assumed to be of some size and significance.

Remote communities all over Canada vied to have post offices as their regions developed and became more populated. Not only because the post office brought people and some measure of activity to a location, not only because someone would be named postmaster and receive a monthly salary, but also because of status. Having a post office made a place much more important and made it, certainly in its own estimation, a place worthy of note, with people to match.

During its nearly fifty years of operation, singular and strange as it was, the Boat Basin Post Office ensured regular delivery and dispatch of mail in this area in a manner that was, broadly speaking, reliable. And such service in a remote area is of incalculable value. Arriving as he did at Hesquiat in 1875, Father Augustin Brabant knew no such luxury, and never dreamed it might be possible. In an article

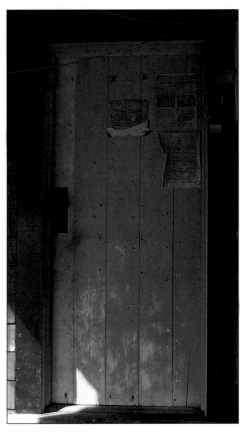

Door leading into Boat Basin Post Office.

written in 1893 he recalls: "There were times when I was five months without receiving news from civilisation. . . . Now the mail comes to within twenty-five miles of the mission. This arrangement was made by the Government to accommodate the crews of a large number of sealing schooners and fur-hunters." Brabant there refers to the delivery of mail to Clayoquot, a mere day's paddle down the exposed and dangerous coast.

His successor had it easier. From 1912 until 1917 Father Charles Moser maintained a post office at Hesquiat Village, and great was his pleasure in the role. He recalls in his memoirs first hearing of his good fortune:

March 23rd 1912: Word was received that Hesquiat would have its own Post Office and that it would open on April 1st. I was to be appointed Post Master. The "Tees" [a coastal steamer] *arrived with all the necessary supplies at the unearthly hour of 2AM, fortunately it was a calm night and it was possible to unload right in the Bay, but at this hour I had to crawl out of bed, go out by canoe to the ship, and take the Post Master's oath before Captain Gillam and went back to bed again a fully-fledged Post Master.*

When the post office started operating the following day, out of Father Moser's house, the first letter he franked with the new postmark was to his sister in Switzerland. Receiving parcels and letters from his distant family in Europe was a great comfort to Moser during his time at Hesquiat. His memoirs frequently give details of good Swiss cheeses safely received, postcards and newspapers from abroad, letters from his dear mother. Certainly this postmaster enjoyed the fruits of his postal labours, although he did perceive that the post office introduced a new form of consumerism that was a mixed blessing. Remarkably soon, shopping by mail order became part of village life. Moser writes of helping Hesquiat people to write out extravagant orders from the catalogues. "They spent their money as fast as they made it," he writes disapprovingly, "and sent huge orders."

In June 1917 when Moser was officially transferred by his bishop to Christie's School at Kakawis, the Hesquiat Post Office closed because, as the Post Office Inspector explained in a letter, "the Department would not sanction the office to be placed in charge of an Indian." Even if such sanction were granted, none of the Hesquiat people would have cared to operate the post office. Despite all the benefits of catalogue shopping, they had protested strongly to Moser about the post office being in the village, because the wireless operators at Estevan had previously paid a Hesquiat man ten dollars a month to get the mail from the steamer and bring it to Estevan. With the post office in the village, this substantial payment had stopped, and much annoyance and ill-feeling ensued.

The Hesquiat Post Office closed, to the great chagrin of the lightkeepers and wireless operators at nearby Estevan Point, for they had enjoyed having a postal outlet so close at hand. Within a month aggrieved letters of protest were in the hands of the Post Office Inspector at Victoria. Eventually a post office opened at

Estevan Point, and continued to operate there for many years, finally closing in 1970.

The post office at Hesquiat Village had little if any impact on the Rae-Arthurs at Boat Basin. By the time of its closure in 1917 they had barely arrived and were facing their hardest years. Later, when their little general store was up and running and when Ada Annie Rae-Arthur's mail order plant and bulb business began to grow, the lack of a local post office became more of a problem. While the children were with her, and while they would do as their mother bid, the awkward and laborious business of delivering carefully wrapped nursery stock and parcels of bulbs to the coastal steamer was a more or less workable arrangement, although extremely hard on the children, who had to row across the harbour to Hesquiat with the parcels to await the arrival of the steamer.

Getting the parcels out to the boat was just the beginning. Special arrangements then had to be made once the parcels of plants and bulbs reached Victoria. A letter surviving from 1930 indicates how cumbersome the arrangements could be. The letter, from postal headquarters in Victoria, is addressed to Mr. W. Rae-Arthur. "As requested in your letter of the 15th March, I have placed postage on two parcels sent by you to Penticton. Postage stamps to the value of 35 cents being balance due to you, are herewith." And at the edge of the letter, some long gummed-together stamps are stuck to the paper— Willie Rae-Arthur's change on an estimated prepayment for two parcels.

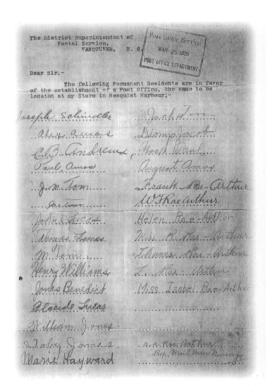

1935 petition for Boat Basin Post Office.

By 1935 Ada Annie Rae-Arthur had had enough of this nonsense. She decided to open a post office at Boat Basin. No amount of government red tape was going to stand in her way. She waded through all the necessary documentation, filled in all the necessary forms, and convinced the bureaucrats to give her application serious consideration. Her husband joined in, applying with her, and insisting furthermore that the steamer delivering the mail to their post office should come right into Boat Basin at least three times a month. Willie was apparently fed up with rowing six miles to the anchorage at Hesquiat to deliver and receive his mail.

Ada Annie Rae-Arthur submitted a petition along with her application to open a post office. She convinced or coerced every available resident in the area to sign a petition declaring that they as "permanent residents" were in favour of establishing a post office at her store. The petition is signed by thirty-six people: by the priest who was then at Hesquiat, Father Joseph Schindler, by many men of Hesquiat Village including Alex Amos, Jack Tom, William Jones, Placide Lucas, Mike Tom, C.B. Andrews, Sylvester Charleson, Jonas Benedict; by several women, including Mrs. Andy Thornberg who usually lived at Clayoquot; by all the Rae-Arthurs imaginable, several of whom were living away from Boat Basin by then. No expert analyst is required to see that several names, perhaps as many as ten, are all in remarkably similar handwriting; some unknown person appears to have signed on behalf of many others. The last signature, under the neatly printed "Miss Isobel Rae-Arthur" is that of A.A. Rae-Arthur herself, and after her signature she specifies "Prop. Mail Order Nursery."

Most annoyingly, the bureaucrats in charge were unmoved by this petition, and refused the application point blank. It was, after all, completely outrageous. There was nowhere near enough business to warrant opening a post office at Boat Basin, and the extra distance for the coastal steamer to travel into Boat Basin—twelve miles return from Hesquiat—would have been unprofitable and time consuming. As J.M. Murray, the District Superintendent, laboriously explains in his report to Ottawa:

> I visited this point on the 21st inst. and find that Rae-Arthur and his family are the only persons residing in the upper basin of Hesquiat Harbour. Evidently the petitioners, except Rae-Arthur, are Indians . . . and would not make use of the proposed office. . . . I might add for your information that Rae-Arthur is operating a shrub and bulb farm, and when shipping by mail, finds it inconvenient to make the trip to and from the steamer, the result of which in many cases is delay in delivery of his nursery stock. In the event of an office being established at this point there would be only the one family making use of it, and under the circumstances would not recommend that it be favourably considered.

To the rescue came George Hippolyte Ignace of Hesquiat Village. Thanks to his offer to transport the mail between Boat Basin and Hesquiat, Ada Annie Rae-Arthur's application was reconsidered. J.M. Murray sent another letter to Ottawa in February of 1936 stating that Mr. Ignace, already contracted to deliver mail between Estevan Point and the steamer at Hesquiat, had offered to "convey mails between the steamer and the proposed post office site three times per month for one year at the rate of $10.00 per month." On receipt of this letter, the Chief Superintendent of Postal Services in Ottawa grudgingly allowed the opening of a post office at Boat Basin in April of 1936, with Mrs. Rae-Arthur as postmistress. Her glee can only be imagined.

Almost immediately howls of protest arose around Hesquiat Peninsula. The postmaster at Estevan Point wrote a wounded letter to the authorities, pointing out that he wanted the residents of Hesquiat Village to buy their stamps from him, not from Mrs. Rae-Arthur. His letter concluded: "The new Post Office should be called Rae-Arthurs or Boat Basin and not Hesquiat. . . ." Father Joseph Schindler also wrote protestingly to the Superintendent of Postal Services in Vancouver, saying that, "Since the new Post Office in our vicinity has been opened there has been considerable confusion in the Hesquiat mail," and pointing out that all the mail for Hesquiat now went in a locked bag to Boat Basin, six miles distant. Having signed the Rae-Arthurs' original petition asking for the new post office at Boat Basin, he now attaches a new petition he has assembled naming nearly sixty Hesquiat people who are, he claims, joining him in his request that their mail not be sent to the new post office, after all.

The local MP, Mr. A.W. Neill, was soon drawn into this postal feud. He received an appeal from the Chief Superintendent of Postal Services in Ottawa, asking him to sort out this local fracas. Neill's reply, dated May 11, 1936 and on House of Commons letterhead, is remarkable for its tone of patient resignation.

The situation is not as bad as represented. I see among the names of those who signed this petition forwarded by the Reverend Joseph Schindler protesting against the present location of Hesquiat Post Office there are at least twenty-one names which appeared on Mrs. Rae-Arthur's petition, including that of Reverend Joseph Schindler himself. Their argument would be sound if the Indians always lived at the Hesquiat Village, but Mrs. Rae-Arthur in one of her letters states that the Indians spend much of their time in what she calls the Harbour, which is comparatively close to where they live, and that therefore it would be more convenient for them to get their mail at Rae-Arthur's place than to have to row back to the village to get it. . . . I would suggest that as the Post Office has been started it be left as at present. . . .

Ada Annie Rae-Arthur won the day. In early June, the name of the Rae-Arthurs' post office was officially changed and became Boat Basin Post Office. Father Schindler was pacified when a private bag containing his mail was guaranteed to be delivered to him directly, presumably by the ever helpful George Ignace, who was embarking on what would prove to be a long career carrying mail back and forth across the harbour to Boat Basin. Ada Annie Rae-Arthur could not have operated her post office at Boat Basin without him, and the two grew old keeping a wary eye on each other over the mail bags, both equally keen to keep the post office open and to benefit from any extra perks the job could offer. In a minor fashion, the post office at Boat Basin became a local gravy train, both for Ignace and the Rae-Arthurs.

From the Daily Colonist, June 28, 1968.

In 1968, George Ignace's work was featured in a full page article in the *Daily Colonist*. "Hesquiat Indian Band's Dedicated Mail Courier" is the headline, and the piece was written by Les Hammer, the Post Office Inspector for the region. Les Hammer fully understood the idiosyncracies of the Boat Basin Post Office, and he had a great liking for George Ignace and for Cougar Annie. His article, laced with superlatives, makes a hero of George.

> *George Ignace remains, still going strong after 34 years as mail courier. He no longer rows a dugout canoe, but runs a sturdy large workboat. . . .*
> *George and his trusty boat must travel several miles through towering waves into the comparative calmness of Boat Basin to exchange mails, receive groceries and other small freight and passengers. He then heads for Boat Basin Post Office, landing on the beach clad in hipwaders, carrying the mails a quarter of a mile through jungle-thick rain forest, over a hand-made split-cedar walkway high on stilts above the swampy forest floor. After delivering his important load to the 79-year-old postmistress, Mrs. Ada Lawson, he returns to the beach and heads towards the open sea. . . . Canada and particularly the rugged west coast are fortunate to have such dedicated men as George Ignace who devotedly carry on their daily dangerous tasks along the storm-wracked coastline, to see that the mails go through.*

Because it boasted a post office from 1936 onwards, Boat Basin was at last given its own entry in the B.C. Directories. These Directories, assembled by a variety of different companies from the 1890s onwards, provided useful inventories of the population of towns and cities in British Columbia. People are listed by name, occupation and address. In larger towns and cities this information was gathered by canvassers, door to door. In remote communities like Boat Basin, reliable residents of the area provided this information—the postmaster, for example.

If the entries for Boat Basin are typical, the Directories are strikingly unreliable. Out in the bush, well beyond official scrutiny, it was easy to fudge the numbers; to overlook countless people or to include many extras just to make the place look more important. If the entries for Boat Basin are to be believed, for decades this dot on the coastal map was home to at least sixty or seventy people, a population the place has certainly never seen.

Until the post office was established at Boat Basin, local honour in the directories went to Hesquiat, which had its own listing as early as 1897 in *Henderson's B.C. Gazetteer*. Then, only two people were listed as resident in Hesquiat, a place described as "A trading station on West Coast of Vancouver Island." These two were "Spring, Chas, general store; Antonio Luckovitz, manager." A classically misleading and misspelled directory entry, this omits all native Hesquiat people entirely, and credits Charles Spring with residing in Hesquiat, which he almost certainly did not. He was in charge of a fleet of sealing vessels operating out of Victoria, and while he established a trading post at Hesquiat, he did not live there.

In 1898, *Henderson's Gazetteer* amends the entry slightly and changes the spelling to "Hesquoit," this time listing the Rev. Father "Breabante" and "Antonio" Lukovich as the two residents, and describing the place as "A trading station on West Coast of Vancouver Island. 40 miles from Clayoquot. 165 miles from Victoria. Has Roman Catholic Mission and Indian school." This entry remained unchanged for many years following.

By 1914 the Directory entry for Hesquiat in what was by then the *Island Gazetteer* adds the triumphant detail that the village has a "Steamer bi-monthly." This Directory expands the population of the village to nine people, including everyone living at Estevan Light, a practice that would continue for several years. A few years later, in *Wrigley's B.C. Directory* for 1918, the description of Hesquiat is more ample, but the population has shrunk to two names: Charles Moser and W.F. Rae-Arthur are the only people credited with living in this place that is "a steamer landing and fishing village on West Coast Vancouver Island, in Alberni Provincial Electoral District, reached by CPR West Coast steamers from Victoria, distant 170 miles. There is a lighthouse at Estevan Point and a Dominion government telegraph office at Hesquiat. Address mail Hesquiat, via Ahousat post office." The ignominy was complete. Hesquiat had lost its post office the previous year and its importance in the Directory from now on greatly diminishes.

The Directory for 1937 sounds the first trumpet for Boat Basin. "Boat Basin: A Post Office and Indian fishing settlement 5m. from Hesquiat, the landing, on west coast of Vancouver Island. Pop. 60." Only five of the putative sixty residents are listed by name and four of the five are variant listings for the same person, one A.A. Rae-Arthur. She is listed separately with each of her jobs, which are described as Postmistress, Telegraphs, General Store and Nurseryman, and again as Postmistress, just in case the first entry went unnoticed. The fifth name on the list is F.S. Rae-Arthur, her son Frank, credited with "farming."

As the years pass in the Directory entries, Boat Basin's population expands, and Cougar Annie continues to be named several times in each listing. Whoever compiled the list cast their net wide, the Boat Basin entry often taking in the priest from Hesquiat, the lightkeepers from Estevan Point, a number of miners and prospectors who were passing through over the years, a few of the older Rae-Arthur children who were long gone, and many residents of Hesquiat. Well-known Hesquiat family names such as Amos and Lucas and Ignace and Charleson appear repeatedly to swell the list of Boat Basin residents, and the declared population stabilizes at a regular figure of

Relics of an earlier postal era.   seventy, reaching its peak in 1942 when a population of seventy-two is declared. Meanwhile the entry for Hesquiat fades into nothingness, year after year being described as "An Indian fishing village six miles from Boat Basin the Post Office."

Yet "Boat Basin the Post Office" was never more than the smallest of operations, serving only a handful of people. Its major customer was without any doubt Cougar Annie herself. The post office was central to her life: a great convenience, a source of income, an essential adjunct to her mail-order nursery business, crucial in enabling her to ship out her countless packages of bulbs and plants and to receive orders for more. As time passed, however, the balance between post office and nursery garden shifted. Cougar Annie realized the post office was far more important than her bulb business: it provided a more reliable source of income, it brought the occasional customers to her little store, and it enabled her to continue indulging in her favourite pastime of raising nursery stock without having to worry overmuch about the logistics involved. Because the post office paid her a monthly stipend, she was happy to keep the prices reasonable for her nursery stock, for what really mattered was that lots of parcels be mailed out, and that the post office do a reasonable amount of business in order to stay open.

The post office provided an undeniable source of entertainment. Not only because it was a small local power base and the scene of many comings and goings over the years, but also because of the very nature of the postal system. Seen from this remote location, the bu- reaucratic carryings-on and the self-important procedures of Canada's postal system were the source of many chuckles. Even now, the chilly, damp, almost pathetic ruins of the Boat Basin Post Office can give rise to laughter.

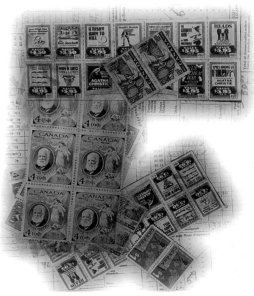

Nothing was ever thrown away here. Year after year, the meticulously bundled piles of communiqués, circulars, memos and directives grew. Postal regulations and circulars still spill from every shelf and drawer in the half-destroyed remains of the building. Such papers accounted for most of the incoming mail here, for nearly fifty years.

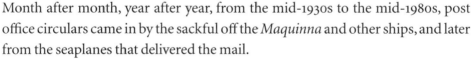

Month after month, year after year, from the mid-1930s to the mid-1980s, post office circulars came in by the sackful off the *Maquinna* and other ships, and later from the seaplanes that delivered the mail.

Although Tommy Rae-Arthur—and Cougar Annie before him— solemnly filed these postal circulars into neat bundles, it is impossible to imagine that he or anyone else would ever read them all. Their number is legion. Their neat, sol- dierly piles, covered now with mildew and white mould, nearly fill the room of the former post office. But these neat piles are misleading; their contents are all mixed up. Money order forms from the 1930s are mysteriously filed in brown manila envelopes along with circulars from 1973 reminding all post office employees of the new postal code system. Invitations to British Columbia postmasters for a conference in Vancouver in 1953 are filed with jolly Christmas posters from 1979 reminding staff to sort all seasonal mail into "Local" and "Out of Town" bundles. Excited publicity announcements dated 1939 proclaim the virtues of the recently introduced Air Mail Service across Canada, and these are bundled up with a letter from the Postal District Director dated 1970.

This letter from the Director soberly proposes that, to "insure continued mail service to Boat Basin Post Office," offers were being sought to establish an air service that would land in the harbour three times a week. During the 1970s the mail

was indeed flown, sometimes twice a week, into Boat Basin, because following the closure of the Estevan Point Post Office, Ottawa was trying to be helpful. Tommy Rae-Arthur received an extra allowance from the post office to walk down to the beach, launch his rowboat, and row out to the plane to collect the mail.

Stewardson logging camp also had a post office in the mid-1970s and sometimes the Boat Basin mail ended up eighteen kilometres down the logging road, at Stewardson. Because collecting it from there would have been very awkward for Tommy, some of the loggers would load the sacks—mostly containing post office circulars—and drop them off in a small shelter Tommy constructed, just outside the entrance to the garden. Unauthorized people are not officially allowed to handle mail, but Boat Basin Post Office operated according to its own rules, and delivery by logging truck seemed entirely reasonable. A log falling from a truck one day crushed the little postal shelter—a pity, because the system had worked quite nicely until then.

Over the years Boat Basin Post Office stayed stubbornly open. The memos and circulars and official literature continued to come thick and fast to the postmistress, Cougar Annie, and to her assistant Tommy, and the postal authorities seemed to turn a blind eye to the oddities of the place. Eventually, someone thought to ask about the age of the postmistress, and on July 23, 1970, when Cougar Annie was eighty-three years old, she received a letter thanking her for "many years of faithful and conscientious service you have given your patrons and the Department while you have been in office," and wishing her health and happiness in her retirement. Much to her chagrin, as she later explained to a newspaper reporter, "The government discovered I was eighty-three and they made me retire."

This did not mean Cougar Annie was giving up the reins. She named her heir apparent, and the Department answered graciously: "Thank you for your letter . . . advising that your son would be prepared to apply for the position of Postmaster at Boat Basin." In this way, Tommy Rae-Arthur became the new Postmaster in 1970 and it fell to him to cope with all the strange instructions from the Department. Like this handwritten memo from 1972: "At 9:15 PM you should clear all mail from your drop boxes, cancel the stamps, sort the mail, and then change the date in the steel dater to that of the next business day." Given that there were no drop boxes and usually no mail, these instructions make engaging reading. Tommy was also in charge when the new postal code came into effect in 1973, a change he accommodated graciously. But when—horror of horrors—the postal system "went metric" in the early 1980s, Tommy was most aggrieved. "He hated it," recalls Chris Marshall with a laugh. "He never even unpacked the new metric scales when they arrived. He would just weigh everything in pounds and ounces and put on the old postage."

As Cougar Annie grew old, and as the mail-order nursery business slackened, and because the population of Hesquiat Harbour had dwindled to almost nil, the always slim revenues of the Boat Basin Post Office became ever slimmer, and the whole operation seemed in peril. It could not be allowed to die because Cougar Annie and Tommy needed the income. In order to keep the post office open, friends and relatives were called into action to help bump up business. Their most important role was to buy stamps, lots of stamps, to give the appearance—at least on paper—of a busy and thriving post office. A visit to Boat Basin, by definition, came to include a moral obligation to buy stamps.

Cougar Annie even sold stamps by mail order when requested to do so. Several of her correspondents sent in orders for stamps regularly. A letter from her devoted admirer Robert Culver reminds her, "Don't forget to send me some more stamps. I've only two left when I stamp this letter." His son Don laughs, thinking of all the stamps his father must have bought from Ada Annie. "For years he was using stamps she sold him, great strips of old outdated stamps and his letters would be covered with them because their value wasn't up to date—he needed lots to post a letter."

The extra sales to friends and family helped, but could not completely remedy the situation. Balancing the post office books, while at the same time giving the impression of a thriving operation, required an ever-increasing amount of imagination and some highly creative accounting. For months on end the post office sometimes saw absolutely no normal business such as collecting money for money orders issued or selling stamps over the counter. No money came in, no sales were made. Nonetheless, month after month more stamps arrived from Ottawa, and they simply had to be sold to reduce month-end inventory. If there were no takers for the excess stamps, they were sold to Cougar Annie's nursery

Inside Boat Basin Post Office.

business, which was called in its latter years "Lawson's Bulb Gardens." An effectively cashless operation evolved, and the postmaster's salary was settled largely with stamps, the balance being paid with money orders made payable to Cougar Annie's bank account.

This arrangement often left Lawson's Bulb Garden with a vast number of stamps. Cougar Annie used them with flair, trying to pay as many of her bills as she could in postage stamps. She even managed to convince stores as large as Buckerfield's in Parksville that this was a reasonable form of payment, and Buckerfield's amiably went along with the plan for several years.

Tommy soldiered on as postmaster throughout the 1970s. He had the help of faithful friends, particularly Joe Balmer, then assistant lightkeeper at Estevan Point, who would hike over to help with the books, and Peter Buckland, who helped regularly on his visits from Vancouver. They would pore over rows of figures by kerosene lamp at the table in Cougar Annie's house, trying to make the books balance, trying to submit convincing accounts, to pay the postmaster, and to give the illusion of day-to-day activity in the post office. Peter Buckland also kept up the noble tradition of fudging the figures of the population of Boat Basin in the annual Directory listings. Every year a form would come to the post office asking for detailed information about who lived in the area, and, realizing that a population of "nil" would spell certain death to the post office, Peter genially included the names of everyone he knew who had so much as visited Boat Basin that year. In this way the names of archaeologists, loggers, hikers, yachters and many short-term visitors found their way into the Directory as Boat Basin residents.

Les Hammer, the Post Office Inspector responsible for the region including

Tommy Rae-Arthur, Boat Basin Postmaster, arriving with the mail, 1973.

Boat Basin, became all too familiar with the quirks of this extraordinary post office, and he was highly tolerant of them. He helped to sort out mistakes, accepted the sometimes impressive sales of stamps without question, and basically allowed the post office to continue as long as he could. He did not want to take Cougar Annie's post office from her, but its days were clearly numbered. Signs of organisational strain at the Boat Basin Post Office became hard to ignore.

In the early 1980s Les Hammer arrived more than once at the post office for an unheralded inspection only to find that the Postmaster had left the place either untended or in the care of unauthorized people. Chris Marshall remembers lying valiantly to cover for Tommy Rae-Arthur's absence when he was away for a length of time, although she is sure she did not fool Les Hammer for a moment. On another occasion Hammer arrived to find that an unauthorized outsider, Barry Lorton, had been co-opted into handling mail and doing post office business. There and then Les Hammer made it all legal and Barry Lorton, much to his astonishment, was sworn in as Assistant Postmaster at Boat Basin. Coming from a family in which his own father had laboured in the Royal Mail in Birmingham, England, for fifty years without coming near to the exalted post of Assistant Postmaster, Barry Lorton could not resist informing his family of his high postal rank, unmerited and unsalaried and short-lived though it was.

The days of the post office formally ended when Cougar Annie was taken out to hospital in 1983. She never returned. Tommy Rae-Arthur also left, and the place fell silent. Eventually two postal officials arrived to remove any valuable post office paraphernalia, leaving the rest to rot. They overlooked a large red and white sign declaring "Boat Basin Post Office", an imposing metal sign as large as those on post offices in major cities across Canada. It remains at Boat Basin, glossy and bright, an incongruous reminder of Cougar Annie's most ingenious operation.

CHAPTER 8

Staying Put

Aᶠᵗᵉʳ ᵃʳʳⁱᵛⁱⁿᵍ ᵃᵗ Boat Basin in 1915, Cougar Annie rarely left. She stayed her ground through thick and thin, paying no heed as others left the coast in droves. Not she. She would not willingly stir a foot from home. She did go out to Victoria once or twice in the late 1920s and—so the rumour goes—to Vancouver in the early 1930s. She did, once in a blue moon, see Tofino. But years could pass—as many as ten, even twenty at a stretch—without her leaving Boat Basin. Why should she? "The place was her life," one of her grandsons says. "She would have died without it."

Her children left willingly, even eagerly. They had had their fill of roughing it in the bush and working all the time for their mother. Their childhood had been harsh: often they had no shoes, no decent blankets, sometimes food was scarce, they worked constantly, they had little company. They fetched and carried mail and provisions from the *Maquinna*, they rowed out to sell produce and sometimes fish and clams to boats visiting the harbour, but their experience of the outside world was extremely limited. Their ways were strange to outsiders. One of the missionaries who travelled the coast remembers the children well: "Once the Rae-Arthur kids knew our boat was coming in they'd be down on the beach, but when we landed they'd all hide—we could see them behind the logs. They were wild little things, completely bushed. When they got older they got out of there as quick as they could."

This was particularly true of the girls. Not one of them stayed on the coast for any length of time; they got away and stayed away, and as the years passed only two of them remained in close contact with their mother. Living out at Boat Basin was harder on the girls than the boys, especially as they grew into teenagers. Fishermen on the coast recall them as beautiful girls, with lovely skin and hair, and "well-proportioned." Naturally they attracted attention, and stories about the Rae-Arthur girls ranged, often unfairly, up and down the coast. Like the story of one of them running away into the bush with a trapper and Cougar Annie sending a search party out to look for them, and the girl easily escaping into the bush, knowing the area so much better than anyone else. Or the story of one of the girls running away to Nanaimo, and Cougar Annie arranging for her to be taken in by some nuns, but the girl tied sheets together and climbed out of the window in the middle of the night and escaped. Or stories of how the girls rowed out to visit fishboats in the harbour, saying almost nothing, just climbing on board and smiling. Or stories about the "wildness" of the girls. Few of these stories are in any sense reliable, they only show why the girls would have wanted to get away from the limited, oppressive world of Boat Basin.

"We all just took off," says the youngest daughter, Helen. She was the last of the girls to leave, making her way to Victoria where she sought out John Hibberson and his family. He was the timber cruiser and keen naturalist who had often

George and Rose Rae-Arthur, late 1920s.

visited the Hesquiat area, the man who had found the dwarf pink trillium that grows beside Hesquiat Lake and brought it to the attention of botanists. Hibberson had often visited the Rae-Arthurs and had told his family how the children were frightened of visitors, running away and hiding when he entered the house. One morning in the late 1930s Hibberson opened the front door of his home in Victoria to find Helen Rae-Arthur on the doorstep, determined to stay in Victoria and never to return to the coast. He and his family found accommodation for her; they helped her to sign up for correspondence courses; they introduced her to new experiences like ice cream and streetcars. She never went back.

Isobel Rae-Arthur also left as soon as she could. As a young teenager she worked for a while at Hesquiat Village, helping Father Joseph Schindler's sister Victoria, who kept house for her brother. Then Isobel made her way to Ahousat, hiking part of the way along the telegraph line with her brother George, who was by that time working as a lineman, a job he held for many years. At Ahousat Isobel worked as the maid for the Gibson family in the big red house where everything was, to her unaccustomed eyes, very fancy—tables were set with proper place settings and she learned to serve from the right. While still in her teens she married Robert Balden, the Gibsons' bookkeeper. "I didn't see much of the family after I left home", she says. "But when my dad died I went back up there for his funeral." She was then twenty-one.

On a July day in 1936, Willie Rae-Arthur died. He was sixty-three years old. Willie drowned—his death certificate says accidentally—while out in his boat in the harbour. Helen and two of her brothers found his boat a short distance along the beach in the early evening. It had drifted ashore and Willie was nowhere to be seen. They secured the boat and went up to the house, anxious and apprehensive, to tell their mother. Darkness was falling when Cougar Annie came down to the beach to look for Willie. Helen recalls that her mother brought a lantern and that she stayed on the beach well into the night holding the light up, straining to see across the dark water, hoping, perhaps, that Willie would see the light and call for help. But the entire family sensed that Willie would not come to shore again. The next day his body was washed up.

A few days after Willie's death, Ian Macleod was one of several men who went to help remove Willie's body from the beach. The body was lying uncovered on some logs. Ian remembers that Cougar Annie either would not, or could not, provide a sheet or blanket to cover the body. The men carried it up to the house and then left the Rae-Arthurs to bury their dead. On July 17, 1936, Willie was buried in Cougar Annie's garden, near the back gate, not far from the graves of the three Rae-Arthur infants. His grave was heaped over with stones to keep animals away.

A smooth blanket of moss now covers the stones, and the grave is half-hidden in the rhododendrons. White heather grows beside the grave.

By the time of Willie Rae-Arthur's death, change was in the wind for people in Hesquiat Harbour. The native Hesquiats were on the move as never before, shifting from their main village to a new location down the coast in the protected waters of Hot Springs Cove. This move to new territory had been discussed for a long time; Hesquiat Village had known much restlessness. Father Moser's memoirs record dissatisfaction in the village as early as 1913: "in March some of the Indians got together and discussed the idea of moving to a new location. The women were very much against it. . . . It was only an idea and soon faded away." Yet in 1915 the debate resurfaced: "The Indians seemed very quarrelsome amongst themselves at this time, and some of them were still wanting to change their location."

The move to Hot Springs Cove took place gradually, led by the increasing number of Hesquiat people who owned motorized boats. Hesquiat Village is ideally located for coming and going in strong dugout canoes, for these could be safely beached and required no moorage. Larger fishing boats and motorboats could not be moored safely near the village, yet this did not deter people from wanting them. The missionaries at Hesquiat were adamant in their demands for a motorized boat. As early as 1906, Father Moser recalls petitioning for funds for a motor launch "which was fast becoming a necessity for a priest in Mission work." Later that year he obtained his desire, but the mission launch *Ave Maria* did not last long on the coast; it sank only five years later in bad weather.

At Hesquiat many costly losses occurred with motor boats. Writing in 1935, Father Joseph Schindler tersely notes that, "Today's storm wrecked two Hesquiat Indian launches here, the one belonging to Chief Benedict is a complete wreck." His predecessor at Hesquiat, Father Moser, repeatedly records his anxiety whenever a motor launch is moored at Hesquiat in rough weather. By degrees, therefore, as motorboats and fishing boats took over from the traditional dugout canoes, Hesquiat Village was virtually abandoned. By the late 1930s only about six families remained.

Across the harbour at Boat Basin, Willie's death had left Ada Annie Rae-Arthur in sole charge. By then her three elder daughters had left, as had her two elder sons. The younger children, Helen, Laurie and Tommy, were still at home. The older boys helped out when they were visiting, but even with their help the family could not keep up with all the work that had to be done. The newly established Boat Basin Post Office, in operation only since April, 1936, demanded a lot of attention, at least at first. Willie had died in the summer when the demands of the garden were at their peak. Harvesting and canning and pickling had to be done; there were goats and chickens and rabbits to tend; the nursery business and the general store required attention; there were traps to set and animals to skin, firewood to chop, and ceaseless other chores.

All of this work was going to be much more difficult for Cougar Annie with Willie gone. He had never been the most diligent of labourers, but he did tend to the house and washed dishes; he sometimes rowed out to Hesquiat to meet the *Maquinna*, built the occasional chicken coop, helped with the animals, wrote letters and tended to business correspondence. Who now could help her? As she explained to a *Vancouver Sun* reporter in 1974 "I didn't want to be left all alone up here, so when my husbands died, I remarried." Meeting a new man was highly unlikely, so she had to advertise.

The *Western Producer* and the *Winnipeg Free Press* were good newspapers to turn to. Both of these papers were Prairie-based, and there were many would-be farm hands on the Prairies. And these newspapers travelled far. "*Producer* Want Ads reach over 100,000 farm homes at a cost of 4 cents a word," declares the *Western Producer* in 1938. This was an impressive circulation, and certainly anyone interested in obtaining nursery stock or farm machinery would be bound to read this paper sooner or later. Similarly, anyone looking for work on a farm would leaf through the "Help Wanted" ads which week after week sought "Experienced Farm Hands for Season," or "Capable Girl for Farm Home," or "Experienced Housekeeper for Farm." Sometimes the ads were more personal: a widowed farmer looking for a housekeeper and/or a wife; an experienced girl (good gardener) who likes little children being sought by a young farmer; or this one, placed by a widow out in British Columbia: "BC Widow with Nursery and orchard wishes partner. Widower preferred. Object matrimony." Cougar Annie was heading into a new era.

Her advertisement attracted letters from several hopeful candidates. Two of them appear to have come up to stay at Boat Basin for a while. One Arnold Keatinge, described in the B.C. Directory as "labourer," was living there in 1938; in 1939 P.B. Smith, labourer, was in residence. By 1940 these names have gone and "Geo. Campbell" appears in the Directory, his occupation described as "general store and assistant Postmaster." George Campbell was to become Cougar Annie's second husband. He was a Scot, sixty years of age. Ada Annie was then fifty-one.

The marriage certificate declares the couple were married in the "Home of the Bride" at Boat Basin on March 18, 1940. Officiating at the ceremony was the United Church minister from Bamfield, who probably came up the coast on a mission boat for the auspicious event, perhaps even bringing the bridegroom with him. Coastal lore has it that George and Ada Annie were married on the very evening of the day he arrived, that they only knew each other through correspondence before they married. Chances are, however, that he was up there before the marriage, or his name would not appear in the 1940 directory, because information for the directories was assembled well in advance of publication.

George Campbell did not last long at Boat Basin. He died in 1944. The circumstances of his death are shrouded in speculation and gossip. He is the husband Cougar Annie is rumoured to have killed. He is also the husband who,

 some say, beat her and tried to terrorize her by saying he would kill her if she did not turn over all her money. Cougar Annie's explanations of Campbell's death varied. She claimed he was cleaning his gun when it went off accidentally; she also claimed he was threatening to kill her, and as he reached for the gun it went off by mistake. Other versions of Campbell's death abound, most of them identifying Cougar Annie, in highly dramatic language, as the one who pulled the trigger and left George Campbell to die. Yet there were no witnesses, there was no evidence, certainly no charges were laid. The doctor who signed the death certificate arrived at Boat Basin several hours after Campbell had died, and in describing the manner of the injury, wrote, "Gun hanging on wall accidentally discharged into left thigh, fractured left femur, massive blood loss." Officially, the case was closed. George Campbell was buried in Cougar Annie's garden on September 14, 1944.

George Campbell had lived at Boat Basin in interesting times. In 1942, the lighthouse at Estevan Point came to international attention as the word spread up and down the coast and all across Canada and into the States that the west coast of Vancouver Island had been shelled by a Japanese submarine. The Second World War came right into Hesquiat Harbour, bringing with it intense excitement and fear.

Robert Lally, the lightkeeper, recorded that he saw more than one hostile warship offshore, as well as the submarine, that night of June 21, 1942. A strange white light came from at least one of the vessels. Lally extinguished the Estevan light and watched in disbelief as salvoes of enemy fire came towards the point. Some twenty-five to thirty shells were fired, the noise terrifying as they exploded near the light or whistled overhead into the bush. Over at Hesquiat the shells were causing such pandemonium that it seemed like the end of the world. People were running out of their houses and heading out to sea in canoes and motorboats to be out of range of the shelling.

Eyewitness reports all agree about the shelling and about the white light, and for years afterwards shells were discovered on the beach. The coastal missionary Harold Peters recalls visiting Hesquiat soon after the attack and finding a shell that measured about sixteen inches by five inches. Over the years many more were found and in 1973, Linda Weeden, who was married to the lightkeeper at Estevan Point, found another shell, the last one to be reported.

Everyone in the vicinity developed a personal version of events. Dramatic stories proliferated. Cougar Annie in later years maintained that a shell from the submarine had hit the beach at Boat Basin, even though this would have been eleven miles off target, assuming that the shells were fired at the lighthouse. According to her son Tommy, Cougar Annie was probably the first to see the enemy submarine, because she claimed it surfaced inside Hesquiat Harbour before firing at the lighthouse.

At the time of the shelling, Tommy Rae-Arthur was working as a fireman on the lighthouse tender *Estevan,* which was anchored at Hesquiat unloading supplies to be taken along the five-mile-long wooden road to the lighthouse. In a letter to a friend, Tommy recalled the exciting events: "The news really was that my

Cougar Annie and George Campbell, early 1940s.

great old mother had seen a real submarine out in Hesquiat Harbour, when she had gone down to the beach, and so she had made a very special phone call on the old land line phone to Estevan Point to let them know." The *Estevan* had nearly finished unloading and, according to Tommy, the ship's captain got wind of this news about a submarine and "told me and all of the ship's whole crew that he was going to go full steam ahead, getting to hell out of Hesquiat." The same night, as they steamed out of harm's way, Tommy kept busy: "The Captain had told me to shovel in the coal and so to keep up the full steam ahead to get on to Tofino." The *Estevan* was well on its way when, in Tommy's words, "This crazy submarine came in and shelled the hell out of the Estevan Point lighthouse."

To the chagrin of local residents and eyewitnesses, their stories of the shelling have often been coolly received by outsiders. The official report of the shelling, submitted to Ottawa by the commanding officer on the Pacific Coast, Commodore J.R. Beech, declares, "It would appear from the reports that the excitement during the bombardment may have caused those present to see and hear things which did not actually occur," and dismisses the mysterious white light as that of a halibut fishboat. The report allows that one submarine alone carried out the attack.

The nature of the attack on Estevan continues to arouse argument. Even though a Japanese submarine commander eventually confessed that his submarine was responsible, his confession does not convince everyone, not least because the Japanese had little real motive to attack a remote lighthouse in Canada. Others believe that the submarine was a United States vessel, bombarding a Canadian site to ensure that Canada's commitment to the war was complete. In the wake of the bombing of Pearl Harbour, the United States may have wanted to boost the Allied war effort, and this attack on the West Coast came, significantly, in the middle of a political debate in Canada about introducing conscription. Following the attack, the pro-conscription lobby in Canada prevailed. And following the attack, according to Frank Rae-Arthur, "War bonds went on sale the next week, and sold out!"

None of Cougar Annie's sons faced conscription. Frank Rae-Arthur served in the "Gumboot Navy" that patrolled the coast, and continued to work as a fisherman out of Tofino. George was at Ahousat, doing his essential work in maintaining the overland telegraph line to Estevan Point. Tommy had suffered an accident as a young man while working on a boat, and his health was not reliable. And Laurie Rae-Arthur was too young, only seventeen when the war ended in 1945.

By 1945, the domestic scene in Cougar Annie's garden had changed yet again. The girls were all long gone, and only the youngest boy Laurie still lived at home.

Estevan Point Lighthouse.

Tommy came and went frequently, and the older sons, Frank and George, were regular visitors. George Campbell had died the year before, and now a new man was on the scene. Esau Arnold is listed in the 1945 Directory as "nurseryman" at Boat Basin.

Esau Arnold had been in touch with Cougar Annie in the late 1930s when he had seen her original advertisement for a partner. Apparently he replied straight-away, and the telegraph records show that she contacted him in September of 1939, a full two months before George Campbell appeared on the scene. He seemed a likely candidate but he became seriously ill and was hospitalized for some time. In the meanwhile, George Campbell appeared, found favour, and married Cougar Annie. Two months after George's death, his widow contacted Esau Arnold to renew their acquaintance and he came up to Boat Basin.

Coming from the small community of Birsay, Saskatchewan, Esau was one of several brothers, all farmers. A bachelor in his sixties, Esau took his family and neighbours entirely by surprise when he upped and left for the coast. "I remember he just left, and then we heard years later that he was married to a woman in some isolated place out on the West Coast," recalls John Kingerlee, who was raised in Birsay and remembers Esau Arnold from childhood. "He used to come and play cards with my parents, and he always cut my hair. I wouldn't say he was simple, not exactly, but he didn't have a lot of education."

Esau Arnold was at Boat Basin for two years before he and Cougar Annie married. Their wedding took place on January 11, 1947, coastal missionary Percy Wills coming in especially to perform the ceremony. Always described as "nurseryman" or "farmer" in the directories of the following years, Esau no doubt provided Cougar Annie with exactly what she needed: a great deal of help around the garden and an assistant who would do her bidding. "Those husbands of hers were basically just hired hands," her daughter Rose says dismissively. "I think she needed a brave to do the hard work," is Harold Peters' assessment of the situation.

Sorrow fell over Boat Basin later in 1947. On September 8th, Laurie Rae-Arthur drowned in Hesquiat Harbour in his boat. Bob Foster, one of Laurie's friends, tells of the death simply: "Laurie went out to get the mail and never came back." Laurie died in rough weather, perhaps having taken a wave over the stern of his small motorboat when he was out meeting the *Maquinna*, anchored just outside Hesquiat Bar. He was then nineteen years old, a bright good-looking young man who had been working on and off on a fishboat. Judging by the death certificate, Laurie's body was not discovered for some time; the burial took place at Boat Basin nearly a month after the death, on October 7, 1947.

A strange story circulates up and down the coast about Laurie's death, another story often repeated but not authenticated, of how Laurie was over at Hesquiat visiting a local girl, and one of the young village men was jealous. He pulled the drain plug from the bottom of Laurie's boat, causing it to sink when Laurie was heading back home across the harbour. Shortly afterwards, the young man was attacked and killed by a cougar, and the next time Cougar Annie killed a cougar, she slit open its stomach to find buttons from the young man's coat and traces of his clothing.

The three surviving Rae-Arthur boys remained on the West Coast. George continued to work as a lineman and telephone operator and lived at Ahousat. Frank lived in Tofino and fished up and down the coast, spending a lot of time at Boat Basin. Tommy, the youngest, held various jobs until he returned to live at Boat Basin in 1956. There he was fated to remain until his mother had to leave in 1983; only then was he able to get away and stay away. He certainly wanted to leave earlier, and sometimes he did manage absences of a couple of months, but Tommy was, towards the end, badly needed by his mother and largely controlled by her.

During the years of Cougar Annie's marriage to Esau Arnold, when she did have reliable help, her sons were reasonably free of her demands. But in December 1954, Esau injured his leg in some kind of accident, probably while chopping wood or felling a tree. Gangrene set in and he became seriously ill, also suffering what may have been a heart attack. Taken out to hospital in Tofino, he lingered for eight days, but he developed pneumonia and on January 18, 1955 he died. A few days later he was buried in the Tofino cemetery. He was seventy years old.

Not quite three months afterwards, on March 3, 1955, a familiar advertisement appeared in the *Western Producer*. "BC Widow with Nursery and orchard wishes partner. Widower around 60 with young children preferred. Object matrimony." This advertisement brought Robert Culver up to Boat Basin. A widower since 1949, Robert Culver was looking for a new start for himself and his three younger children. Originally a Prairie farmer, he was living in Salmon Arm and working

on a poultry farm when he saw the advertisement. He came to Boat Basin for a couple of months in the spring, on reconnaissance, liked what he saw and decided to try to make a go of it. He returned to Salmon Arm to fetch the three children, and together they all made the trip to Boat Basin—six days of travelling by train and ferry, bus and fishboat.

Stuart Culver is the eldest of the three who went with their father that summer. Just thirteen at the time, he recalls Mrs. Arnold saying that "boys who come to the West Coast don't usually want to leave—they fall in love with it." Stuart and his younger brother Don did love it, the summer was an extended adventure for them, marred only by the correspondence courses their father and Mrs. Arnold insisted they do.

The boys were kept busy in other ways during their months on the coast. They were chief goatherds, in charge of the flock of seven or eight goats, and every day their job was to take the animals down to the grassy foreshore at Yahksis to graze. Armed with pot lids to bang together to make a lot of clatter, they were responsible for keeping the cougars at bay. Any loud noise would do; they sang and shouted and banged for a couple of hours every day while the goats cheerfully grazed. Whenever possible, the boys were off, scrambling over the rocks on the beach, and making their way into Rae Basin. "We weren't supposed to go that far—Rae Basin was a place of deep mystery to us, so of course we went as often as we could," recalls Don.

Entering the garden, 1973.

Their young sister Nairne, who was nine years old, spent more of her time in the garden and in the house. While the boys slept in one of the outbuildings, she was privileged to share Mrs. Arnold's bed. "It was a wooden cot in a corner of the kitchen-living-room-bedroom, the main room in the house. I spent most of the time diving under the covers because I was scared of the bats flying through the house." Other fears troubled her; having heard of the cougars prowling about she would not go near the high fences around the garden, fences she remembers her father was always mending.

Robert Culver's memoirs also recall the fences and all the work they caused: "Ada's garden, as she called it, was . . . surrounded by a 5-foot woven wire fence which enclosed all her garden space, orchard, buildings and so forth. Outside was almost solid bush and forest. This fence needed constant repairing, due to animals trying to get in, ravages to the fence due to wet weather, rusting and so forth."

The gardens were a delight to Nairne. "I can still taste those transparent apples. Never in my life, never again, has an apple tasted so good. And there were flowers everywhere. I learned pretty fast not to step on the flowers when I was

roaming around, those flowers were important. And I sure remember all those dahlias and the endless digging." Mrs. Arnold was kind, but always busy, working every hour of daylight out in the garden, and keeping everyone else busy, giving the children jobs to do. Nairne's great delight was to leaf through the collection of old catalogues she discovered in one of the sheds; catalogues she recalls being over thirty years old, from the mid-1920s. She would spend hours looking at them, enthralled by the old-fashioned clothes.

"I remember Dad took us to the beach one day," Nairne recalls, "and we sat in an old boat and talked about what we should call this woman. Would she be Mrs. Arnold, or Aunt Ada, or Mum—and I can't remember what we decided but I know we talked about it. Ever since my mother died, my dad wanted a mother for us kids, especially for me, I guess because I was the youngest."

A kindly, soft-spoken man, always willing to help others, hard-working and highly inventive with machinery and tools, Robert Culver was devoted to his children. They remember him with the greatest affection and respect. The summer at Boat Basin was a valiant effort on his part to establish a new life for them all. "I think he was searching for companionship and a purpose in life," says Don Culver reflectively. "And a good place for us."

But by November of that year, the dream had died. Robert Culver felt he could not stay. Three medical emergencies had alarmed him during the summer and autumn: one after the other his children had to be taken out for medical treatment in Tofino. To stay seemed unworkable and Robert Culver reluctantly abandoned Boat Basin. He left the West Coast and turned his sights elsewhere, eventually settling up north, in Terrace. He never forgot Mrs. Arnold. In their later years, Robert Culver and Ada Annie Lawson were destined to spend long stretches of time together and he was to become her most devoted admirer. But in 1955 neither of them could foresee the future, and their goodbyes had a sense of finality.

Cougar Annie still needed someone at Boat Basin. By the late 1950s Tommy Rae-Arthur was living at home again, but there was more work than he could handle. "Oh, she had some boyfriends in between the husbands, I guess," her daughter Rose says. "She needed the help. But they didn't amount to much."

By 1960, George Lawson had arrived on the scene. A dry note from a lawyer in Victoria addressed to Mr. G. Lawson at Boat Basin, dated September 19, 1960, announces that his divorce decree is enclosed, adding, "You have to wait 45 days to get married but remember that if Mrs. Arnold has made a Will, this must be re-drawn after marriage...." They waited a bit longer than required, and on July 3, 1961, Ada Annie Arnold, aged 72, married George Lawson, aged 60. Once again the coastal missionary Percy Wills made a special trip to Boat Basin to perform the ceremony.

This was not a marriage made in heaven. Lawson reportedly drank, stole money from the store, and sometimes beat Cougar Annie. He appears to have been convinced that she was wealthy, and that she was determined not to let him have a penny. By 1967, or perhaps even earlier, Lawson left Boat Basin never to return. Rumour has it that his angry wife drove him off at gunpoint; also that she sent for the police to take him away. Whatever the circumstances of his departure, this was not a graceful leave-taking and Lawson left behind a much-relieved Cougar Annie. She did not have a good word to say of him, and she expressed grim satisfaction when she learned of his death in the early 1980s.

A letter Robert Culver wrote to Ada Annie Lawson in 1977 says, "It's a tough world for women. Providence seems to make them so they don't know the difference between a good man and a bad one before marriage. Too bad, but that is the way it seems to be." Robert Culver was a gentler and more idealistic soul than Ada Annie; he cherished high hopes concerning marriage and partnerships. Ada Annie appears to have been altogether more pragmatic about such matters.

One of the more striking moments in Frank Harper's play "Cougar Annie," performed in Tofino in 1996, comes when the elderly stage-version Cougar Annie is being quizzed about her husbands. "Well," she says, "there were two George-husbands, I know that, even though I get them mixed up in memory. Because my father was George too. And so was one of my sons a George. And we once had a duck named George. A big white drake with black eyes who used to eat slugs, used to search for them under logs. Smartest duck I ever lived with." As she drifts into George-the-duck memories, another character on stage intervenes.

"There was George Campbell and George Lawson. And Esau Arnold."

"Esau!", exclaims the stage Cougar Annie. "Yes, I remember him. Shot himself cleaning his gun. . . . Least I think it was Esau who shot himself. Maybe it was one of the Georges. Maybe it was George Campbell. Maybe Esau died of a heart attack. Could've been him. Or got pneumonia. . . . Or was *that* George Campbell? . . . . I remember for sure! George Lawson died from strangulation. . . . Either that or he was the one I ran off the place for trying to strangle *me*. One thing I know, they all read my advertisements. . . ."

In this play, Frank Harper makes abundantly clear that his stage version of Cougar Annie is having the last laugh. She is not about to explain herself or provide details, even if she can remember. Why should she? The evidence points to a pretty obvious conclusion, after all. In order to stay put at Boat Basin, she saw a need to marry, however difficult the marriages might have been. The marriages were not of primary importance. Staying put was.

Animal Tales

WHEN YOU SHOOT *a cougar, sight fast and aim for his chest. That way you hit the giant cat's heart. And that means you'll kill him dead. The woman who gave me this advice Friday offered it as she would a cookie recipe. Fortunately it is a recipe of sudden death she has used with fantastic success since the 1920s. Ada Arnold is 65-ish . . . She says she has killed 62 cougars and "about 80" black bears near her home on the west coast of Vancouver Island. She killed the first in the 1920s, the last in September. She still has the pelt of the last victim ready for shipping to the game warden's office. As cougar trouble-shooter for her area, Ada gets double the bounty for a kill. Once, in 1955, she killed 10 cats and earned $400.*

In the *Vancouver Sun* dated October 19, 1957 an article appears with the headline, "Woman Sniper Kills Cats." More than forty years after writing this article, Alex McGillivray still recalls both Cougar Annie and her garden. "It was pretty overgrown. The place looked like it had been an orchard. I remember she said she wanted someone to come and stay there to work the property, and an older gentleman was there who was a widower and had answered an ad she'd placed in the paper. But he wasn't too impressed with the place. I don't know if he stayed." In his article McGillivray wrote:

Nature has begun to reclaim parts of [the garden] *despite the 16 and 18 hour days Ada puts in milking goats, feeding rabbits and collecting eggs.*

*Ada Arnold admits Boat Basin is lonely now. Except for the cougars. Aren't
you afraid out here in this lonely home with only the whipping of the Pacific
and the silence of the forest for company? she was asked. The clear blue eyes
of this remarkable woman reflected surprise at the question. "I love to meet
a cougar if I have a gun," she said.*

When Alex McGillivray heard about Cougar Annie he was a staff reporter at the
Vancouver Sun. The ingredients of the story were irresistible. He knew that this
cougar bounty hunter, this woman alone in the bush, would have tales of adventure to delight readers' hearts. She did not disappoint him.

> *The last cougar that raided Mrs. Arnold's goat barn killed nine goats. Now
> he is dead. It took her three days to get the big, orange-coloured beast into a
> trap. One day, about seven weeks ago, she found the goats dead in the barn.
> There was a hole in the roof where the cougar and possibly a companion
> had jumped through. They had tried to drag a half-eaten goat back out but
> failed.*
>
> *Mrs. Arnold put large iron traps in the barn and near the fence that
> night. She put the skin and part of the half-eaten goat on the fence. Two
> nights later she caught her cougar. He was caught by two toes. He had
> thrashed and knocked the fence down. He saw Mrs. Arnold coming, turned
> to go but almost ran into a stump. "Then he turned and came for me. I
> sighted fast and shot. He staggered and fell eight feet from me. . . ."*
>
> *One night her husband cried out that a cougar had carried away a goat
> from the barn. "I got my flashlight and rifle and went after him. He had
> dragged that goat quite a way into the forest, heavy as it was. I saw him,
> though. He was hiding down near a stump atop the goat. He saw me, too,
> and was just ready to spring. His mouth was wide open. I don't usually
> shoot in the mouth, but I could see this would go down his throat. I shot
> quickly. He dropped on the spot and rolled back."*

Killing cougars was always, for Cougar Annie, a straightforward necessity to protect her livestock, but she was no doubt influenced by a strong financial incentive
as well. A bounty had been offered on cougars by the provincial government
since the 1870s, when a sum of ten dollars per animal was paid. Vilified as "nox-
ious predators" and greatly feared, particularly by farmers who were concerned
for their livestock, this bounty on cougars continued for nearly a hundred years.
In the 1920s the bounty was increased to forty dollars, and over the ensuing years

the sum fluctuated between ten dollars and thirty dollars. Apart from the bounty, each cougar killed represented a valuable skin to be sold to the raw fur dealers. For a hunter, these creatures were well worth the kill.

Tales of Ada Annie as a cougar hunter and markswoman are by any standard remarkable. Never mind the rest of her achievements, never mind the coastal gossip about husbands and family, never mind any other feature of her life—by her reputation as a cougar hunter this woman achieved near-mythic status. Cougar hunters always do; they stand head and shoulders over other hunters; their exploits seem particularly dangerous and thrilling. Once Ada Annie's fame as a cougar hunter began to spread, the name "Cougar Annie" came gradually into circulation. Some of her friends say she did not like the name; others believe it pleased her. Either way, it stuck, and with this title she joined the ranks of other famous cougar hunters of Vancouver Island: Cougar Smith of Black Creek, Cougar Joan of Metchosin, Cougar Brown of Port Alberni, Cougar Charlie of Cowichan Lake and others.

Cougar Annie's arsenal.

Ada Annie's methods of hunting did not follow the norm. Cougar hunters generally used highly trained dogs whose job was to tree a cougar, enabling the hunter to shoot it easily. Cougar Annie used her goats as bait, tethering them near cougar traps, enticing the big cats to come right into the garden. Orthodox or not, the system certainly worked. In her lifetime she killed some seventy cougars, although the exact number is unknown. In George Nicholson's history of Vancouver Island's west coast, published in 1965, he writes of how "sixty-two of these predatory animals have fallen to the expert marksmanship of the Rae-Arthur family since...1914. Of this total, forty were shot by the thrice-widowed mother—now Mrs. George Lawson, the last on her 73rd birthday." This total of forty is paltry compared to Cougar Annie's later claims. The numbers crept up gradually over the years. Various friends and visitors recall hearing of eighty, or ninety, perhaps as many as a hundred cougars killed by Ada Annie Lawson. "I remember that the number kept going up even after she was practically blind," remembers a regular visitor with a chuckle. "'My eyesight is failing pretty fast, but I can still hit the target,' she would say."

Ian Macleod was, like so many others, intrigued by Cougar Annie's method of attracting and killing cougars. He saw this at close quarters on a memorable visit to Boat Basin in 1952, when he had taken three prospectors up to Hesquiat Harbour in his boat and had anchored in Rae Basin. A severe gale blew up; they were stuck for several days and ran out of food. Ian went up to Cougar Annie's to buy some canned meat and eggs. She was there alone and did not want to let him leave; she even closed the door and stood in front of it, insisting that he help her set the large bear trap which she used for cougars. She had arthritis and could not set the trap herself. "We set it inside a huge hollowed out tree outside the front gate," Ian remembers. "She must have used that place before, because there was a

ring bolt inside the hollow part of the tree, on the back wall. She tied a baby goat to the ring bolt, on a short leash so it'd be out of reach of the trap and the cougar. I spread the trap and set the trigger catch and we left the goat bleating away."

The following morning Ian hiked back up to the garden to see what had happened and sure enough, there was a cougar in the trap, caught only by one of the pads on its foot. He went up to the house and found Cougar Annie sleeping on a straw mattress in her clothes. When he woke her up, she bolted right out of bed and they went to investigate. She shot the cougar with her twenty-gauge shotgun, and the terrified goat lived to bleat another day.

In his memoirs, Robert Culver includes many accounts of Ada Annie trapping and killing cougars. He prefaces these with an explanation he felt impelled to make:

Ada does not attempt to kill or destroy any animals unless they are interfering with her birds or animals. The traps she uses are bear traps. She covers the traps in the daytime so her goats can safely browse in the forest. Then when the goats are safely in the barn for the night, she uncovers the traps for overnight, inspecting in the morning to see if any animals have been caught, and covering the traps again for the day. She uses three traps set at suitably spaced intervals around the [garden] enclosure.

Many visitors recall these traps in the garden, and Cougar Annie's untroubled assumption that such massive jaw traps were a normal feature of the place. You just had to be on the lookout, that was all. For the sake of visitors, however, she did place painted signs declaring, '*Beware Cougar Trap*.' Ed Arnet recalls, with awe, a tour of the garden with Cougar Annie and how, as they went along the narrow boardwalks and around the dahlia beds, she warned him to watch his step. "We were just walking along looking at the flowers and she'd say 'Now be careful, right here by this stump there's a cougar trap' like it was the most normal thing in the world, and sure enough there it was, only thirty or forty feet from the house."

Robert Culver was also impressed by the way in which Ada Annie coolly tackled cougars as part of a day's work.

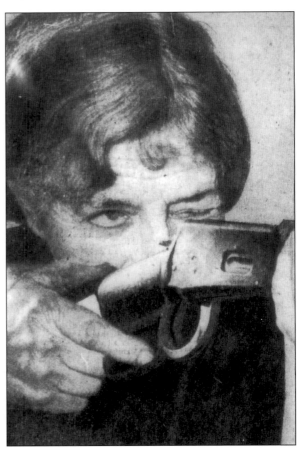

Cougar Annie, 1957.

Cougars would circle around outside of the fence, but didn't seem to realize how easily they could have torn it down, though she did one time catch two cougars trying to get through underneath a fence where it was weak. She said she took a stick, yelled at them and chased them off. That woman was absolutely fearless. . . . I was present one time when Ada was getting ready to shoot a cougar that had been caught in a trap. The sky was overcast and dull, and I noticed from a distance that the cougar's eyes seemed to shine with a green luminous light . . . she disposed of what was probably the largest cougar she had bagged in all the years she was there. It was just two inches short of seven feet (82 inches) from tip of nose to tip of tail. She always had standing orders for any cougar skins she could get. As I remember they were valued at some ten to twenty-five dollars each. At the time I left, she had bagged a total of 72 cougars since she moved up there in 1915.

As Cougar Annie's daughter Isobel recalls, cougars were all over the place when she was young. They were always after the goats. Once a cougar killed ten at one time, baby goats that had just arrived in a crate on the *Maquinna*. "They were fancy brown ones, really cute, they looked a bit like baby deer. Mother was real mad when the cougar got them." More than once Isobel recalls a cougar taking several goats at a time, on at least one occasion leaving the Rae-Arthurs with no goats at all, which meant no milk.

Once, walking along the beach, Isobel found a cougar in a trap, caught by the toe. She ran across the beach logs and up to the house, calling her mother. Cougar Annie picked up her gun and came at once. When they reached the trap, she rested the gun on Isobel's shoulder, took aim and fired, killing the beast instantly. "Mostly she got cougars like that, shooting them in traps in the bush. The odd one was treed and then she'd shoot it."

In an article in the Vancouver *Province* dated June 30, 1934 and headlined "Cats Bite the Dust," George Nicholson claims that on the west coast of Vancouver Island fifty cougars had been shot already that year, and the bounty claimed. According to Nicholson, the coast was infested with cougars, and he clearly favours the idea that hunters should shoot the animals on sight and claim what was then a ten-dollar bounty. He writes, "In every district now it seems the cougar is coming right into the settlements looking for cats, dogs, calves and other domestic animals, for they no longer have deer to eat, deer being practically extinct the entire length of the west coast of Vancouver Island."

When deer were scarce on the coast, cougars went hungry. Then they would be driven wild by the scent of the goats in Cougar Annie's garden; then she would have to be on the alert. She explained to Robert Culver how the deer and cougar populations on the coast seemed to go in cycles, and how these cycles affected her goats.

In that country existence was a seesaw business between the deer and the cougar. It ran in cycles of about twelve years. When the deer were plentiful, the cougars didn't bother Ada's goats much, but as time went on and the cougars increased, the deer would diminish and the cougars would go for the goats. . . . Due to these cycles, Ada sometimes had as many as forty goats running out, and she has had as few as three.

After one particular slaughter in the goat shed, Cougar Annie began to use two lanterns at the corners of the shed at night because a cougar will not approach a light. Robert Culver clung fast to this bit of cougar lore the night she sent him out into the dark to fetch a nanny goat tethered at a distant corner of the garden. They had forgotten to bring her in earlier.

I took a lantern out on the chance that a cougar might attack me. When I came near to where I knew the goat was tied, I called to it to reassure it. I was too late; I just saw the flash of something disappearing. It was the cougar that had just killed it and tried to drag it away, but couldn't because it was still tied to the stake with its rope.

Sometimes when Cougar Annie tethered a goat out as cougar bait, she would stay alert well into the night, listening for it to start bleating with fear. As soon as she heard the goat bleat she would go out armed with a lantern and her gun. She killed many cougars at night. According to some stories, she was able to take aim, shoot, and kill a cougar without even putting the lantern down. In later years she would align a flashlight along the gun barrel, and when she saw the luminous eyes of the cougar, she would fire.

"She could sure handle a gun," was the comment of the coastal missionary Harold Peters, reflecting on Cougar Annie's skills. Everyone who saw her in action concurs. Robert Culver was simply astonished by her abilities.

One time Ada was down near the shore with her gun when she saw four wild ducks coming in from over the water. She had her gun up waiting for just the moment for a favourable shot when she noticed that the ducks were aligning themselves one behind the other so that it looked like just one duck coming in. Just at the right time she fired. All four ducks dropped as one into the water. Several Indians were in their boat, just coming in to the shore. As they landed, they said to Ada, "Mrs. Lawson, how d'you get four ducks with one shot?" She didn't tell them, of course, that it was part luck. The incident just further enhanced her already wide reputation as a dead shot.

With such a mother, her sons could not compete. Even though Frank Rae-Arthur bagged a good number of cougars in his time and often helped his mother to skin the cougars she caught, and even though Tommy Rae-Arthur was called into action to set and check the traps, the Rae-Arthur men were completely outshone by their mother when it came to hunting, particularly hunting cougars. Wisely, they let her have all the glory. Ron Dalziel tells a story about this in his memoirs.

Tommy told me of an incident that occurred when he was a bit younger. "Went out into our garden," he said, "and saw a cougar down in the far corner of the fence."

"So what did you do," I asked, "go for your gun?"

"Oh, heavens no. That was a job for mother." She, I understand, quickly dispatched the creature, and skinned it out herself.

As for the dangers of hunting cougars, Robert Culver writes admiringly:

Ada has lived in that country sixty-five years, and she told me that on two occasions cougars pretty nearly got her. She said one time she was coming up the wooden trail and felt certain there was a cougar a short distance away. She had her gun loaded and ready and sure enough saw one spring at her. She fired and it dropped dead at her feet. It is very rarely that a cougar will attack a human being, but there was one other occasion . . . that one did. This time she couldn't take aim quickly enough. It sprang at her and knocked her down. She said she screamed and after it knocked her down it kept on running instead of killing her as it could have done.

Stellar's jay.

While cougars were without any doubt the most exciting and challenging prey in the area, the smaller prey probably took up far more of Cougar Annie's time and attention over the years. She trapped and shot any creature that posed any kind of threat to her garden production or to her livestock. She particularly disliked mink and marten, hawks, owls and Stellar's jays, giving them all short shrift. Mice were also on her hit list, especially if they raided her grain. To outwit the mice, she would leave the lid off a grain bin for several nights and then play a cruel trick. The bin with its rich pickings would be replaced by a bin full of water, covered with a thick layer of floating grain. Dozens of mice in one night would confidently jump into the barrel for a snack, only to meet a watery grave.

On the occasions when a hawk swooped down and seized a chicken, Cougar Annie would be on the attack instantly. As the hawk crouched over the squawking chicken, pinning it to the ground and stripping feathers off its neck prior to killing it, she would go straight for her gun. Robert Culver saw this happen more than once.

> *When the hawk sees Ada, it rises up on the hen, preparatory to flying out of danger. Ada takes quick and careful aim, aiming at the upper part of the hawk, and fires. The hawk falls over dead, and the hen, very badly scared, races for the hen-house, stays there the rest of that day. . . . Ada says men are apt to get in such a flutter when they shoot a hawk, they shoot right in the middle and kill both hen and hawk, and as Ada says, there is no sense in killing a hen just to get a hawk!*

Cougar Annie also became adept at blasting owls out of her garden with careful and hostile aim. They always had an eye on her chickens.

> *Owls were likely to carry them off in the night if left outside. Ada told me the way owls did it was to fly down and land on a branch next to a hen, on the side towards the tree trunk. The owl would then start crowding the hen further out on the branch. The hen would soon lose its balance and start fluttering to the ground. The owl would immediately swoop down and catch the hen in mid-air before it reached the ground and carry it on and up in the air.*

Trap for jay hanging from a fencepost.

Stellar's jays were a particular pest in the garden, and they met a grim fate if they stayed around. Puzzled by the fact that for several years after planting her azaleas they would not flower, Cougar Annie was determined to solve the problem. She kept careful watch and was outraged to discover that jays were making off with the buds. Her solution was simple. Trap the jays. Until the end of her days she set small leghold traps for jays, on fenceposts, on stumps, anywhere in the garden where she suspected they were taking her produce, eating buds or digging up newly planted seeds. Ron Dalziel remembers how repelled he was to find a crippled jay flapping around in a trap set on a stump. He freed the bird, hoping the old lady would not notice. She would have had little time for such sentiment, having no mercy for these birds. Their corpses were regularly flung into the pot bubbling on the back of the stove, a sight Robert Culver often observed. He mentions her dislike for jays more than once in his memoirs:

> The bluejays seemed to be about the most trouble in the garden, digging up sweet potatoes and carrying them off. She said she found potatoes up on the mountainside, which had taken root and grown there. She said the bluejays seemed to be about the most unintelligent of birds, walking right into a trap that had no camouflage at all. Catching a bluejay in a trap doesn't frighten away the others at all, but if one migrating robin is caught in a trap, the rest of the flock will move on right away. She said the raven seems to be the most wary of birds . . . if a raven is flying overhead and sees a person setting a trap it will avoid that spot, and if you have caught a raven in a trap, its mate will keep it fed as long as it is alive.

Ruffed grouse, another endangered visitor to the garden.

An intriguing traffic in animals came and went within Cougar Annie's garden. She brought in goats, many kinds of chickens, pigs, rabbits, ducks, geese, hares, and even mink. These animals had to take their chances coming up the coast; they arrived in crates on the *Maquinna*, braving all kinds of weather, only to be offloaded into a canoe and then paddled across to Boat Basin. By the time they were uncrated, some were no doubt in a state of complete shock. The process of getting the animals to shore was tough for everyone concerned. Stuart Culver recalls vividly being put to work fetching some goats during the summer of 1955:

> We had to take delivery of some goats one night, there must have been two or three of them. We rowed out to the boat at two in the morning—it was the one that took over after the Maquinna—and we only had a ten-foot rowboat. All the way out there, great big dogfish were nipping at the end of the oars, and I remember thinking I must be awfully careful not to rock the boat. And somehow or other we got the goats into the rowboat and then we rowed over to a fishboat and spent the rest of the night there waiting for the light, and then we went back to Boat Basin with the goats.

For a number of years Cougar Annie experimented with raising pedigreed fur-bearing stock, particularly rabbits, exchanging and selling good breeders with J.A. Ransford's fur farm in Steveston, and sometimes sending Mr. Ransford marten and mink as well. In one of his friendly and rambling letters Mr. Ransford writes: "Of course we want healthy stock, no snuffles or colds, Mrs. Rae-Arthur. . . . They must not be in young." He looks forward to expanding their trade, and says he awaits the next boat down with interest.

Cougar Annie doubtless enjoyed this trade in live animals and the challenge of breeding pedigreed stock, but such ventures came and went, seldom lasting long. On the whole dead animals were more lucrative. Fur trapping was part of her life at Boat Basin from the outset. Even when she was elderly and half-blind, her daily routine started with checking her traps, setting and resetting them in and around the garden. Large and small, the traps are still there, rusted and useless now, but lethal in their day. The small ones put an end to the lives of countless mink and marten who stalked the garden furtively, yearning to sink their teeth into a chicken. The larger ones captured bear and cougar. Some of the wooden boards used for skinning and drying and stretching the pelts are still in Cougar Annie's garden: even some of the old pelts remain. Decade after decade, she shipped out countless pelts and sold them to raw fur dealers, usually through the Hudson's Bay Company.

Bear in a pear tree

While she had little time to indulge in unprofitable sentiment towards her animals, Cougar Annie genuinely had a soft spot for her goats and chickens—and for any young creature, if Robert Culver is to be believed. He describes the uncanny affinity she sometimes developed with young animals and how she would befriend kid goats or any kind of new life, chickens or geese or rabbits. He tells how flocks of young chicks closely followed her wherever she went, and how the geese waddled around the garden, trailing after her in a possessive fashion. Young kids would "come running up to her, put their feet on her and show every sign of remembering her and being glad to see her."

The goats were a constant presence, and a constant concern. Never happier than when they went down to the grassy beach at Yahksis to graze, they caused, over the years, a great deal of trouble when they were out and about. A cryptic note inside the Rae-Arthurs' one and only medical book, *The Doctor at Home*, appears on the page where the entry for "Arsenic Poisoning" is outlined in pencil. A scribbled note in the margin in Willie Rae-Arthur's handwriting says, "Indians put soda biscuits spread with butter and arsenic at IR [Indian Reserve], 19/1/1921. One Billy died of poisoning 21/1/1921, another of the results of poisoning 27/2/1921." Why anyone would want to poison these goats is a mystery; perhaps their presence in the area attracted cougars and wolves, and the native people living nearby saw no reason why they should tolerate this.

Apple tree ravaged by a bear.

Isobel Rae-Arthur's memories of growing up at Boat Basin include many adventures with the goats that strayed far from home. "I remember being out overnight looking for the goats, and huddling up during the night in one of the Indian shacks along the shore. I milked the goats and drank their milk from a clamshell." Her mother was not overly concerned. "She never seemed to worry about us, she was too busy."

Sometimes if the goats went too far, and if there was no child available to be sent to the rescue, a marine operation would be put into effect. Harold Peters recalls that on one visit to Boat Basin in the mission boat, the *Shantyman*, before he knew what was happening he had been talked into going along the beach with Cougar Annie to rescue her goats. He helped her load them on board, and back they all went to Boat Basin where "we read a little Scripture together, but I think her mind was on the goats." Another time when the goats had gone too far to be rounded up on foot, Robert Culver remembers that:

Ada and her son Frank went down on his fishboat, dragging the rowboat behind. When they arrived where the goats were, Ada went on shore, called the goats to her, and Frank loaded a number of them at a time into the

rowboat and transferred them to the deck of the fishboat. When they were
all loaded, they all went back home on the fishboat. Ada said that the goats
stood quietly and appeared to enjoy the ride and the scenery.

Entertaining as they are, however, none of these tales about Cougar Annie and her various animals can begin to compete with stories of the local cattle. The wild cows and bulls of the Hesquiat Peninsula enjoy an enormous reputation. Elusive and fierce and fleet of foot, these beasts are greatly feared and rarely seen, but like Ogopogo or the Sasquatch, their very absence from general view makes them all the more fascinating. Only the bravest of hunters will go after them. Cougar Annie is reputed to have hunted and shot wild cattle in her early years at Boat Basin, when food was scarce. By the time she arrived in 1915, cattle had been roaming the peninsula for decades.

Ever since Father Brabant brought his original cattle to this area in 1875 and built sheds and fences to contain them, the cattle of Hesquiat developed their own ideas about where they wanted to be. They paid scant attention to the fences and barricades, and the relatively safe environs of Hesquiat Village were not to their liking either. The mission cattle continually escaped into the surrounding forest; first from Father Brabant's care, later from Father Moser's. The creatures enjoyed wandering freely around Hesquiat on the winding little trails they soon established, and they particularly enjoyed making their way over to Estevan Point along the five miles of wooden road, grazing happily all the way. Writing in 1915, Moser comments fretfully that he began the winter with twenty-four head of cattle and now had only fifteen. The others had simply wandered off and stayed away, joining forces with other forest cattle that roamed wild.

References to the wild cattle appear as early as 1894 in an article in the *Province*, and the wild cattle were an accepted local phenomenon by the time Estevan Lighthouse was under construction in 1907. The construction workers at the lighthouse, thoroughly disgusted with the rations provided for them, petitioned their employers to buy decent meat from the mission at Hesquiat and failing that, declared they would go out to hunt wild cattle. One of many angry letters about the food supplies points out that "the Indian Storekeeper in Hesquiat, who acted for the Rev Father Brabant during the latter's absence, offered . . . fat steers or cows for 10 cents a pound slaughtered out, and any wild bull or cow, for $10."

For a number of years the mission priests tried to keep tabs on the wild cattle, claiming and occasionally selling these creatures as their own, but this was a losing battle. The cattle were off and running and the issue of ownership gradually became a futile discussion. However, Father Moser never admitted defeat; he never gave up trying to control the cattle, even when he no longer lived full-time at Hesquiat Village. In the mid-1920s, after much discussion with the authorities at Estevan Lighthouse, he erected a fence across the wooden roadway to Estevan in the hope that "his" wild cattle would not meet and mingle with the other wild cattle from the opposite side of the peninsula.

As Hesquiat Village was gradually abandoned, the cattle were left entirely to their own devices. They became famous on the coast, although they were not unique. An article dated December 27, 1928 in *Farm and Home* is entitled "Bands of Wild Cattle roam on West Coast of Vancouver Island," and it describes three bands of wild cattle: two roaming around Nootka, Estevan and Hesquiat and one in the Long Beach area. "These cattle, although originally of domestic stock, brought in by some of the earliest settlers, have ranged over this locality for over thirty years and are now truly creatures of the forest. They are as wild as any wild animal of the woods," declares this article, going on to describe spectacular fights between the wild bulls and telling how the cattle roam in bands of ten or twelve along their established and well-hidden routes through the thick underbrush.

Cows on the beach at Hesquiat Village, about 1917

When Diane Ignace arrived at Hesquiat Village in 1975 there were seven wild cattle roaming the beach at Hesquiat, providing excitement and entertainment and plenty of fearsome stories. Everyone was frightened of the cattle, even the men who hunted them. Ian Macleod hunted cattle at Hesquiat in the late 1940s, but only once succeeded in killing an animal. "They were twice as wild as deer to hunt, especially the bulls. If they heard as much as a twig snap they'd run for two or three miles without stopping. And they could run like hell." Hunters usually went after the cattle in September, the dry time of the year, because then they could hike through the swampy areas on Hesquiat Peninsula.

Dave Ignace has done his share of hunting Hesquiat cattle, and he is convinced some cattle are still out there on the peninsula, although no one has sighted any of them for years. "They're scary, those bulls, real fast and mean. Sometimes when we were out hunting them and we actually found one, the guys were so scared they'd drop their rifles and run right up the nearest tree." Jim Haggarty can understand this reaction; his brief encounters with Hesquiat cattle during the 1970s remain vivid in his memory. "Those things were incredibly mean-looking, with huge horns," he says. "And they were so tough. I once had some of the beef to eat and twenty years later I'm still picking the sinew out from between my teeth."

The Ignace family can tell many a story of the cattle. How during the rutting season one of the bulls would storm through the village, steam coming out of his nostrils, bellowing and screaming. How the bulls fought with each other, almost ripping each other to bits with their horns. How George Ignace was brave enough to pat the great black bull but the rest of them were too frightened. That black bull sometimes came "roaring down the beach, just roaring" according to Diane Ignace, and if anyone was in the way complete panic and pandemonium would ensue. Once the black bull came charging when they were having a marshmallow roast on the beach, and everyone scattered in all directions. One little boy was so overwhelmed he ran straight into the sea still holding his marshmallow on its stick high over his head. Another younger bull was also a regular on the beach for many years. The Ignaces called it the "hippy bull" because of the white curly hair hanging like bangs on its forehead. This bull came to a sad end when grazing on the edge of the forest. A pack of wolves backed it off a cliff edge and it crashed onto its back on the rocks below, ivy still in its mouth.

Many fishermen and other visitors to the harbour delight in describing the incongruous appearances of the Hesquiat cattle along the shore. A huge bull—sometimes a white one—would loom out of the forest onto the beach, followed by a herd of seven or eight cows. These creatures were a regular feature of the landscape until the late 1970s when sightings became more rare. And although rumours still drift up and down the coast about a sighting last year, or a couple of summers ago, or about something strange that appeared on the beach when a low-flying aircraft skimmed the shoreline recently, the Hesquiat cattle have faded from sight. "They're still out there, though. Absolutely. You can bet on it," say diehard believers. And why not? With steaming nostrils and the light of battle in their eye, these Hesquiat cattle could well be lurking in the shadowy forest, rebuilding their numbers, about to emerge onto the beach once again, as awesome as before.

Low Tide 1/94: Hesquiat Bay, *by Takao Tanabe.*
Acrylic on canvas 55" × 120"

CHAPTER 10

Around the Harbour

Leaving cougar annie's garden and heading down to the beach takes you into a patch of old-growth forest. The open light of the clearing gives way to dark enfolding trees. On bright days, shafts of sunshine filter through the canopy overhead, sometimes lighting on traces of human activity in this silent and seemingly undisturbed space.

A large cedar windfall, lying across a barely visible pathway through the forest, has been cut and a section removed from the log to leave a gap for people to pass through. The cut ends are now thick with moss and ferns and fungi, while out of the log a large hemlock grows, along with many smaller trees and bushes. This cedar fell centuries ago and the cuts were made over eighty years ago, requiring hours of work with a crosscut saw. This was the path from the beach used by Cougar Annie and her family when they first arrived, before they built the raised boardwalk through the woods.

Not far from this boardwalk, now shaky and frail, are many far older signs of people at work. If you venture into the forest, you will come upon a number of giant red cedars with markings from untold years ago. From some of the living trees, boards have been split off and the trees have continued to grow around the cuts. Great swathes of bark have been stripped from other trees for making baskets and ropes and for weaving cedar fabric, and the long straight scars left behind extend high up the tree trunks. Even more dramatic are the canoe trees. Overgrown now, grey with age and covered with moss and fern, these tall angled cedar stumps appear intermittently in the patch of old-growth forest between Cougar

Annie's garden and the beach. From these stumps grew the straightest and strongest trees, which were cut down with infinite labour and care, chip by chip, using hand-held stone adzes. The dugout canoes made from these trees were the most valued of possessions, beautifully crafted vessels, perfectly designed for the wild waters of the coast. Father Augustin Brabant, describing the slow and painstaking art of making dugout canoes in his diary in 1876, was astonished by the absolute perfection of the craft. "All the work is done without instruments to go by or measure. Yet most of these canoes are so true and so well shaped and proportioned that not even an expert could detect the least flaw or imperfection."

In the deep salal in the forest near the beach lies a dugout canoe, hidden. Last used several decades ago, it belonged to Rose Rae-Arthur when she was young—she bought it from some Hesquiat children for twelve dollars. "We called it *Tippy*," she remembers. *Tippy* lasted many years before being laid to rest. Now slowly rotting into the bush, this canoe is almost invisible. Alders and salal grow out of it, moss covers the sides, small cedars are sprouting in the prow as the forest reclaims its own.

After walking through the forest, emerging into the open light of the beach brings a wide horizon into view and a silvered curving shoreline on either side. Seen from the head of the inner bay at Boat Basin, Hesquiat Harbour seems vast and empty, its shores deserted. No sign of human activity disturbs the scene unless a boat comes into view, or unless at night you can see a light at Hesquiat Village far across the way. If there is a light, it shines from only one house. Dave Ignace and his family are the only ones living there now.

Yet the Rae-Arthur children, growing up here in the 1920s, saw the harbour differently. Canoes were crossing the water and skimming along the shore constantly as they had done for generations, some laden with cedar bark or salal berries, some with baskets full of the traditionally valued cinquefoil or wild clover root, others perhaps laden with clams, salmon, or fish oil. The harbour was lined with small encampments on the beaches, and if the Rae-Arthur children ventured far along the beach looking for goats, as they often did, before long they would come across a settlement or encampment. Rose well remembers being helped by Hesquiat people camped along the northwest shore of the harbour. "They gave me hardtack biscuits and let me stay the night, I remember. And I was sure glad to have those biscuits." she recalls. As a boy, George Rae-Arthur made a habit of walking along the beach and dropping in to see his Hesquiat friends at Yahksis, usually around suppertime. Ruth Tom's grandmother became accustomed to his arrivals and to his appetite. "I guess I've got to feed this one, too," she would say kindly.

Long before the Rae-Arthurs arrived, an article in *The Province* dated December 1, 1894, described the scene in the harbour. "Along [Hesquiat Harbour's] shores appear Indian houses standing alone in little patches of cleared ground: all telling of prosperity and civilization." This article also takes note of the Roman Catholic mission at Hesquiat Village, its large white-painted church dominating one end of the village. White clapboard houses—twenty or thirty of them according to *The Province*—were scattered through the village, and a number of traditional longhouses still stood, grand and imposing, near the shore. Over at Anton's Spit stood the Luckovich home and store; no trace of it now remains. At Maahpe stood another long-forgotten house, its brick chimney now collapsed in a heap of rubble in the fast-growing bush.

"This was a very busy place earlier this century and as far as we can tell throughout the nineteenth century," says archaeologist Jim Haggarty. "There has been an extraordinary amount of change in a very short time." Haggarty is an archaeologist who worked in Hesquiat Harbour in the 1970s doing research into earlier settlement and population movements in the area. His findings and those of others in his field indicate that the population of the Hesquiats, in keeping with other native populations on the coast, has dropped by about half since the time of the arrival of white people in the latter part of the eighteenth century. The combined effects of smallpox epidemics, tuberculosis and other diseases were catastrophic for the native people. And even before the Spaniards and the British arrived on the west coast of Vancouver Island, the smallpox had preceded them. Early records from the Spanish priests who travelled with the explorer Juan Perez

Hesquiat Village, 1914.

Hesquiat Village from the water, about 1912.

describe the all-too-familiar scarring of smallpox on the faces of native people in this "undiscovered" part of the world. Traffic up and down the Pacific Coast probably ensured that the disease reached here some time before, spreading from the Spanish-held territories to the south.

A group of Hesquiat people was the first to witness white people on the west coast of Vancouver Island. In 1774 near Estevan Point, on the western shore of Hesquiat Peninsula, the *Santiago*, the Spanish sailing ship commanded by Juan Perez, came within sight of an encampment of Hesquiat people on shore. With fear and wonder, the Hesquiats saw a cloud of sail above what appeared to be a huge floating house, and sensed the presence of spirits from another world. After observing the ship cautiously, a collection of brave men ventured near the *Santiago* in their canoes, and were able to do some trade with the Spaniards, bringing back to shore such exotic goods as cloth, hooks, knives and silver spoons. The crew of the ship did not come ashore, and the *Santiago* sailed off as mysteriously as it had arrived. Proud to have been singled out as the first to encounter these strangers from another world, the Hesquiats told and retold their story, assuming a new importance in the eyes of neighbouring tribes.

Four years later, in 1778, Captain James Cook sailed into Nootka Sound and went ashore at Friendly Cove, northwest of Hesquiat. He raised the Union Jack and claimed this part of the coast for Great Britain, a claim energetically opposed by Spain. This led to a dispute that came perilously close to war, forestalled by the Nootka Convention of 1790. From the time of Cook's arrival, the dubious honour of early contact with white men rests with the native people of Nootka Sound. A cairn erected at Friendly Cove commemorates Cook's "discovery" of this place. No plaque has ever appeared on Hesquiat territory to commemorate their earlier contact with Perez.

During the 1970s, at the request of the Hesquiat people, extensive archaeological investigations went on in Hesquiat Harbour. The work was carried out by the staff of what was then the British Columbia Provincial Museum, and became known as the Hesquiat Archaeological Project. The Hesquiats were incensed because some of their burial sites within the harbour had been desecrated by visitors and curiosity seekers. They feared that the remains of their ancestors in certain burial caves had been wilfully disturbed and treated with complete disrespect, and that cultural artifacts within the caves were being stolen. Such fears were well founded, and the Hesquiat people had every reason to be alarmed.

Rumours and stories abound of how outsiders had gone into burial caves and rummaged around without compunction, not only taking away coins and beads and anything else considered valuable or interesting, but breaking open cedar boxes, upending mummified bodies, putting cigarettes in their mouths and playing games with skeletal remains. Small wonder the Hesquiat people were outraged. A committee of concerned individuals, called the Hesquiat Cultural Committee, approached the Provincial Museum for assistance.

After much consultation, archaeological work began in 1971. Its main purpose was to remove skeletal remains and cultural artifacts from some eleven burial caves and rock shelters along the coastline of the harbour. By the end of that summer work had been completed on nine of these caves, and materials from the remaining two were removed two years later. By the time the experts had finished, they concluded that at least 108 people had been buried in these caves and shelters, some of them as long ago as early in the nineteenth century. Most of the caves sheltered only a few bodies, but one of them in the inner harbour contained the remains of 57 people. Thousands and thousands of cultural items had been placed in the caves along with the deceased: cedar bark mats, cedar baskets, cedar plank boxes, kelp cords, combs, mirrors, trade beads, knives, harpoons, and so on.

Jim Haggarty, who worked on the excavations, recalls with awe the time he spent, often flat on his belly, in the burial caves, painstakingly removing every object and every trace of human remains. "To do that work was a great privilege," he comments. He also remembers how in one burial cave the archaeologists came across the skeleton of one of Cougar Annie's goats. It had wandered in and found its final resting place in the company of long-dead human beings, and there it lay, the bell still around its neck.

On and off, archaeological investigations continued within Hesquiat Harbour and at Hesquiat Village throughout the 1970s. The work amounted to a thorough archaeological reconnaissance of traditional Hesquiat territory, locating, recording and photographing twenty-eight different archaeological sites. Since then, more sites have been discovered, mapped and classified. The focus of the work shifted from salvage work within the caves to studying early occupation within the harbour, including summer and winter village sites, fishing stations, and caves where people had lived, some of which were later used as burial caves. In the same cave that had sheltered fifty-seven bodies, there are signs of habitation dating back to between 100 and 400 A.D. While little is yet known of the civilisations represented by these early layers of archaeological evidence, it is abundantly clear that the history of people living in this harbour stretches back very far indeed.

From the late eighteenth century onwards, even though the evidence is admittedly patchy, a reasonably coherent picture emerges of settlement within Hesquiat Harbour. According to some estimates, as many as five hundred people lived in and around Hesquiat Harbour by the early nineteenth century. Hesquiat Village was the site of the largest winter village, but most of the population was scattered along the nearby shores, both inside and outside the harbour. The First Nations people known now as the Hesquiat band can trace their origins to five small and distinct local groups, each with its own ancestral and family structures, its own hereditary chiefs and its own traditional territory for hunting, fishing and root gathering. The different groups occupied various sites, usually including a winter village and one or more seasonal camps located near easily available resources such as salmon streams and clam beds. Two of the five Hesquiat groups were based on the outer coast of the harbour; three were inside the harbour.

These local groups were far from static. Their numbers fluctuated with alliances and marriages, with the availability of food, the severity of the weather, the damage caused by local warfare and with the prevalence of illnesses. Evidence shows that some sites around the harbour were occupied for as long as two or three centuries at a stretch, and were then abandoned for equally long periods of time; that occupation was intermittent and patchy in other sites; that seasonal patterns of occupation changed over time.

Hesquiat, the largest winter village site, had as many as eight imposing long-houses, the largest of which measured 95 feet long and 45 feet wide. Depressions in the ground where the support posts stood can still be discerned. In the mid-nineteenth century, this village and its population expanded considerably when the five local groups amalgamated, coming together as a large and loosely defined band in order to strengthen their position on the coast. As a larger group they could better withstand the new pressures and the social changes surrounding them. Faced with the ineradicable presence of white strangers in their midst, faced with the terrible threat of smallpox sweeping up and down the coast, faced with a radically changing economic scene, hemmed in as they were by more powerful tribes to the north and to the south, the traditional small local groupings of people around Hesquiat Harbour needed to support each other. Even together their numbers were not great, having diminished considerably during the 1800s. In a letter written in 1886, when the Hesquiat Indian Reserves were established, Mr. P. O'Reilly of the Indian Reserve Commission declares in flowing handwriting that, "The Hesquiat tribe number 221 viz 70 men, 66 women, and 85 children...."

Looking at any map of Hesquiat Harbour from the late nineteenth century onwards, five small blocks of land can be seen around the harbour, numbered IR1 through IR5. These are the reserves of land set aside for the Hesquiat people in 1886; five reserves crudely intended to delineate limited territory for the five local groupings of the Hesquiat people. The anglicized names of these reserves are Maahpe (150 acres) and Iusuk (33 acres) in the inner harbour; Teahmit (113 acres) in the middle of the western shore of the harbour; Hesquiat (232 acres) at the harbour entrance, and Homais (88 acres), a seasonal fishing village site on the western shore of Hesquiat Peninsula, around from Estevan Point.

Maps of this area usually show at least a few of the place names in and around Hesquiat Harbour: Rondeault and Leclaire Points, Anton's Spit, Boat Basin, Rae Basin generally appear, as well as Matlahaw Point and Hesquiat Village, and sometimes the names of the reserves. Yet the names of landmarks in this harbour are far more deeply rooted than any map can show. There is an entirely different

148

layer of names, names unknown to most people, names ancient and gentle in tone used by generation upon generation of the Hesquiat people. These names bear a story or several stories, they give character and history to boulders and sandy beaches and small streams all around the harbour, they describe resources, family histories, mythology. Such names characterize features such as the large flat rock visible only at low tide near Matlahaw Point, a rock known as *ch'ihlhaa*. According to tradition, Thunderbird left scratches on this rock when landing here with claws outstretched. Nearby, some say, there is a rock called *tl'isimyis*, bearing a white mark. Thunderbird landed here also, leaving behind a white feather that marks the rock to this day.

The Hesquiat names are challenging to frame in English: the name for Rae Lake is written as *t'icha7am*; the name for an area at the top of Mount Seghers is *kwa7ahulhh*; the site of Hesquiat Village is *hishkwii*. With each name comes a story. Rae Lake was a place where people went to train for spiritual power, where bats attacked a man whose name was *chuntsuxws* while he underwent spiritual training. He swam to the whitish-coloured reef in the lake, and because the reef rose like a monster, others always feared to go there. And near the top of Mount Seghers there is a cave, a place of power: birds die when they fly past, birds' feathers litter the floor of the cave, and strange sounds emerge from it when bad weather is coming. Men went here to receive special whaling powers. As for the main village site of Hesquiat, this name comes from the word *hiishhiisha* which describes the sound of eating herring roe on sea-grass, the sound made by running this grass through teeth and lips to remove the eggs.

The earliest attempt in this century to record place names and history of the Hesquiat people appears in Philip Drucker's *The Northern and Central Nootkan Tribes*, published in 1951. For his information Drucker drew on data gathered through fieldwork and discussions with two Hesquiat elders. Then came the

Homais, about 1912, with visitors from Estevan Point Lighthouse.

Hesquiat Project during the 1970s, which involved extensive fieldwork by museum staff in collaboration with the Hesquiat Cultural Committee, and which relied heavily on interviews granted by Hesquiat elders. This work of the 1970s directly and indirectly led to several publications and theses, including work by archaeologist Jim Haggarty, anthropologist Jerome Cybulski, the detailed studies of ethnobotanists Nancy Turner and Barbara Efrat, and the work of ethnologists Randy Bouchard and Dorothy Kennedy.

Bouchard and Kennedy prepared a report in 1990 entitled *Clayoquot Sound Indian Land Use* in which they named, mapped and documented many locations along the coast. All their information comes from interviews with native elders. In the Hesquiat area they methodically list, under "Hesquiat Place Names," 129 sites of traditional significance around or near Hesquiat Harbour. Relying on what the elders told them, Bouchard and Kennedy provide descriptions of who lived at these locations, the varieties of fish or clams or birds there, and the different stories associated with the places. They move from Split Cape on the western side of Hesquiat Peninsula around to Hesquiat Village, all along the northwest coastline of the inner harbour, up to Rae and Hesquiat Lakes, back along the southeast coastline, and stop at Hesquiat Point.

Their report pays scant attention to the boundaries of the five Hesquiat reserves, because such boundaries do not resonate with stories or carry traditional authority. Being imposed on the map in the late 1880s, the reserve boundaries reveal little about the Hesquiat people and much about the administrative procedures of a government determined to take control of native people and their traditional territories. O'Reilly of the Indian Reserve Commission appears to have been largely responsible for deciding what land should be set aside for the Hesquiat people and he did so without noticeable enthusiasm. He was certainly not interested in the place himself nor was he impressed by what he saw. This was not O'Reilly's idea of a decent place to live:

> *The soil on these allotments is of the poorest description and unsuitable for agriculture, the situation being exposed and bleak; the only real value of the reserves is their proximity to the fishing and sealing grounds from which the Indians derive their livelihood. There is no white settlement in the neighborhood, nor is any likely to take place.*

Strictly speaking, O'Reilly was mistaken. If the permanent presence of a missionary, and the intermittent presence of sealers and traders and law enforcers can be considered white settlement, then such settlement was firmly established at

Hesquiat. Father Brabant had arrived in 1875, the coastal merchants and sealers had been active since well before then, and the justice system of the white man had been memorably imposed upon the Hesquiat people after the shipwreck of the *John Bright* in 1869. By the time the Indian Reserves were set aside in 1886, the Hesquiats were probably only too well accustomed to the presence of white people in their territory. The number of whites was not great, but their impact had already been huge.

Just around from Estevan Point, near Homais Cove, a tragic shipwreck occurred in October 1882 when the American ship *Malleville* struck one of the offshore reefs. The wreck was visible to the Hesquiats staying at Homais, and when the first body washed up on shore they set out at once to Hesquiat Village to inform Father Brabant of the tragedy. With a large number of people from the village, Brabant set out at once to hike from Hesquiat to Homais, finding along the route signs of the disaster. A trunk full of ladies' dresses, and children's clothing were amongst the first signs on the beach, then the body of a young man, then the body of a young woman "dressed gorgeously," according to Brabant. This was Mrs. Harlow, the captain's wife. The bodies of her two young children were not recovered, nor were the bodies of most of the twenty-two people on board. Children's toys and letter blocks washed up on shore, even the body of a pet pig, but only eight bodies in total. "It was the saddest thing I ever saw in my life," Brabant wrote, though he took comfort from "the noble work of the Indians. I had seen them up to their necks in the sea and surf, drag the bodies on shore and hand them over to me for burial."

Later, the Hesquiat people were honoured by the American government for the assistance rendered at the time of the wreck. *The Colonist* of Victoria noted, on November 16, 1883, that the Hesquiat chief had been awarded "a suitably inscribed gold medal and a cheque for $300.00. The money to be distributed amongst his humane and kindly hearted people in recognition of their honesty and Christian-like behaviour...."

This is a far cry from the sentiments of the *Colonist* in 1869, at the time of another shipwreck near Hesquiat. Then, the newspaper was baying for the blood of the "wretched savages" at Hesquiat, accusing them of "cruel butchery," and even demanding the whole tribe "be made food for crows."

The *John Bright,* a British barque heading for Australia with a load of lumber, foundered on the rocks near Matlahaw Point in February 1869. This wreck was a disaster with many faces. All fourteen people on board perished and a tangled and terrible web of fear and vengeance and betrayal arose during the following weeks and months, along with a mass of contradictory, often hysterically exaggerated, information about the wreck. The outcome of the *John Bright* disaster was a public hanging, right on the beach near Hesquiat Village. Two Hesquiat men were put to death, having been found guilty of murdering the supposed survivors of the shipwreck.

The story of the disaster is complex. Shortly after the wreck was discovered, Captain James Christiansen of the sealing schooner *Surprise* took his own tale of the disaster to Victoria, claiming he had seen evidence of theft and butchery and even dismemberment of bodies on the beach near the wreck, and he demanded that a warship be sent up to investigate. His story attracted much attention in the newspapers, but some time passed before any investigation took place. Meanwhile Christiansen returned to Hesquiat himself and purportedly discovered more mutilated bodies, and several Hesquiat men who were behaving guiltily.

So agitated was the response of the public in Victoria to Christiansen's story, which emphasised the supposed mutilation of the captain's wife and hinted at the possible rape of a young Englishwoman on board the *John Bright*, that an enraged group of fifty citizens formed a vigilante group and offered to go up the coast to wreak vengeance on the Hesquiat people. To avert this, the governor agreed to send a warship to Hesquiat, with heavily armed marines and a coroner on board. The bodies of some victims of the wreck were exhumed, a verdict of wilful murder was declared and several Hesquiat men were arrested on suspicion of murder. In the end two were charged and stood trial. They were found guilty and sentenced to death.

The hanging took place on June 29, 1869 on a hastily erected gallows on the beach. The warship *HMS Sparrowhawk* stood at anchor in the harbour; scarlet-coated marines stood at attention; Father Charles Seghers—later Bishop Seghers—attended; the High Sheriff Andrew Elliott directed operations, and summoned all the native people in the area to witness the event. The two frightened Hesquiat men mounted the platform to have black squares placed on their heads and nooses around their necks. Some accounts of the hanging say that a cannon was fired from the *Sparrowhawk*, resounding around the harbour, and that drums rolled as the men met their death.

Contemporary accounts of the *John Bright* disaster and its aftermath admit to no uncertainty about the guilt of the two men, but uncertainty abounds now, in reading the documents of the case. A critical examination of the court records suggests the trial was by no means fair, that there was not even a reliable interpreter for the two accused. The truth of what happened at Hesquiat after the wreck of the *John Bright* is not evident in these records, but the lack of clarity in the court proceedings is painfully obvious.

In later years, the most vehement defender of the two men hanged for murder was Father Brabant. The *John Bright* affair predated his arrival by six years, but the events cast a long shadow over Hesquiat, and Brabant examined the case as closely as he could. It preyed on his mind for years. He prepared a lengthy hand-written document about the case which begins by citing a Latin motto:

> Neminem Time—Neminem Laede. *Be afraid of nobody—hurt no one.*
> *When I landed in Hesquiat . . . one of the first things which attracted my at-*
> *tention was the above inscription on a piece of board nailed above the door*
> *of the house of one of the petty chiefs of the tribe. It was the signboard of the*
> *barque John Bright. . . .*

Page after closely written page follows, detailing all of Brabant's objections to how the case of the *John Bright* had been handled. He maintains that Captain Christiansen had not come ashore at Hesquiat to investigate the wreck of the *John Bright* at all, but had "cowardly sailed away." According to Brabant, Christiansen had gleaned his inflammatory stories from other native villages along the coast, peopled by tribes hostile towards the Hesquiats. Brabant also suggests that the interpreter who was employed when the bodies were exhumed was influenced by Christiansen's version of events, and that this man was entirely untrustworthy: "he could not be relied upon to interpret anything which did not agree with his own ideas, and as his tribes-men were the sworn enemies of the Hesquiats it was more than probable that his interpretation would be defective if not manifestly false."

In this document, Brabant also comes to the defense of the accused, saying that one of them, "an intelligent and quiet Indian," was condemned simply because he was the first to see the wreck, and that the other was a mere scapegoat. Initially, the Hesquiat chief had been arrested and accused of murder, and, in order to free him, his people offered a replacement.

> *Foolishly . . . they decided to sacrifice a man called Katkinna expecting*
> *thereby to appease the spirit for revenge of the white visitors and thus se-*
> *cure the release of their brother and chief. The man Katkinna was a simple-*
> *ton of inferior rank and considered so worthless that not one woman of the*
> *tribe would have him as a husband.*

In 1904 an article in the *Colonist* recalled the *John Bright* disaster, exaggerating and embellishing all of the most lurid details, including the supposed rape of the young Englishwoman: "The pretty English maid was delivered up to the young men of the tribe who dragged her into the bush. Her cries filled the air for hours and when she was seen again . . . the poor girl was dead and her head had disappeared!" Father Brabant was so outraged by this article and its condemnation of the Hesquiats, he wrote to the editor of the paper—and author of the article—Mr. D.W. Higgins. His agitated handwriting covers several pages, and he begins by declaring of Higgins' article: "There is hardly one statement that I cannot disprove!"

Brabant goes on to cite a witness who saw Christiansen leave Hesquiat in a panic rather than come ashore to investigate the wreck; he refers to Bishop Seghers' account of the events; he stresses that he has lived thirty years amongst the Hesquiats and speaks their language; he suggests that Katkinna had a solid alibi; he again insists that the court interpreter was unreliable and hostile; and he hopes that "for the sake of truth and justice" Higgins will "very materially correct" his account. Higgins was unmoved by this appeal. In his carelessly scrawled reply he says:

> *I never had the slightest doubt that the people were murdered. . . . I would not do an injustice to anyone, wilfully, not even to that unfortunate race who have been destroyed by the acts of vicious men of our own race and if the men who suffered went to their last account unjustly it is a most regretful circumstance. It is too late now to recall them, and while I would gladly alter the circumstances as told in the story, in the face of the evidence and the . . . condemnation of the judges, I cannot do so.*

Following the hanging in Hesquiat Harbour, the gallows was left intact on the beach as a lesson to all potential miscreants. It must have been a grim reminder while it lasted. Officially, the case of the *John Bright* closed well over a century ago, but it is haunted by many uneasy questions. Perhaps they cannot ever be answered or perhaps, somewhere in the mass of conflicting documents relating to the case, a few answers still may, one day, be found.

When Father Brabant arrived to establish his mission at Hesquiat in 1875 he arrived amongst people who already had acquired—sometimes at bitter cost—considerable knowledge of the white man and his ways. Not only because of the

John Bright disaster and other shipwrecks, but because of the rampant spread of disease, the expanding interest in trade and commerce, the increasing traffic of sailing vessels on the coast. The native people of the coast had for some time been trading sealskins and dogfish oil with merchants on the coast, and by the time of Brabant's arrival, the sealskin trade was expanding rapidly. This trade, significantly, relied on native hunters for its success.

In the late 1860s the coastal trader Captain Charles Spring realized that the international demand for furs was increasing and he came up with the idea of increasing his sealskin trade by taking native hunters and their canoes with him on his sealing schooners, to hunt seals farther afield. Spring, along with several other entrepeneurs, established a formidable fleet of these schooners, based in Victoria, and the ships travelled to sealing grounds up and down the Pacific coast. Each ship would call at coastal villages and take on board about a dozen native hunters and about the same number of boatmen, and sometimes their wives would come along as cooks. The canoes would be heaved onto the decks and secured in place, farewells would be said and the sealing season began. Father Brabant, writing in 1876, speaks of "a dozen or more sealing schooners" coming to call at Hesquiat, occasioning the annual separation of families.

After 1883, the sealing ships began to go even farther, all the way north to the rich seal hunting grounds in the Bering Sea. When they reached these foggy and treacherous waters, the hunters would launch their canoes, paddle close to the seals and start harpooning. The killing was plentiful. On their return journeys down the coast, some of the schooners would carry up to a thousand, even two thousand sealskins on board. Father Charles Moser's memoirs repeatedly mention ships with eight or nine hundred sealskins on board, and he was writing later, in the years when the sealing trade was falling off.

Sealers from Hesquiat were amongst the best on the coast, and regularly headed north to the Bering Sea. New recruits were always welcome, for the work was plentiful. According to Father Brabant's diary in 1883: "From the beginning their success [as sealers] was such that they now seem determined to prosecute this lucrative work and leave the dog-fish business to the old people."

Adventures in the sealing trade were extraordinary and often tragic, for it was highly dangerous work. Many canoes were swept out to sea, many lives were lost. In 1886, two Hesquiat men who had been given up for dead defied the odds and reappeared many weeks later in the village. Up in the Bering Sea they had become separated from their sealing schooner in the fog, and had drifted a long way in their canoe, landing eventually on one of the Aleutian Islands where they met a native who directed them to a trading post. From there, they made their way to a remote bay where some American fishboats were moored, and on one of these boats the men went to a bigger trading post, and eventually travelled by steamer to San Francisco. The two Hesquiats were then put in touch with the British consul who shipped them up to Victoria where the Catholic bishop contacted with the owner of the schooner which had lost them in the Bering Sea. Provided with a new canoe, they paddled victoriously back up to Hesquiat where, according to Father Brabant, "They now excite the wonder of all the Indians" and "pose as heroes."

Another famous sealing adventure involving Hesquiat hunters occurred in 1893, when the schooner *Ainoko* from Victoria, commanded by Captain George Heater, was in the western waters of the Bering Sea. It encountered a Russian gunboat which ordered it to stop, allegedly for violating a zone in which the Russian and British governments had prohibited all sealing. Captain Heater protested his innocence, explaining that bad weather and strong winds were to blame, but nonetheless the Russian captain seized the *Ainoko*'s papers and ordered Heater to report to the nearest British consulate, which happened to be in Yokohama, Japan. Reluctantly, Heater complied and set his boat on a southwest course to Japan. But the fifteen Hesquiat natives on board could read the ship's compass and realized the ship was heading towards Japan. They absolutely refused to continue. Because there were only four other people on board, because he did not want to risk outright mutiny, and at least partly because he did not want to go to Yokohama anyway, Heater changed course and set sail for home. He delivered his disgruntled crew back to Hesquiat and then headed down the coast to argue his case in Victoria, rather than in Yokohama.

By 1910, many years of wholesale slaughter had gravely endangered the seals on the Pacific Coast. In 1911 an international treaty between Canada, Russia, the United States and Japan prohibited fur-sealing in the North Pacific to allow the herds to build up again. The sealing industry out of Victoria came to a halt. The fleet of sealers remained at anchor, and the days of Hesquiat hunters travelling to distant and dangerous waters in small sailing ships came to an end.

CHAPTER 11

The
Mission

A PAINTING HUNG FOR many years inside Cougar Annie's house. It showed
a lighthouse beaming forth golden rays, and a text declaiming "Jesus the
Light of the World." Along with a sodden Bible, a volume entitled *Family Prayers,*
a handful of Jehovah's Witness books, a few publications from the mission boats
that plied the West Coast, and a couple of parish magazines from England—one
from St. Matthew's Church in Bolton, the other from All Souls' Langham Place in
London—this painting is one of a handful of vaguely religious relics in the
house. Nothing here hints at a connection with the Roman Catholic church; if the
Rae-Arthurs had any church affiliation it was casually Presbyterian, or perhaps
offhandedly Anglican, but not Roman Catholic.

Yet the only church within reach was Roman Catholic. Perhaps the Rae-
Arthurs never even entered the historic Catholic church across the harbour at
Hesquiat Village. After all, why should they bother? The church made no effort to
address the needs of the one non-Catholic white family in the area. The services
were mostly conducted in Latin, and the sermons were preached in Chinook or
in the Hesquiat language, as well as the priests were able, though sometimes they
reverted to English. By all accounts, the priests paid scant attention to the Rae-
Arthurs, and received little or no attention in return. In this way two mutually
indifferent sets of white people, at opposite ends of Hesquiat Harbour, more or
less managed to ignore each other, decade after decade.

Curiosity may have led the Rae-Arthur children, on their trips across the harbour, to investigate this tall, imposing church, to cross over the small stream on the footbridge leading up to the large front doors of the white-painted church, to open the doors and warily to look inside. Here was a silent, lofty, interior; the high arched windows shedding light on row after row of pews, on carved wooden altar railings, on statues of the Virgin, on the holy water stand near the door.

By the time the Rae-Arthur children were growing up at Boat Basin, this church had stood for decades, a leading symbol of the missionary work of the Roman Catholic Church on the West Coast. Here, according to the instructions of the church, the priest was to "devote himself chiefly and directly to the salvation and spiritual progress of the Indians." Such devotion found vigorous expression.

Here in this church, the priests thundered out their condemnations of native religious ceremonies; here elaborate processions made their way up the nave on special saints' days; here as punishment for fornication, men sometimes stood at the altar railing and faced the congregation throughout a long Sunday service, forbidden to sit down; here on many occasions over a hundred people packed the church as they attended Mass and sang hymns; here sometimes the priest would come to say Mass and find the place empty. Candlelit processions illuminated the building for Midnight Mass; weddings and baptisms and funerals beyond count took place here, and lonely priests from distant countries knelt here in solitary prayer. As the years passed, here also many Hesquiat people observed dispassionately as the roof began to leak and the building began to decay.

Perhaps if the Rae-Arthur children were inside the church in the late 1920s or early 1930s they would have noticed the signs of this decay, for by then the church was in trouble. Or perhaps the children would have just wandered around, cautiously investigating the place. The temptation to ring the bell next to the confessional would have been great, just to see if it would bring the priest running. Or to open the closet and look at the array of vestments: stoles and chasubles, copes and cassocks, hanging solemnly in the vestry. Best of all, the children might have made their way up the tall bell tower to see—or even to sound—the large brass bell inscribed "St. Antonin —A.J. Brabant—1884." But to do so may have roused

The church at Hesquiat in the 1920s.

too many people; raised too many ghosts. Father Brabant was not one to tolerate levity in his church, and his would be a stern ghost to appease.

On a Tuesday afternoon in May 1875, the sailing sloop *Thornton* entered Hesquiat Harbour and anchored in the inner bay. Onlookers from the beach at Boat Basin, had there been any, would have seen an imposing figure, over six feet tall, standing on the deck, assessing the scene around him. The weather was stormy and unwelcoming, but this large man with the strong jaw had other matters on his mind.

Augustin Brabant had arrived at Hesquiat, this time to stay. Two brief visits had previously introduced him to this harbour and to the people living in Hesquiat Village. He had, by his own estimation, been welcomed, he had said he would return to stay, and true to his word he had arrived, a man possessed of terrible energy and zeal, a man determined to put his mark on this place. He had come to establish his mission church.

The impact this one man was to have on Hesquiat and the surrounding area was huge. The historian Charles Lillard puts it bluntly: "almost single-handedly," he writes, "Father Brabant changed a civilisation. How many men can say that?" Another question might well be posed: "How many men—or women—would *want* to say that?" But Father Augustin Brabant was not prone to question or to doubt the course of his own actions. In common with nineteenth-century missionaries in recently colonised lands all around the world, he was convinced that God was on his side and he had come to rescue an indigenous people he regarded as brute savages, to civilise them, and to convert them to his own religion. His fervour was immense; his determination awesome; his humility non existent. Later, he recorded his feelings on first arriving:

Father Augustin Brabant in the late 1870s.

. . . there are no words to convey how monotonous it is, and how lonesome one would feel were it not for the thought of the sacredness of the object for which he is here. Nothing in the world could tempt me to come and spend my life here were it not that the inhabitants of these inhospitable shores have a claim on the charity and zeal of a Catholic priest.

A Belgian, then in his early thirties, Father Brabant was about to establish the first Catholic mission on the West Coast. Another priest with him, Father Rondeault from Quamichan, was to help construct the first mission buildings, along with a French Canadian carpenter, Noel Leclaire. Two points of land in Hesquiat Harbour now bear the names of these early church-builders. These men also brought "three small calves, one bull and two heifers, which were destined to become the pioneer cattle in this part of the country," as well as a Newfoundland dog who for years was Brabant's close companion.

On Brabant's two previous visits to Hesquiat, he had been in the company of his bishop, Charles Seghers. The first visit early in 1874 was brief, but on the second, later that year, both Seghers and Brabant stayed for four days in the village as part of an extensive voyage along the coast. They were seeking the best place to establish a mission, and their travels excited a great deal of interested curiosity amongst the native people living there. In September 1874 the two Catholic fathers approached Hesquiat from the north, travelling by canoe with a Muchalat crew. Brabant's description of their arrival at Hesquiat is vivid.

> When off Perez Rock we met a Hesquiat canoe crowded with young men, who were on the lookout for our expected arrival. As soon as they recognized us, they put about, intending to precede us and warn the tribe. However, our Muchalat crew took to their paddles, and a regular race between the two canoes took place. There was no wind, and the sea ran mountains high. We had not met such a heavy swell in all our travels. Although in company with the Hesquiats, we would lose sight of them for several minutes to see them again rise on the crest of the heavy waves, whilst we were, as it were, in the abyss of the ocean. It was really a grand piece of sailing we had on that day from Perez Rock to Hesquiat Harbour. We at last lost sight of the Hesquiats in the fog, but we could hear them fire off their guns ahead of us as a signal to the tribe to be ready. We found the Chief's house, where we stayed for four days, cleanly swept out, and mats laid all over the floor. The Indians were full of joy to see us again.

Exhilarated by their trip, Brabant and Seghers set straight to work teaching the "Lord's Prayer, Hail Mary, Creed, Ten Commandments and Seven Sacraments, all of which the Indians learned with much zeal. Here it struck the Bishop that this tribe would be a good place to start a Mission, being the most central and the Indians of the best good-will." Eight months later, Brabant arrived aboard the *Thornton*.

An odd procession, it must have been, when Brabant arrived in Hesquiat Village in May of 1875. With Rondeault and Leclaire, with Captain George Brown of the *Thornton*, perhaps with some Hesquiat people who may have come to greet them, certainly with an incongruous array of animals, Brabant made his way along the beach to the village. The cattle "followed us like dogs, sometimes forgetting themselves when amidst good pasture, and then running up to us with the utmost speed."

Once at Hesquiat, deliberations and arguments began at once about where to build the church and mission buildings. The chief, Matlahaw, was away, and none of the Hesquiats "dared or was willing to point a suitable place out to us." With the support of Captain Brown and after much argument with the Indians, Brabant selected a site, overriding all objections, and began construction. This was the first of many tactless and arrogant actions that caused the brooding, dangerous resentment of Chief Matlahaw who, one year later, made a murderous attack on Brabant, nearly killing him. Brabant survived, thanks to the help of the Hesquiat people and the arrival of a rescue party from Victoria. Matlahaw fled into the bush never to return, and his body was found the following year by Brabant and his assistant Father Nicolaye, who arrived shortly after the mission was established.

From the outset Brabant was oblivious to anything but his own aims. "Our orders had been," he writes, "to put up a church of 60 × 26 feet and a small residence for the priest. Everything was to be done as cheaply as possible, as the establishment of a Mission was only an experiment. Later on, say five years, if the Mission was successful, more substantial buildings would be put up." In keeping with this spirit of economy, the first church at Hesquiat was made mostly of wood sal-

The priest's house at Hesquiat in the 1920s. On the porch is Father Charles Moser

vaged from a shipwreck. A year earlier the barque *Edwin,* loaded with lumber for Australia, had foundered near Hesquiat. The captain's wife and two children and the Chinese cook had all perished, but thanks to Chief Matlahaw and several Hesquiat men who launched their canoes in heavy seas and went to the rescue, the rest of the crew had been saved.

The lumber from the *Edwin* was piled up on the beach a mile along the shore from Hesquiat Village, and with typical energy Brabant soon managed to obtain most of it for his church. Working alongside the carpenter Noel Leclaire and Father Rondeault and several Indian builders, Brabant laboured long days to ensure the church went up quickly, although Leclaire did his best to slow the project down by complaining of illness, picking arguments, and refusing to speak to his co-workers for days on end. "Everything considered," Brabant concludes, "the first Mission buildings on this coast were put up amidst much unpleasantness."

The new church was dedicated to St. Antonine, and the first Mass was celebrated on July 5, 1875. According to Brabant all the Hesquiats were present, including Chief Matlahaw, as well as a crowd of Muchalat Indians from just up the coast. The very next morning Father Rondeault and Noel Leclaire set out in a canoe for Victoria, no doubt glad to get away as fast as they could, leaving Brabant in sole charge of this extraordinary, isolated mission. Over the following years Brabant was to learn much about isolation. At first he could not even talk to anyone, not then knowing the Hesquiat language and having no one in the village who could act as interpreter. Undaunted, he recalls that he simply "made up my mind to study the language, which I found no easy matter, for I had no books to consult and there was no one who could give me any information about it." In later life, Brabant compiled a dictionary of the Hesquiat language. Handwritten, closely annotated, never published, this work is 134 pages long, a meticulously detailed study carried out by a man who was unquestionably a gifted linguist. His abiding interest in words, place names and linguistic variations is reflected in his correspondence and in his diary, as well as in this dictionary.

Brabant was a formidable man. The energy he devoted to every aspect of his mission at Hesquiat overwhelmed everyone in his path. Buoyed up with enormous physical strength, he never looked back, never let up, never faltered. He set out to "convert the heathen" and he gave the people of Hesquiat no peace until they acquiesced, at least nominally, at least temporarily, to his demands: that they attend Mass, that they wear "proper" clothes, that they abandon their superstitions, that they have Christian marriages.

Charles Morin, a carpenter who worked with Brabant in 1877 building another mission in Barclay Sound, wrote in his diary:

[Father Brabant] is a Belgian priest, 34 years old . . . a man of massive build, six feet tall and weighing around 200 pounds. He had a very young and handsome face, very interesting to talk to and with health to match. He could survive on dry fish and biscuits, could sleep outdoors and could pass days out in the open, rain or shine, as nothing seemed to bother him.

Morin is open in his admiration for Brabant's ability to endure discomfort. On one disastrous canoe trip on the open ocean when they were swamped by huge waves and unable to manoeuvre the waterlogged canoe, they tossed around helplessly hour after hour as it grew dark. Completely lost, they finally made it to shore, managed to hike to a native encampment and from there made it back to the mission site, utterly exhausted and chilled to the bone. "Father Brabant had not said one word during our ordeal on the open sea," Morin writes, going on to say that according to Brabant this was the worst storm he had ever experienced. And Morin continues: "He then sang me a little song he always sang to me when I had been in bad humour. 'In this world everything is fine, I don't know of anyone to blame, except the one who grumbles!'"

Father Brabant in his later years.

Although the mission at Hesquiat was intended to be the jewel in the crown of the Roman Catholic Church on the West Coast, its supremacy as a mission began to fade almost as soon as Father Brabant left, some thirty years after his arrival. The energies of the Catholic authorities increasingly focused on Christie's School, the residential school down the coast at Kakawis. As a result the handful of Catholic mission churches on the coast received less attention, and even less money.

Christie's School had been founded in 1900 by Father Brabant, largely in response to the presence of Protestant missionaries on the coast. He had campaigned strenuously to establish this school in order to protect what he considered exclusively Catholic territory from the increasing number of Presbyterians and Methodists on the coast. Writing as early as 1895, Brabant declares gloomily: "Their efforts to invade the coast are very pronounced," adding scornfully that these Protestants have only started to arrive because the coast is now more accessible, thanks to the monthly steamer travelling to the Scandinavian settlement at Cape Scott.

When a man's life was in danger and when the only means of travelling was an Indian canoe, when the mails reached us only once or twice a year . . . we were welcome to do alone the work of converting the natives. Now with the present facilities . . . the ministers come in sight to give us trouble and pervert our Indian children.

Brabant was delighted when the school was built, for this, he believed, was the ultimate key for controlling the native people on the coast, more important even than his original mission.

By the time the Rae-Arthurs arrived to live in Boat Basin in 1915 the mission was starting to change, to move past its heyday. In any real sense, it was always a one-man show and that man was gone. Augustin Brabant left Hesquiat in 1908 and died in Victoria in 1912. None of his successors were cut from the same cloth, none so dominant and powerful. Brabant had, with extraordinary force of personality, imposed his will and his ways upon the village and its surroundings; he had done so at a time when radical and frightening changes were sweeping up and down the coast. Smallpox was commonplace, tuberculosis was spreading, government agents were forcing Indian people onto small land reserves, a cash-based economy was developing, white settlers were appearing for the first time — and in this maelstrom of social change, Brabant remained in Hesquiat for over three decades, solid as a rock. Arrogant and dictatorial and insensitive as he was, he stayed put, exuding confidence and authority in a world seeming, to the native people of the coast, to be increasingly chaotic and out of control. He set himself up as an intermediary between the Hesquiat people and the forces of the outside world. The captains of sealing vessels, the Indian agent, the coastal traders, the doctors—all of these people had to deal first and foremost with Brabant when coming to Hesquiat.

Father Charles Moser in his early days at Hesquiat.

By the time Father Charles Moser came to live permanently at Hesquiat in 1910, the mission was well into its second generation. The tidal wave of change that had swept the coast in the late nineteenth century had subsided to a mere tempest. Traders and missionaries and government agents were, for better or worse, an established part of the scene, and while the scene kept changing steadily, change was now expected. Near to Hesquiat Village, the large and imposing lighthouse at Estevan Point had been built in 1908; many more white people were coming and going; more and faster transport plied the coast; a telegraph line in the village; settlers were arriving and claiming bits of land; some were even staying.

Father Moser was definitely no Brabant. From Switzerland, he was a simpler and less forceful individual, greatly in awe of his predecessor. He did his best to emulate Brabant, dutifully preaching about morality, repeatedly—and futilely—banning native religious ceremonies, baptising and marrying and burying the people of Hesquiat in what he considered proper Christian fashion. He kept careful tally of all the religious rituals he performed, every year counting the numbers of baptisms and funerals and weddings. He also kept track of communions: 894 in 1912; 1911 in 1914; 1356 in 1915. He seems anxious to keep these numbers up as proof of his adequate performance as a priest.

Moser seems to have been far happier in his garden than in the pulpit. In his memoirs he writes contentedly of manuring the garden, hilling the potatoes, planting apple trees. He was also happy with his cattle. Moser took the raising of these Hesquiat cows—the descendants of the original cattle brought in by Brabant—most seriously, frequently pursuing them through the bush when they strayed, constantly building and repairing fences to contain them, cheerfully butchering them and preparing feasts for the village or sending the meat down the coast to the residential school at Kakawis. Moser was better suited, probably, to life as a farmer or butcher than to the life of a priest. He was far more human than Father Brabant, certainly more interested in and more attached to the people with whom he lived. Repeatedly in his memoirs Moser records his grief at the time of a death, his sorrow in a tragic event befalling a family, his respect and liking for individuals, his enjoyment of simple pleasures such as playing cards, lighting fireworks, cooking meals.

After 1917, when he was sent to work at Christie's School, Moser continued to visit Hesquiat, clearly considering it his own mission, his own special place. As the years passed, however, the Hesquiat people did not welcome him as they once had. Christmas of 1920 was a particularly bad time for him:

Dec. 22nd I went up to Hesquiat, at least I intended to go there but as no canoes came out when the steamer blew, I was obliged to go on to Nootka. I was not a bit happy about this, and had to remain at the cannery as I had

no keys to the church or the house at Friendly Cove. Christmas was the
most miserable day I think I have ever spent. No Mass, no church, I
returned on the steamer back to Kakawis.

This refusal of the Hesquiat people to come out to the steamer to fetch Father Moser was a first; his earlier memoirs tell of many such arrivals by steamer when he was faithfully met and greeted warmly after an absence. But in his later years on the coast, Moser was based at Christie's School, and his reputation at Hesquiat was no doubt tainted by this.

Never a reflective man, at least not in his memoirs, Moser seems incapable of understanding that the enforced attendance at this residential school was completely intolerable to many of the students and to their parents. Back at Hesquiat in 1921, he is delighted to discover a new candidate for the school, though his visit to the village sounds rather like a trophy hunt: "I went to Hesquiat early in January and returned with a new girl for the school, also with 370 pounds of baby beef also for the school." All up and down the coast, children were being taken or sent to Christie's School whether or not they wanted to go. Moser tells several times in his memoirs how the Indian Agent and the local policeman would visit groups of people on the coast, telling them that unless their children go to school "the Indian Act would be enforced," and their children would be removed from their care.

The deep unhappiness of some of the students is crystal clear in Moser's memoirs, as is the unapologetic use of force to keep them at the school. Time and again, children were cruelly disciplined; time and again the wishes of their parents were ignored; time and again children who tried to run away were brought back. Many children from Hesquiat were at Christie's School. Those wanting to run away had a long and dangerous journey home by canoe, but despite the dangers, some of them made it home, so great was their determination to get away. Not for long though, because usually the escapees were tracked down by a constable and brought back to school. On their return they faced certain punishment. Sometimes they were beaten; they might be confined in the school jail; their hair might be shaved off; they could be put on rations of bread and water. In one instance when some boys filed through a lock, took two sides of bacon and other food and made off with some of the girls in a canoe belonging to the school, they were caught and charged with abduction of the girls and theft. Even though the abduction charge was dropped, the charges of theft were pursued and the boys served two years in Reform School in Vancouver.

Writing in 1922, Father Moser sounds bewildered:

We were very perturbed to hear that complaints had been made to Ottawa re our school, and it was suggested that the school be closed. It made one feel that ours was a very thankless job for in spite of all we had done it seemed so little appreciated. It was to our credit that the school was still standing for so many of the schools in other places had gone up in smoke, to the delight of the natives.

Despite this threat to close the school, it continued year after year without further challenges. As time passes Moser's memoirs become increasingly troubled and defensive, his good natured zest of earlier years dulled. Ever more problems beset him, both at the school and in the mission field as he struggled to maintain churches in Nootka Sound and at Hesquiat and to keep in touch with other communities on the coast. Recalling events in 1926, he writes:

Back at Hesquiat I ran into trouble. I was accused of giving poison for medicine to a sick child, also of poisoning dogs so that I could enter houses without fear of them, such nonsense. Apparently the Indians were really very annoyed with me because I had recently spoken against their dances, I also heard over the phone that more boys had run away from the school, so it was with a dull heart that I boarded the steamer back to Kakawis.

On his regular visits to Hesquiat throughout the 1920s, Moser kept a close eye on the village, always vigilant for signs of immorality and vice, for returns to "pagan" ways, or for the incursions into "his" territory of the dreaded Protestant missionaries. In August 1928 he returned to Hesquiat to find the very worst of his fears had been realized, worse even than Presbyterians and Methodists coming to visit: "On my next visit to Hesquiat I found that one of the Jehovah Witnesses had been there and had sold a number of their books to the Indians, all blasphemous against our faith and church; he was also reported to have sold books further on up the coast...." Later he writes: "I told the people to bring me all the books they had bought from the Jehovah's Witness man, for a public burning..."

In 1929, when instructed to hand over control of Hesquiat mission to a newly arrived Father Victor, Father Moser was both hurt and horrified, not least because for some unknown reason Father Victor cut down all his apple trees. But the newcomer did not last long, and Moser was soon told to return to Hesquiat. Resignedly, he set off up the coast from Kakawis on the maiden voyage of the new CPR ship the *Princess Norah*, with a full complement of distinguished guests, including Lord and Lady Willingdon, the Governor General of Canada and his wife, out seeing the sights of the West Coast. Back at Hesquiat Moser set to work building a new barn and tried to find some lost cattle, but his heart was weary. "I was not feeling very happy about the mission any more and wrote to the Abbott asking him to allow me to go back home." Perhaps in an effort to raise his spirits, he burned a few more of the Jehovah's Witness books in a big bonfire on the beach.

A few books in the vicinity escaped his attention. Over at Boat Basin, the Jehovah's Witnesses had also provided the Rae-Arthurs with a number of books. Neatly inscribed "A.A. Rae-Arthur, Hesquiat, Sept. 30 1928,", the book entitled *Creation* (Watch Tower Bible and Tract Society) is one of several Jehovah's Witness publications still in Cougar Annie's house, along with *The Harp of God*, no doubt delivered to her at the same time as the Witnesses were making their visit to Hesquiat, and doing their best to convert the "Catholic" natives to a new way of thinking. The success of their brief visit to Hesquiat Harbour was minimal; no converts emerged from either Boat Basin or Hesquiat, but Father Moser thoroughly enjoyed his bonfires.

Later in the year, Moser again wrote to the Abbott asking to be allowed to go home. "I felt that my time on the coast was finished and I needed a change, nothing seemed quite the same as it used to be." At last the Abbott agreed to let Moser leave. He celebrated his last Christmas at Hesquiat where he enjoyed a truce, a happy time. He finally reached an agreement concerning the ever-roaming cattle with the wireless operator from the lighthouse; he assisted at a childbirth and baptised the new infant; he enjoyed an evening of bridge with several men from the Estevan Point Lighthouse; and on December 27, 1929, "I said my last Mass in the little Church, and in the pouring rain, so typical of the West Coast, left on the *Maquinna*, many of the Indians came down the beach to see me go." Further down the coast, Moser bade farewell to Kakawis: "With the Captain's permission I blew three long whistles as a salute and goodbye, and left behind me many memories happy and sad."

When Moser refers to the "little Church" where he said his last Mass, his mind was perhaps wandering to another church on the coast. Whatever the church at Hesquiat may have been, it was not little. The original church built by Brabant in 1875 was replaced in 1891 with a far grander building, financed by Father Brabant's energetic fund-raising in Belgium. This church was designed by Stephen Donovan of Victoria and was an elaborate Gothic structure complete with buttresses and gables and an octagonal bell tower topped with a high pointed roof. Damaged by fire in 1897, the church was promptly rebuilt along similar lines. It endured wind and weather without misadventure until the early 1920s, when the tall spire was removed because of decay and replaced with a small domed roof atop the bell tower. The decay gradually affected other parts of the building, however, and slowly the whole structure fell into disrepair. Eventually this church was razed to the ground in the late 1930s, and a humbler and smaller church erected on the same site. By then the future of the mission was highly questionable.

Following Father Charles Moser, first Father Anthony Terhaar and then Father Joseph Schindler was stationed at Hesquiat during the 1930s. These priests found themselves in a village slowly being abandoned by its own people as the Hesquiats left to take up residence down the coast at Hot Springs Cove, where they could safely moor their fishboats and motor launches. The glory days of the village as a thriving, productive location on the West Coast were over. In the face of such change, the mission could not possibly survive. No longer the preserve of the Benedictine Order, the mission now was the responsibility of another monastic order, the Oblates, but, as a series of priests were to discover, the church was fighting a rearguard action in maintaining any kind of presence at Hesquiat.

By the 1950s priests came and went only periodically to Hesquiat, always lamenting the state of the church, trying to raise money to fix it or paint it, and

Father Joseph Schindler, his sister Victoria and visiting priests at Hesquiat, mid 1930s.

generally moving on before they could do much. A few memorable letters from the late 1950s chronicle the graceless decline of the building and, by inference, the mission itself. Father Brabant's high-reaching ambitions to establish a model Catholic village on this "heathen" coast collapsed, ingloriously, into the ground.

Writing in 1957, Father Fred Miller describes his first visit to Hesquiat, in language laced with superlatives. "Hesquiat is the storied reserve; the remote and often inaccessible reserve," he begins, saying how he had often flown over the peninsula, "that low-lying featureless terrain with its marshes and pools and scrubby forest, and wondered at its silence and the unquiet seas that storm upon its rocky shores." Landing for the first time by water, he says:

> *My excitement turned to amazement when I saw the approach. I had always imagined the beach as a beautiful arc of sand, but instead I found great fields of kelp floating in the shallow water and a field of boulders stretching like the devil's potato field for at least a hundred yards to the tall grass on shore. It was an eerie sight in the early morning light. . . . In a dugout canoe we paddled towards shore till we were halted by the boulders. We stepped out into the thick sea grass and the slimy rocks, the pungent odour of low tide in our nostrils.*

The church at Hesquiat, early 1970s.

Miller was visiting Hesquiat to investigate the state of the church. "Hesquiaht's front doors are falling to pieces. The Church windows from the original church are all rotten." Yet the place cast a strong spell over Miller for he was thrilled to be standing where his hero Father Brabant, whom he calls "that prince of missionaries," had stood. "The great church he built, the pride of the Coast, has long since been replaced by a more modest building. His great . . . house has fallen into decay and the great herd of cattle he started now roams wild through the woods. But the air is pregnant with the presence of the spirit of this great Belgian priest."

Inside the church, sanctuary lights were missing, mildew covered the vestments and the smell of decay was thick in the air. But Miller's letter does not dwell on these points. He has come in search of what was to him a heroic missionary past, and he finds it. "But the climax of it all came when I pulled the bell rope and all the ghosts of past glories started from their graves! For the sound of the bell was deep and majestic and it sent a thrill through me. It bears the stamp "St. Antoninus—A.J. Brabant—1884.""

Two years later Miller again wrote of a visit to Hesquiat:

Poor old Hesquiaht. It was a little the worse for wear. Two old houses had given in to the inevitable and laid down in the sallal brush. . . . I fixed my eyes on the church as I crossed the bridge, sizing it up apprehensively. How had it come through the winter. . . . Billy Ambrose pointed out the places where the rain had come through the roof making pools upon the floor. . . . Brown rats had found their way into the vestment cupboard and destroyed the numeral veil and other vestments.

The church became hopelessly derelict. Windows were broken, furnishings and vestments rotted, mice and rats ate the books. Anything of value was either taken away by the diocesan authorities or fell into the hands of curiosity seekers. Hikers and visitors tell of discovering weird artifacts as they roamed cautiously inside the church: a soggy diary of an unknown priest, decapitated statues, indecipherable documents in Latin, a sorry mess of beer cans and garbage. And so the building surrendered to the elements. Doors came unhinged, the walls sagged, the floor buckled and the whole structure sank gently and slowly to the forest floor. It lies there still, flattened and almost completely overgrown with salmonberries and salal. Traces of the church will soon disappear altogether.

The large brass bell so proudly installed by Father Brabant in his church in 1884, brought up from Victoria on the schooner *Favourite*, laboriously loaded into a canoe and taken ashore, remains in Hesquiat village. Like the remains of shipwrecks along the coast, it is a curious, eerie relic. The people for whom this bell tolled are long gone; the hubristic plans and ambitions of the missionary who brought it here are long silent. The bell could still be sounded, could still ring out over the harbour, but its voice would sound strange now, its context lost. If it were now to toll, it would toll hauntingly, a voice from the past that does not resound easily in Hesquiat Harbour.

CHAPTER 12

Land Lines

ALL AROUND COUGAR ANNIE'S garden the land is overlaid with a fine tracery of lines, lines both visible and invisible, lines that in many different ways identify and delineate land use and title, the land's resources and its potential. This area, seemingly uninhabited and isolated, has been explored and used and mapped and surveyed and demarcated in countless ways. Tangibly and intangibly, people have imposed their lines and their marks on the land in order to define the land and to express particular understandings of the land.

These land lines are sometimes glaring and harsh, impossible to overlook, like the logging roads twisting up the mountainsides, or the sharp outlines of clearcuts. Sometimes the lines are barely discernable, like the old telegraph line through the bush, or the blazes notched into trees alongside traplines, or the small copper plates marking the posts of long-forgotten mining claims. And many lines leave virtually no mark on the land but carry considerable authority, like the lines defining the traditional territories of the Hesquiat people, or the lines setting out recently declared parks, or the seemingly arbitrary lines surveyed through the bush, dividing some of the land into small, legally defined parcels for pre-emption or purchase. Some of these marks are ancient, like the smoke stains on roofs of caves along the shore; some are recent, like the signs posted along the logging road numbering the kilometres.

In visualising these lines and marks on the land, human activity in this apparently isolated area can be re-imagined in a new way. It may be remote and the population may now be negligible, but over many years people have laid their real or imaginary lines on this land for complex reasons. Each and every line bears its own stories, some of which are scarcely known while others are readily traced.

Surveyors tramped through the bush up all along this coast in the 1880s and 1890s when certain tracts, notably the Indian reserves in this area, were first surveyed. Their job was to impose physically onto the land the lines already laid out on a map. This meant marking the boundary lines of reserves and of other legally defined parcels of land by blazing trees and setting wooden posts in the corners. The position of these important corner posts was recorded with reference to "bearing trees" nearby; these were blazed trees onto which letters and figures were carved giving the distance to the corner post. To this day, blazes made by the original surveyors are visible in the forest. As the trees grew, the blazes became large blurred scars on which the original carved letters and figures still appear, now distorted by the tree's growth. Surveyors working on the coast still rely on finding the original blazes and the bearing trees to be sure of their ground.

Jack Gisborne's surveying firm was asked to resurvey the Homais Indian reserve in 1987, and he recalled this experience in an article in *Pacific Yachting* in August 1998. Armed with the original survey notes of Mr. F.A. Devereux, who surveyed Homais in 1893, Gisborne and his crew first had to determine at least one of the corners of the reserve.

> *Even in undisturbed forest a good deal of detective work is required to find bearing trees blazed 100 years ago. Trees are masters of transformation. A clearly carved blaze becomes nearly invisible as the wound in the bark heals. Trees die, fall and rot—or grow enormously. It takes concentration and imagination to detect an old bearing tree, and careful ax work to reveal the hidden message left a century before. We were fortunate to find Devereux's tree. Whoops of excitement echoed in the forest.*

Similarly, when Dave Ignace worked alongside survey crews in Hesquiat Village trying to determine the original boundaries of the lands pre-empted by Anton Luckovich and by the Roman Catholic church, he joined the search for trees bearing blazes from almost a hundred years ago. Again, the crew was successful in finding the bearing trees. "They're big now," says Dave. "Maybe two and a half feet across, and they were probably just little trees when the blaze was made, maybe only eight inches or so."

The original surveyors on the coast left remarkable records in their survey notes. Not only did they provide intensely detailed notes of the topography, they did so in exquisite handwriting complete with numerous little maps showing interesting features of the land. In 1922, Mr. A.W. Harvey surveyed the Rae-Arthurs' pre-emption and the adjacent property which was still at that time held in Allan Wheeler's name. Mr. Harvey's report for the two properties runs to twenty-four pages of copperplate notes, noting every rise and descent in the land, every change in vegetation, every stream, every rocky formation, along with neatly worded descriptions of every corner and portion of the property. "Rough Broken Country," he remarks of one area. "Brushy," of another, adding on the next page "Thick sallal brush." Comments such as "Steep rocky shore" and "Flat Swampy" are interspersed with lists of the trees he comes across and comments about their size. Cedar, hemlock, yew, balsam, pine and fir appear repeatedly and once Mr. Harvey notes "Crab Apple," the indigenous crabapple of the lower slopes. If a similar survey were now to be conducted, a modern-day Mr. Harvey would find a wider variety of vegetation in the area. The forest and shoreline near Cougar Annie's garden are peppered with unexpected plants and shrubs and even some trees which have escaped from the garden to establish themselves in the forest.

Cotoneaster, for instance, has travelled far and wide, appearing regularly along the shore, spread there presumably by birds. Broom, that indestructible invader, has also gone forth and multiplied, particularly along the logging road near the garden. Foxgloves bloom cheerfully on the dusty verge of the road, and several types of heather have jumped the garden fence and frequently appear in the area of bog pine forest adjacent to the garden. Rhododendrons and hollies also show up in the forest near the garden, flourishing in the heavy growth of young conifers that now dominate the perimeter zone once cleared by Cougar Annie just outside her five acres of fenced garden. Buddleia flowers near the logging road high on Mount Seghers and, according to Cougar Annie, potato plants appeared on that same mountainside many years ago. A solitary clump of Michaelmas daisies blooms above the high-tide mark at Rae Basin, rooted in the debris of driftwood, and just outside Cougar Annie's garden a small cherry tree is almost invisible amongst the conifers.

Near Rae Basin, for one season only in the early 1970s, an incongruous display of gladioli bulbs flowered gaudy and bright on a large fallen cedar poised horizontally over the beach. Although they came from Cougar Annie's garden, these gladioli were not escapees. They were planted on the log by Peter Buckland and Bus Hansen, near a smaller tree growing out of the decaying wood of the log. This small tree became the final post of one of their mining claims. "The most ecologically friendly claim post on the coast," Peter claims. "We planted the flowers to see if anyone would notice." No one did.

With or without gladioli, claim posts are hard for an untrained eye to spot in the forest. Small metal plates, half obscured by the growth of the forest, mark the initial and final posts of a mining claim. They impose a line on the land demarcating an area that could, just could, contain untold riches, but which often provides little more than a recreational dream for the prospector. Many prospectors have come and gone in the area around Cougar Annie's garden, usually leaving only slight traces of their passage. Hikers and loggers occasionally come across old claim posts out in the bush, and a prospector's cabin is reportedly rotting in the forest on the eastern slopes above Rae Lake, but generally the prospectors pass invisibly through the bush. Their incurable optimism leaves no footprint.

Claim post.

Part-time prospecting first brought Peter Buckland to Boat Basin in the 1960s. He came with Bus Hansen, who had been prospecting in the area for many years. A huge man, a great storyteller, a true prospector, Bus knew this area as well as anyone. He had tramped far through the bush around here, his eye on the rocks, officially in search of minerals, but basically just glad to be here far away from everything, free to hike around, dreaming dreams, doing what he loved best. In Rae Basin, on one of his claims, Bus built a small shack, and this became not only his but Peter's base camp when either of them was in the area. They staked several groups of claims in the region, concentrating mostly on the geology of the "Brown Jug" claims near Hesquiat Lake, an area that has interested prospectors since the 1890s.

The rock in this overall region intrigues geologists and prospectors. Any geological survey map will show dramatic and unpredictable formations all over Vancouver Island and its coast. On such maps, the lay of the land is described in a complex explosion of lines illustrating how fantastically the ground has heaved and shifted over millions of years, thrusting up various rock formations into unpredictable outcrops. All around Hesquiat Harbour the evidence is clear. High on the flank of Mount Seghers, dramatic layerings of sedimentary rock, formed below sea level, jut almost vertically from the surrounding formations. This sedimentary occurrence—the Escalante formation—underlies all of Hesquiat Peninsula, emerging on the foreshore of Leclaire and Hesquiat Points in jagged and colourful layers. Another rarely occurring formation undercuts Hesquiat Lake and outcrops spasmodically down to Stewardson Inlet. Known as the Sicker Group formation, usually found very deep within the earth, this rock is often rich in minerals.

The Sicker formation in Stewardson Inlet was extensively explored in the late nineteenth century, and led to the development of an active copper mine. This mine operated in fits and starts from 1904 until 1938, shipping out more than 70,000 tons of ore during that period. Some of the books from the library of the mine have found their way up to Boat Basin and remain in Cougar Annie's house, stamped "Tidewater Copper" inside the front cover. While traces of the mine's tramway are still visible on the northern slopes of the inlet, the intense bustle of industry during the years of production is hard to imagine in the now silent landscape. Yet Stewardson Inlet and the adjoining Sydney Inlet were lively places during the 1920s and 1930s; the copper mine was going strong and the pilchard reduction plants were also active. Captain George Heater, who had commanded sealing schooners on the coast for many years, owned a herring saltery in Sydney Inlet. He hired a bevy of girls from Aberdeen, Scotland to work at his fish plant and to enliven the local scene. He housed them on the *Favourite*, a sailing schooner converted into a dormitory. According to George Nicholson's history of the West Coast, this was "a popular rendezvous for halibut and cod fishermen who called there regularly for bait."

Around Hesquiat Lake the rock formations seemed, in the early years of the twentieth century, at least as promising as those at Stewardson. The B.C. Ministry of Mines report for 1899 states that in the "Hesquoit" area "Considerable work has been done in this section of the division, the claims proving very satisfactory; copper ore predominating." A few years later, the 1902 report provides more detail about the work around the lake, describing some new claims on the eastern lakeshore: "175 feet above and some 4,000 feet back from the water, reached at present by a blazed trail only," and another on the west side of the lake "about 300 feet up and less than a quarter of a mile back from the water, reached by a steep trail." The report describes an open cut into the hillside, twelve feet long and four to five feet deep at the face, showing up "very clean and solid ore."

After 1902 not much activity is reported and by 1917 the mining recorder reports, in tones of great irritation, that he could not even *find* the earlier mining claims near Hesquiat Lake. With two native guides he spent a day searching for the claims, "but was unable to find any trace of trails or blazes leading to outcroppings, nor could any one be found who had any knowledge of any work having been done in recent years."

Work on the claims around Hesquiat Lake waned and by 1925, according to the Ministry of Mines report, no work was being done at all. Interest in the claims flickered on and off for many years following, keeping a number of prospectors coming and going. In 1983 some exploratory diamond drilling was done on the "Brown Jug"claims, but no further action has since been taken, largely because increasing environmental concerns have discouraged exploration investment. These claims are surrounded by one of the so-called "scenic corridors" created by the Clayoquot Sound Land Use Decision of 1993: areas which are—ironically—still open to logging and mining activity.

Checking the telegraph line at Hesquiat, about 1920.

Cougar Annie often hinted that valuable mineral deposits were plentiful on her own land. Up at Rae Lake, she repeatedly claimed, she had "seen something glittering." In the mid-1970s she asked Peter Buckland to stake a claim for her from the shoreline of Boat Basin up to the lake. He obligingly set the initial post in place near the lake and flagged the line of the claim. The exercise degenerated into comedy when he realized the line would go straight through the chicken coop. The would-be claim caused additional confusion because when Tommy Rae-Arthur saw the flagging tapes running down the fence of his vegetable garden he was outraged, believing the flagging was there to mark the route of the proposed logging road. He was determined to defend his valuable turnips against all comers, be they prospectors or loggers.

☙

In Cougar Annie's house, a disintegrating map entitled *South Western British Columbia*, issued by the B.C. Department of Lands and dated 1912, emerges from a pile of damp papers. At first glance the map is unremarkable, but on closer examination the finest pencilled handwriting appears at the head of Hesquiat Harbour. These minuscule copperplate letters declare "WF Arthur's Land" on the site of the Rae-Arthur pre-emption, and other faint lines have been drawn on the map. The pathway to the beach is marked, and another much longer line runs all the way from Rondeault Point to Stewardson Inlet. "Proposed trail," the writing declares.

This was the route of the telegraph trail stretching overland—and occasionally underwater—from Tofino to Nootka. Although wireless radio had been installed at the Estevan Point Lighthouse and started operating there in 1908, this new telegraph line was to improve communications greatly for the scattered settlers on the coast. In the autumn of 1913, as Father Charles Moser recalls in his memoirs, "Next time the steamer came in it brought... heavy coils of telegraph wire as it had been decided to establish the telegraph from Clayoquot to Nootka. Hitherto we had been terribly cut off, the only news from the outside world coming from the wireless station at Estevan Point, several miles away."

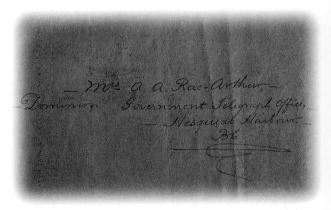

In June 1914, the telegraph construction crew arrived and pitched their big tents behind the church at Hesquiat. By July 8th all the cables had been laid and the Dominion Government Telegraph was installed, its headquarters being in the priest's house, which had the one and only telephone for the village. In August, Moser comments, "It is now possible for me to get the latest war news on the telephone, although many of the reports conflicted one with the other."

An early map shows the telegraph line crossing underwater from Rondeault Point to Leclaire Point, bypassing Boat Basin entirely, but according to Father Moser the newly arrived Rae-Arthurs definitely had a telephone in 1915, for that was when Willie called Moser on the telephone when Ada Annie was having difficulties in labour. The Rae-Arthurs later became agents for the Dominion Government Telegraph; for a fee their telephone was available to anyone in the locality who wanted to send telegrams or make phone calls

The telegraph line on the coast became a legend in its own time. Mike Hamilton was the "agent and linesman" responsible for the forty miles of land line between Ahousat and Hesquiat Harbour from 1915 to 1918. He records in his memoirs that his job was "no lazy man's task...it was nothing unusual to have miles of line hopelessly wrecked by one big storm." The line was strung mostly along the shoreline, stretching from tree to tree, held in place with oak brackets and scantily protected with porcelain insulators. Sometimes the line stretched across the open and exposed water of small bays; sometimes it went across a neck of land between two bays. The men who tended the line built small cabins along the route so they could shelter from bad weather. Their job took them out in all weather and at all hours, mending the fragile and vulnerable line, travelling dangerously close to shore in their boats to view the damage, seeking safe anchorages so they could go ashore and hike through the bush to do the necessary repairs. As Mike Hamilton recalls: "It must be understood that there was not a single foot of what might be called a road or even a good walkable trail...the sea was and still is the only highway."

Nearly sixty years after Mike Hamilton's time, this line was still functioning. In his memoirs Ron Dalziel recalls how the line intrigued road builders and loggers at Stewardson Camp in the 1970s.

There was an old telephone line ran through that camp, reaching from Ahousat down to Estevan Point. There probably wasn't a half dozen subscribers on it in total, when we hooked into it. We had a little crank phone on the wall in the bunkhouse. We just hung the wire from tree to tree with little insulators. Sometimes a high load logging truck would catch the line and tear it down. We'd just stick it back up again...there was a guy [Frank Rae-Arthur] working almost steady keeping that phone line up. Running along the beach in some places, it went out over the water as it crossed a bay. Sometimes when tides were extremely high the phone wouldn't work because the line was under water. Didn't seem to be bothered if it was under a fresh water mud puddle, but the saltchuck would shut it down. The maintenance guy would go out in the middle of the night to keep the phones operating. I've never seen anything like it. There were little shacks along the beaches every mile or two where the lineman stayed. There were phones in them also, so if anyone as in trouble at sea, he could hit the beach and hook into the phone line for assistance."

Robert Culver describes the line in his memoirs with equal fascination. "The telephones are of the old magneto cranking type, and the current is in the form of a pair of #6 dry cells for each phone. The signal tones are usually very weak and the service a few hours a day. This was in the years I was there. A few years ago, radio-telephones were installed, but I've never been able to get Ada on the phone since then."

The ringing of the telephone in Cougar Annie's house was a noteworthy event. "It was so exciting to hear from anyone" recalls Nairne Carter, looking back to her summer at Boat Basin in 1955. Others along the line felt the same; they were keenly attuned to the familiar rings. Two shorts and three long was the ring for Ivan Clarke in Hot Springs Cove. One long and three shorts was the ring for Ahousat General Store. One long, one short, one long, two shorts was the signal for Bus Hansen's cabin in Rae Basin. Three shorts was for Boat Basin Store.

Insulator bracket from old telephone line.

Cougar Annie liked talking on the phone—this was one of her few entertainments, and the temptation to eavesdrop on other peoples' calls added spice to life. In her later years, the fun ended when the old line, looping haphazardly through the forest, was replaced with new technology needing no line at all.

Out in the bush, the old line died. Falling trees and bad weather demolished most of it, the linemen's cabins gradually decayed into the forest, the rough pathways they had made through parts of the forest were quickly overgrown. Coastal scavengers gathered up much of the valuable copper wire and the porcelain insulators made their way into collectors' hands. Hikers still come across vestiges of the line, sometimes tripping over it on barely visible inland trails. Just back from the beach at Boat Basin a tree bears one of the old oak brackets that once held the line in place, a reminder of the communications system linking hundred of trees and a scattering of cabins with a single fragile wire.

Around Estevan Point various lines that once marked the land have fallen into dramatic disuse as communications along the coast have changed. All supplies are now helicoptered into the lighthouse, a luxury undreamed of when the light began operation in 1908. Then a track of wooden rails, two and a quarter miles long, linked Estevan Point to Homais where supplies were landed. An unfortunate horse had to haul supplies along the track back to Estevan, a tricky operation taking anywhere up to four hours, depending how often the horse fell off its plank walkway between the wooden rails, how many times the load was upset, and how frequently the horse had to rest. Walking along the wooden track, frequently elevated over marshy ground, on two twelve-inch wooden planks was exceedingly difficult for the horse who was, according to an understated report in 1915, "not accustomed to walking on two planks and is in a nervous condition."

Truck used for many years to take supplies from Hesquiat to Estevan.

In 1925, when the track was virtually beyond repair, a suggestion came from a bureaucrat in Ottawa that the route to Homais be "filled in and graded for a macadam road." Mercifully the marine agent in Victoria was able to forestall this lunatic idea, pointing out wearily and repeatedly that most of the route was made up of ravines and "seven marshes varying from 50 feet to 1900 feet each." Meanwhile the wooden "Government Road," as Father Moser terms it in his memoirs, was constructed. This roadway extended for five miles between Estevan Point and Hesquiat Village and for several decades it saw a considerable amount of use thanks to the regular arrivals of personnel and mail and supplies on the *Maquinna*. Gradually this became the main supply line for the lighthouse, supplanting the narrow-gauge tracks completely.

A pickup truck from the lighthouse travelled the wooden road between Estevan and Hesquiat, balancing carefully along the planks hammered in place above the hefty cedar crosspieces. To be able to negotiate the entire roadway without slipping off the planks was a considerable feat. The last truck that regularly travelled the roadway has long since ceased to function. Frank Rae-Arthur bought this truck in the late 1970s after the wooden road was abandoned in favour of supplying the lighthouse by helicopter. Now a derelict wreck, abandoned alongside the logging road near Cougar Annie's garden, the old truck is almost invisible, completely overgrown with salmonberries. Across the harbour the wooden road is also disappearing into the bush, and few traces now remain of the two and a quarter miles of narrow-gauge track that once led out to Homais. As these old land lines disappear, helicopters beat their way overhead, slicing the air noisily as they carry fuel and supplies ashore from the Coast Guard tender to the lighthouse.

Amongst the many lines, real and imaginary, criss-crossing the area surrounding Cougar Annie's garden are lines that reveal the movements of animals and birds as they consistently follow their same routes, year after year. Wolves pace along the beaches at night, leaving clear fine prints on the sand. Black bears follow their accustomed routes through the forest, along the sides of logging roads, along the shoreline, predictably appearing and reappearing at the same streams, the same rocks, the same grassy patches. Mink and marten race, small and fierce, through the same territory, along the same routes, season in and season out. Traplines marked by blazes on trees generally follow the routes taken by animals across the land. All around Hesquiat Harbour traplines are registered, some of them remaining in the same families for generations. Cougar Annie had two traplines, one extending through the bog forest just to the north of her garden and the other up to Rae Lake. Marked by Tommy Rae-Arthur's handwritten signs, "Beware: Cougar Traps," this second trapline was known as "Cougar Alley."

Blaze marking Cougar Annie's trapline.

High overhead, many habitual flight paths intersect the sky, flight paths strange and mysterious to people watching from below, yet familiar as air and water to the birds following their timeless routes. Perhaps most remarkable of all the birds etching their paths across the sky is the marbled murrelet, that small rainforest bird famed for nesting exclusively in old-growth forest. These birds attract intensive research in Clayoquot Sound. When a research team arrived in Boat Basin in the summer of 1998 for their second season of field research, their Beaver aircraft was heavy with large marine batteries and high-frequency radar equipment, including the specially adapted six-foot-long receiver, and a barrage of other equipment. Once they had set up camp, the crew worked late and early tracking their birds on a green glowing radar screen. The birds show on the screen as a series of little blips as they speed unseen directly over Cougar Annie's garden. They can fly up to 160 kilometres per hour and are extremely difficult to see with the naked eye as they make their way towards their nesting grounds. Occasionally they are heard, their high-pitched squawks sounding for all the world like a strangled seagull.

Research into another small and little-known species—in this case a flower—has come to the defense of a specific patch of land near Hesquiat Lake. Hesquiat Lake Park was formed to protect the dwarf pink trillium found clinging to the rocks near the lake. The *Trillium Hibbersonii* was brought to botanical attention in the 1920s when John Hibberson, a keen naturalist who was timber cruising in the area, discovered it beside Hesquiat Lake. He prised it out from the rocks using a miner's pick and took it to Victoria for identification. The small trillium now bears his name. Although recent research has shown that the trillium grows in other locations on the West Coast as well as near Hesquiat Lake, botanists and naturalists speak guardedly about its precise locations, hoping to protect the flower, still considered a rarity, from collectors.

Gathering data about the flora and fauna in this area, as elsewhere on the West Coast, contributes to an ever-increasing body of knowledge about the delicate ecosystem of this region of temperate rainforest. Time and again, the findings of researchers have asserted the overwhelming importance of retaining old-growth forest along the coast, not only to protect the trees themselves but the watersheds, the salmon streams, the clam beds, the nesting birds, the animals, the complex undergrowth. Strand after strand of research has created a powerful line of defense of these old forests, a mass of scientific evidence impossible to dismiss or to deny. Yet looking around Hesquiat Harbour, looking around the mountains near Cougar Annie's garden, many observers bleakly wonder if this carefully amassed defense has come altogether too late. Some of the more recent lines imposed on the land have been devastating.

CHAPTER 13

Above the Garden

A<small>N UNEXPECTED GLINT</small> of light flashes high on Mount Seghers above Cougar Annie's garden. It is the summer of 1997. The upper reaches of this mountainside stand naked, as they have been for many years now, a barren expanse of steep rock littered with dead trees. From below, the litter of lost trees appears like white matchsticks strewn on the slopes.

Since being logged some twenty years ago, no trees remain on the higher elevations of this mountain. One lone survivor stands on the summit, a tall spar, stark and white, clearly visible against the grey West Coast skies. Beneath this tree the mountainside drops away, scarred with small slides, ringed with logging roads now disused and dangerous.

In the mid-1990s work resumed on these slopes, on these roads. Heavy machines once again appeared, grinding up and down the crumbling, precipitous inclines, to deactivate the roads, to remove culverts, to try to re-establish the natural shape and watershed of the mountainside in order to prevent landslips. The view from here is magnificent, on a fine day Hesquiat Harbour stretches blue and beautiful around lazy curving beaches, all the way out to Estevan and beyond, across the Pacific, until the horizon disappears in a haze. But working up here leaves no time to admire the view; the men and machines toiling on this steep mountainside need to concentrate fiercely on the job in hand.

The flash of light on the hillside, seen from the garden below, is at first inexplicable. Then comes news of the accident. The sun is reflecting on the glass windscreens of an excavator, a huge road-building machine, that has crashed terribly and fatally down the mountain. The machine and its operator were working on an insecure bit of road on the cliff edge when the road gave way. They plummeted three hundred metres down the mountainside. The excavator came to rest on its side, splayed and broken. The operator, trapped inside, could not be saved. He died of his injuries.

For a fortnight or so the ungainly, contorted body of the machine remained on the slope before being salvaged. While it awaited the winches and cables, it was visible on clear days from the garden far below, a reminder, yet another reminder, of the messy wreckage of dreams and schemes that constitutes the history of logging out here.

Such reminders are scarcely necessary. Any eyes uplifted to the hills can see the damage. No witness can escape the conclusion that much of this area has been, by any standard, desecrated. Visitors are silenced by what lies before them. Road builders and tree planters, brought in to try to repair some of the damage, often can only shake their heads.

One mountainside after another has been logged. From the peaceful waters of Rae Lake, look to the east, then look to the west. In both directions, slopes have been scoured of trees. Small and perfect, this lake borders the back line of Willie Rae-Arthur's original land pre-emption. Three major landslides have dumped large quantities of silt into the lake; the roadbeds inching up the mountains have visibly collapsed.

If you fly over the area around Cougar Annie's garden, just look down. No need to look far or look hard. Just circle for a while, taking in Rae Lake, Hesquiat Harbour, Hesquiat Lake. A parcel of land to the south of the garden, across the harbour from Boat Basin, has been logged. To the west, the area behind the beach at Yahksis, part of the Maahpe reserve, has been logged—the fresh growth of alder attests to that. North of the garden, the slopes of Mount Seghers have been logged, and the mountain above Rae Basin to the east has also been logged. Jagged slashes of bare mountainside have become the norm around here, and anyone spending any time in this area cannot help but witness the impact of such logging.

Position yourself on the logging road, on the sturdy bridge crossing the tidal river leading from Hesquiat Lake down to the sea at Rae Basin. The date: March 1997. The weather: stormy and wild. This river only travels some 150 metres before entering tidewater in the basin. It is entirely clogged with logs and debris left here by a recent disastrous slide. When this jam eventually breaks, logs will move with slow and insistent force to create such pressure that some of them will be tossed into the air like kindling. As they move they will scour the chum salmon

Clearcut above Rae Basin.

spawning beds under the bridge; when they reach Rae Basin they will dump vast quantitites of sand and gravel and wood debris and choke the rich clam beds. As you watch, the first of the densely packed logs begins, ominously, to move.

As you stand on the bridge, far above, on a nearby slope, sharp loud cracks like gunshots are sounding. Every few moments, the same sound recurs. These are trees snapping, breaking off, in the unlogged area bordering the clearcut. They now have no protection from the wind. The logging above Rae Basin was done in such a fashion that the wind tunnels in fiercely, its velocity increasing as it focuses on this slope. The trees snap like twigs in almost every high wind.

You have seen enough. The tale of West Coast logging is clear, right here. You could go farther afield, leave the area immediately around the garden, and see more. You could travel some twenty kilometres up the logging road to the famous, much photographed clearcut of the Escalante watershed, and you would there see far worse slides, far larger clearcuts. There you would see what looks like the irreversible death of whole mountainsides, sights which have earned this coast the title "Brazil of the North." Or you could view any number of other clearcuts in the old-growth throughout Clayoquot Sound. But there is enough to see right here.

ॐ

The logging road passes directly in front of Cougar Annie's property. When the road was first punched through this area of old-growth forest in 1974, she and her son Tommy were the only ones living at Boat Basin. They were nervous of the loggers and road builders at first, yet at the same time determined not to be out-manoeuvred in their own territory.

Cougar Annie refused point blank to sell any of her land to the logging companies for road access or for use as a logging camp. She entertained offers, let the road builders and the loggers present their cases, and made them wait for a while. But the final answer was a resounding "no"; she would sell not one square inch of her property. As a result, the road runs right along the edge of the Rae-Arthur property, about two hundred metres up from and parallel to the beach.

If an early scheme had borne fruit, Cougar Annie would have had the logging camp close at hand. It would have opened onto the beach right in front of her house, a little to the east of her raised walkway through the forest. According to Ron Dalziel, this is the site where the base camp, the one that became Stewardson Camp eighteen kilometres away, should have gone; the travelling for loggers would have been greatly reduced, the logistics of building the camp much simpler. Had this plan been carried out, Cougar Annie could have just walked down

View of the logging road bordering Cougar Annie's garden.

Mount Seghers.

to the beach to witness all the action, while up in her garden she would have heard the large diesel generators used to power the camp, and the garden would have resounded with the noise of big road-building machines all day long. She would undoubtedly have had many more visitors, many more curious seekers and intruders, many more potential helpers: after all, she would have had up to seventy men within hailing range.

In his memoirs, Ron Dalziel, who was in charge of the road-building gang, recalls the "Cougar Lady" had not been very friendly at first: "As a matter of fact," he writes, "she was sort of spooky—she'd run for the house when she saw us coming up the beach from the plane." But as time passed she became friendlier, no doubt because Ron Dalziel and several other men took a genuine interest in her, and they were openly impressed by her reputation as a hunter. Dalziel recalls visiting her to ask for advice about "the best way to bag a cougar." He writes, "When I arrived at the old girl's place, I noticed something hanging in the woodshed. Thought it might have been a deer, but later learned that it was indeed a tawny cougar. She'd tell me, 'Oh yes, I eat a bit of cougar meat, feed some to my cats [this should read chickens, she had no cats], and even can a little.'"

In 1974 the road came in, and soon the logging trucks began rolling by.

190

Reaction from people who knew the area was mixed. Walter Guppy, when visiting Hesquiat Lake to check his mining claims, was taken aback by the new road. "We landed at the lake, at the old lineman's cabin near there, it's quiet you know, really quiet. Suddenly there was a terrific roaring, and a cloud of dust. We were right near the new logging road. I hadn't seen it before —this had been pristine wilderness last time I was up." Barry Lorton, who happened to be visiting on the day that the big machines first arrived in front of Cougar Annie's garden, remembers how the old boardwalk down to the beach was ripped asunder, how the splintered grey cedar boards flew in the air as the machine made its first pass. Peter Buckland recalls his growing sense of foreboding on visit after visit to the area, as he saw the lines of surveyor's tape stretching ever farther through the forest, flagging the route the road was to take, bright slashes of colour marking big trees that would soon be gone.

But this was development, and the Rae-Arthur family had awaited development from the outset. Ada Annie and Willie Rae-Arthur had arrived as part of a wave of coastal settlers, many of whom had fanned extraordinary enterprises and ambitions into life, peppering the coast with various types of development. Cougar Annie had lived to see most of these fade into extinction. She had outlived the rise and fall of the copper mine in Stewardson Inlet, not to mention the rise and fall of numerous pilchard reduction plants, including the one just around the corner at Riley's Cove. She had outlived the frenzy of gold fever that had seized Zeballos, and she no doubt knew of many fish canneries that had come and gone on the coast. She knew of the whaling industry that had been and gone, of the vain ambitions that had inspired the unlikely agricultural settlement at Cape Scott early in the twentieth century, of the many small-scale logging operations that came and then disappeared. All these undertakings enjoyed their moments of hope and glory, however hard won, however fleeting, however misguided, but Boat Basin had known nothing of the kind. Now, surely it was their turn. The loggers had come and so had the road—high time.

Yes, it meant their solitude was broken. Yes, it meant their boardwalk was broken. Yes, it meant noise from the trucks and dust on the road and the racket of huge chainsaws at work. And yes, it meant the loss of trees, some of them so old and so large they were here long before Columbus set foot in the Americas. But it also meant more people, more company, more help, it meant more stamps to sell from the post office, more potential purchasers of eggs from the ever-obliging chickens, more cigarettes and sometimes stale chocolate bars to sell at the store. Most of all it meant a road.

The dream of a road had finally come true, the road longed for by Father

Charles Moser in his lonely musings in his earliest days at Hesquiat, the imminently awaited road he excitedly discussed years later, in 1924, in letters to his bishop, the road the Rae-Arthurs and other early settlers had been hoping to see from the moment of their arrival, the road so wistfully desired by Ada Annie's faithful admirer Robert Culver in the late 1960s. This was progress, at last. A faded snapshot taken in the summer of 1974 shows Cougar Annie with her daughter Rose standing in front of a large machine on the new, raw road in front of the garden, both smiling broadly, with a handwritten sign posted jauntily behind them saying "Boat Basin Highway."

This road never became a highway. To this day it remains a closed circuit road, connecting one logging camp to another, stretching from Stewardson Inlet to Mooyah Bay on Nootka Sound. It remains a logging road, not leading to the outside world at all, a road much used for over twenty years, but now carrying little traffic of any kind. Given the great changes in logging practices and the reduction in allowable cut resulting from pressure by the environmental movement, the road has fallen silent, most of the time at least.

Yet this road remains an abiding preoccupation out here, even though its use has radically changed and its continued existence is under question. For the road even now continues to inspire hopes and dreams. To this day rumours waft through the bush that the road will be made to join up with Hot Springs Cove, or Gold River, or anywhere at all that leads to anywhere else at all. To this day, people stubbornly hold onto their hopes for this road, not least Ron Dalziel, who, having built it with so much extraordinarily hard work, cannot bear to think of it falling into disrepair.

The logging road in winter.

He writes yearningly of this stretch of road in his memoirs. "It seems to me there is a great future for bus tours from Stewardson to Mooyah Bay. Tourists could get on the *Uchuck* (the freight boat) at Gold River and enjoy the ride to Mooyah Bay. Then they could get on a bus with their box lunches and ride down to Hesquiat Harbour...." From there, according to Dalziel, another bus would take them to Stewardson and then a boat would take them out to Tofino, and the next day they would head back to Gold River the same way. "Along the way, by land and sea, those tourists would see a vast expanse of unexplored wilderness."

Looking around at the clearcuts and the landslides on the mountains, and given the silence and the isolation here, this notion of tour buses full of jolly visitors careering happily up and down a logging road to enjoy "unexplored wilderness" seems odd, out of joint. The arrival of this logging road and the subsequent logging activity in the area has not, after all, augured well for tourism and recreation. An earlier dream for this area, one that was cherished for a while by the Parks Branch of the provincial government, was put to rest because of the road and the logging.

Two cultures at work: cedar tree near the logging road.

Just as the road building was getting underway, just as the plans for logging were becoming a reality, the Parks Branch was exploring the notion of creating "Ecoreserve #61" at Hesquiat Harbour, and was even for a while contemplating a provincial park in the area. Official correspondence dating between 1974 and 1976 discusses many aspects of this potential "ecoreserve" and/or park, particularly its ecological value and its potential for recreation. Early and optimistic correspondence between the Parks Branch and the Ministry of Forests describes a "recreational reconnaissance" of the area and concludes that the "foreshore and immediate backshore have significant recreational potential."

But by the spring of 1976, the Parks Branch was abandoning hope for this area. "We were interested in the area because we thought it may have possibilities as another 'West Coast Trail,'" a disappointed official declared at the time. "However, a logging company has constructed a road...and the slashes and road have destroyed the wilderness qualities of this bay. Presumably, this is also why the ecoreserve proposal was dropped."

If this dream of a second West Coast Trail had gone through, the area around Hesquiat would have become widely known to hikers and boaters as an area open to a broad range of recreational activity, one admittedly hard to access, but untouched and unspoiled. This is a dream hard to credit now when looking up at the naked mountainsides; hard to credit when faced with the scoured watershed of the Escalante River; hard to credit when watching a log jam break up in a flooded creek. But it was, for a while, an active and promising dream.

If this land had been protected for recreation before the logging occurred, Cougar Annie would never have seen a road come anywhere near her garden, nor would she have enjoyed her friendships with the men in the logging camp. Instead she would have seen only the occasional hiker and her later years at Boat Basin would have been much harsher. Whatever the logging has meant to the surrounding area, it was a godsend to Cougar Annie. Her final years at Boat Basin were tough enough; without the loggers she would have known even more hardship.

Back in the 1970s, Cougar Annie was as wily as a fox in her dealings with the loggers and road builders. Here were men, strong men, and strong men were always useful. They could fix things, bring her things. "Now boys," she would say after one of them had mended a fence, dug a ditch, or patched her roof. "Now boys, I can't pay you today, but I'll give you some eggs," or canned fish, or produce from the garden.

Enkianthus tree: Mount Seghers in the background.

With great good nature the men from the logging camps willingly obliged, year after year through the 1970s and 1980s, keeping an eye on her. After all, she was a little old lady out in the bush in a house slowly falling apart, and she lived right by the logging road, and they went past her house every day in their great big trucks. Many of the men took a real interest in Cougar Annie. They would check as they drove by to make sure smoke was coming out of the chimney; they would deliver firewood right to the front gate, dropping off entire logs and returning to buck up the wood and split it. They would stop to visit, bringing treats from the logging camp. Ice cream was her special favourite; she could not get enough ice cream. "Oh, Granny would have had ice cream for every meal if she could have. She just loved it." recalls one of the men with a chuckle.

"Just call me Granny," she would say to the men. They all did, and so did the handful of women in the logging camps. Occasionally Cougar Annie was invited down to the camp at Stewardson Inlet for dinner, jolting over the gravel road for thirty minutes in one of the trucks and arriving at the camp to be greeted as a special guest, a local heroine. The women in camp would make a fuss over her, comb her hair and lend her lipstick. These were big nights out for Cougar Annie.

For some of the men travelling along the dusty logging road, stopping at the garden to visit Cougar Annie became a regular and special event, even something of a treat. This garden was, after all, the only habitation along the entire forty kilometres of road, and a visit was never dull, even if it did mean chopping wood or fixing a fence. Leo Mattson was always happy to drop in.

Oh, I loved visiting Granny. She would talk and talk, you had to follow her around as she talked, because she never stopped working. And she knew every flower and every stick in the place. She was going blind, but she could tell you everything that was going on, warn you about every trap in the garden, she'd know when a marten was near the chickens. And she'd still go for her gun, even when she said she couldn't see. She just knew if some critter was nearby.

Because she was going blind, Cougar Annie never did see the results of the logging around her garden. What would she have made of it? She leaves no record. But she was a woman of an entirely practical and self-serving nature, and she was a product of her times. Her generation had come to the coast with the notion of taming the wilderness, subduing it—an attitude shared by countless settlers. Several of the novels in Cougar Annie's house tell larger-than-life stories of gallant pioneers whose axes flash proudly in the sunlight as they fell giant trees to build their farms and clear the forest to allow "civilisation" to take root in the wilderness.

In the remarkable period-piece *The Redemption of David Corson*, one of several novels that has survived the decay in Cougar Annie's house, the hero's breast swells with pride as he works: "It is one of the most impressive spectacles of human life to see a man enter a primeval forest and set himself to subdue nature with no implement but an axe!" And a tattered collection of verse by one Donald A. Fraser falls open at a poem called "The Song of the Axe."

I am the tooth of the human race,
Biting its way through the forest vast,
Chip by chip, and tree by tree,
'Til the fields gleam forth at last
Eating its heart with keen delight,
Into the groaning tree I bite.
Every stroke the land doth bless,
And joy o'erflows the wilderness.

Sentiments like these were shared by many on the West Coast, often without the agricultural intent. The Rae-Arthurs wanted to settle and clear some land and start a garden and raise their family here, but many of the so-called settlers held hand-logging licenses or were prepared to wheel and deal with loggers to sell timber from their newly acquired tracts of land. They were there for the trees, not the land.

The small-scale loggers of the early twentieth century were an anarchic bunch. Theirs was a world of hit-and-run logging, sometimes taking out choice big trees, sometimes logging for cedar poles, sometimes looking for trees to make "shingle bolts" or shakes. Seen now with the benefit of hindsight, knowing the devastation of modern logging methods, this early style of logging along the coast seems positively enlightened because it was by definition selective. Loggers did not have the technology required to strip entire mountain-sides; instead they chose individual trees care-fully, sometimes ranging far in search of the best. On the slopes above Hesquiat Lake, at elevations over two hundred metres, stumps of great Dou-glas firs, over two metres in diameter, appear un-expectedly at a few locations in the thick forest. The work of sawing down such a tree by hand and the business of easing, levering and sliding it down the slope to the water with the help of ropes and pulleys, was both arduous and dangerous.

Evidence of early logging is also clear right at Boat Basin in the stretch of forest between Cougar Annie's garden and the beach. Entering the forest from the beach, when you push your way through the high salal, depending where you have landed, you either find yourself dwarfed by a stand of old-growth forest, with cedars up to a thou-sand years old, or you will be in second-growth stands of hemlock and balsam, airier and lighter than the huge old forest. The logging done here early in the twentieth century was selective horse logging, taking out only the most valuable and accessible trees near the shore. Occasional huge stumps, thick with moss and rich with new growth, stand high from the ground, reminders of this long-for-gotten way of logging. An old horse collar rotting in the bush nearby is another reminder of the hard work undertaken by some entrepeneur who landed his animals and equipment here on the beach, staked out the most valuable logs, and went to work, probably with no more than a six-foot crosscut saw and a couple of helpers.

The well-known Gibsons were behind some, if not all, of the logging in Boat Basin. The father of the family and the founder of their coastal enterprises, William F. Gibson, had a keen interest in this area, and he took pains to ensure that the place was settled by the Rae-Arthurs and Wheelers. No doubt it suited him to have amenable settlers here, possibly to safeguard his interest in the area. The Gibsons were famed along the coast for their early timber-seeking; their shingle mill at Ahousat required a lot of wood and in the early days men hungry for timber could range more or less freely along the coast to take what they fancied. As Gordon Gibson explains in his autobiography *Bull of the Woods*, "In those days most of the timber on the waterfront of Clayoquot Sound was owned by the Crown. If a man took out a hand-logging license it was unofficially but generally assumed that he could take Crown trees at any spot along the hundreds of miles of coastline in the sound. . . ."

Gibson describes exploring the steep hillsides all around Clayoquot Sound, looking for trees that could be felled so they would slide into the water under their own momentum. On the west side of the main arm of Sydney Inlet, one thousand feet up a hillside, he found the tree of his dreams, a red cedar, perfectly symmetrical, fourteen feet in diameter with a forty-five-foot circumference, two hundred and twenty-five feet tall, going one hundred feet into the air before its first limb branched away from the trunk. Starting with a six-foot crosscut saw, later using a ten-foot saw, he and his men worked all day to bring this giant down. It began to fall at dusk, groaning and crashing through smaller trees. Watching this tree plummet down the mountain was, for Gibson, pure poetry.

> It seemed to pause in the air for a moment like an eagle in slow motion, before starting down the mountainside, cartwheeling end over end and disappearing into the water at a 45-degree angle. After what seemed to be a five-minute lapse, it suddenly emerged on the surface like a giant whale breaching from the depths. It was completely devoid of branches and most of its bark had been stripped away by the 1000 foot passage over rocks and windfalls.

This one tree provided Gibson with a month's supply of wood for his shingle mill. In his sixty years' experience of logging, this tree was the most outstanding and profitable tree he had ever seen. And while he recalls it with a kind of awe, cutting it down was all in a day's work. Years later the outspoken British Columbia politician, Phil Gagliardi, summed up this attitude towards the great trees with his memorable comment: "Those trees weren't put on that mountain by God to be praised, they were put there to be chopped down."

All around Cougar Annie's garden, the trees have been chopped down in a manner that would no doubt have pleased Gagliardi. As some loggers put it, the mountains have been "given a haircut." The outcome is that forestry work in the area in recent years has been costly and endless and largely aimed at repairing the ongoing damage caused by such logging practices. Along with the tree planting on stripped hillsides, along with the work of spacing and thinning young trees planted some years ago, along with the risky work of deactivating the logging roads that snake around the mountains, new initiatives are introduced constantly in the hope of greening over or stabilizing the slide areas: grass seed mixed with fertilizer dumped from helicopters, huge bales of hay hauled up to the mountain roads to absorb silt, quick-growing alder, a non indigenous variety, planted on slide areas, as well as webs of cuttings from willows, buried in the earth to sprout in the hope that the fast-growing roots will help stabilise the slopes. The success of such initiatives is, at best, mixed—or as yet unknown—because the technologies of repairing such ecological damage are in their infancy.

Perhaps some year the mountains and watersheds around Cougar Annie's garden will look less ugly, perhaps the pale scars of the slides will green over with fresh growth of grass and alder and willow, perhaps the native earth will stop slipping away as new trees take over and their roots slowly find their way down to bedrock and eventually hold firm and strong. Perhaps all this will happen. But the topsoil on these slopes—in most places less than half a metre in depth—was formed over thousands of years since the last ice age. It has been eroded drastically in many places—in some, lost entirely—and without this soil the intricate ecosystem producing the soft dark growth of old forests on these slopes has gone forever. Such forests, once clear-cut, do not return.

CHAPTER 14

Down by the Sea

Follow the wooden walkway from garden to beach, through the deep damp forest quickening with the new growth of early March, and the harbour emerges through the trees, steel-grey against a water-coloured sky. It is electrified, clamouring with life. The calm of only a few hours earlier has gone. A spawn of herring has come in. In the early spring, the herring come and go in waves, transforming the harbour when they arrive.

Scores of eagles wheel above the water and dive, talons stretched out, rising triumphant with a small silver fish, or angry in defeat having missed their prey. Count twenty, count up to fifty at a glance—they leave their perches high in the trees and swoop with strange quivering cries towards the water. They mingle with the flocks of gulls and seabirds, all hovering chaotically, a cacophony of life. The water is alive. Schools of herring shift around the harbour, swiftly moving from one area to another. They spawn near the shore, laying their roe offshore on long strands of kelp or near the shore on eel grass or on the seaweed clinging to the rocks in front of the walkway to the garden.

Seen from the air, the herring spawn curves around the shorelines in milky waves, followed by flocks of sea birds, by all sea creatures great and small. An abundant spawn of herring is a happy event. The roe was harvested by Hesquiat people for years beyond number. Fresh roe on kelp is a delicacy; run it through your teeth and a fat, fishy mouthful explodes in your mouth. Dried herring roe was a traditional staple of the West Coast diet. "The Indians were very busy

Boat Basin from Mount Seghers.

drying herring eggs," Father Charles Moser writes of this annual event, "the herring came into the bay in myriads and were shovelled up in canvas and wheelbarrow."

Hesquiat Harbour is famous for its herring, but the herring fishery is now closed here. The abundance of herring was radically reduced by the vigorous fishery that went on here in the 1970s. Ed Arnet recalls that in 1974 up to a hundred gillnets were in the harbour for four or five days of the herring spawn; the boats spread from Matlahaw Point all the way into Boat Basin. A huge scow was anchored in Boat Basin; this was the buying station. The boats would offload their fish and sell them for cash and go straight back to take more herring. Frank Rae-Arthur once claimed that in thirty minutes of herring fishing he had made forty thousand dollars. It was a gold rush for fishermen while it lasted; they were always paid in cash and the money was flown in to the buyers by the suitcaseful. "You couldn't find any bill larger than twenty dollars west of Winnipeg in those days," Frank declared. "The buyers needed all the cash they could get." Few species can withstand such systematic and large-scale harvesting for long.

The impact of heavy fishing, combined with unexplained fluctuations in some marine populations, has taken its toll on many species in this area. The pilchard fishery, once so abundant, is now non existent. Ian Macleod, who fished for pilchards in the 1930s, recalls following huge schools of these little fish on the coast: "They looked like a great big shadow moving on the water, mile after mile of them." A deep-water fish, the pilchards never entered Hesquiat Harbour, but the fishery was a major industry for about twenty years, profoundly affecting the coast. Pilchard reduction plants sprang up everywhere: in Nootka Sound, Sidney Inlet, Riley's Cove, Stewardson Inlet, Esperanza, Queen Cove, Barclay Sound, Quatsino. The pilchards were processed into fish meal and fish oil; when Ian Macleod was a young man, pilchard oil cost only twelve dollars for fifty gallons. He recalls a common use for the oil was to mix it with red or yellow ochre for use as a wood stain and preservative.

The massive runs of pilchards were never predictable. Sometimes the plants lay idle, waiting for the fish. Recalling a trip up the coast in 1926, Father Moser writes:

On the return journey home the Princess Maquinna *was packed, there wasn't room to move. All the Reduction Plants had closed down and their crews were on their way home. The pilchards which had been running in myriads had suddenly ceased to run, so the plants were closed. These Reduction Plants were almost as odiferous as the whaling stations. For a time fish reduction was quite a West Coast industry, every particle of the fish was used either for oil or meal or some other valuable product.*

The pilchard industry was virtually finished by the Second World War. Ed Arnet remembers one pilchard plant still working in the late 1940s, but after that the show was completely over. Pilchards have never reappeared in such numbers on the coast.

Another fish whose abundance has been phenomenal is the spiny dogfish. These small sharks have always come into Hesquiat Harbour in great numbers. Tales are told of the water being thick with them, at times so thick that anyone rowing would strike dogfish with the oars on almost every stroke. Writing in 1876, Father Brabant describes how the Hesquiat people made use of this resource:

> [They] *availed themselves of the presence of large schools of dog-fish to make dog-fish oil, which they sold to coasting schooners, receiving in exchange flour, molasses, tobacco, print-calico, and articles of dress. The old people who did most of the work objected to the buying of clothing, but the young people, especially the women . . . invested most of their earnings in the purchase of decent wearing apparel.*

Forty years later, the dogfish oil trade still continued. In July 1916 Father Moser notes that "Many of the Indians had been to Clayoquot with tins of dog-fish oil for which they got $1.00 per tin (one old coal oil can) and came back laden with [wares] and very pleased with themselves."

Seabirds in Boat Basin during a herring spawn.

Dogfish oil was widely used as an industrial lubricant and for lighting. The open-flame pitlamps used in the coal mines of Nanaimo and elsewhere on Vancouver Island were all fuelled with dogfish oil. The clear oil was extracted from the livers of the fish, a process involving both pressure and heat. The extraction was traditionally done on a small scale by native people all over the coast, and traces of this industry are still in evidence around Hesquiat Harbour. Two old wooden barrels containing long-forgotten and rancid dogfish oil, barrels probably sixty or seventy years old, are hidden in the bush along the shore inside Rae Basin.

A short-lived but extremely intense commercial fishery developed for dogfish during the late 1930s and 1940s. It was known as the liver fishery. The high vitamin A content of dogfish livers and the rocketing demand for vitamin A products and capsules turned this industry into a bonanza for fishermen. They flocked to join the action. The invention of synthetic vitamin A came about just in time to save the dogfish, for their numbers had become radically depleted all over the coast in only a few years. With the cheaper synthetic product readily available, the fishery collapsed completely. George Ignace spent some time on a dogfish boat in the 1930s and he described how, as the fish came on board, they

Dogfish longliner in Boat Basin.

were slit open, their livers flicked into a container, and the bodies dumped overboard. Ron Dalziel also writes of this in his memoirs, recalling that the "accepted practice was to dump dogfish carcasses at the mouth of a deserted bay."

For a long time after the liver fishery ended, dogfish were left alone and the population re-established itself. In the mid-to-late 1970s a thriving food fishery began, as an international market developed in Europe and Asia for dogfish. Initially this food fishery concentrated on the east coast of Vancouver Island, but in the last decade dogfish longliners have been coming into Hesquiat Harbour. These boats set baited hooks every two metres on lines stretching up to six kilometres in length. The pickings have been rich. On one occasion a huge factory ship came into Hesquiat Harbour and remained for several days, working around the clock. At night the dazzlingly bright halide lights of the factory ship lit up the beaches around the harbour so intensely that anyone on shore could easily have read a book at midnight. Each morning the beaches were littered with the bones and skin of the processed dogfish.

Dave Ignace, who has observed the results close at hand, is convinced that only small dogfish can now be found in the harbour, and nothing like the numbers of earlier times. Because dogfish are slow-growing and long-lived, a considerable time will be needed for the population to reassert itself. A three-foot-long dogfish, formerly a common sight here as elsewhere on the coast, is around sixty years old. Such old-timers are becoming hard to find.

Crabs too, are reportedly becoming smaller in Hesquiat Harbour. For years this harbour boasted the best Dungeness crabs on the coast, and these crabs have been ruthlessly fished. The numbers of crab taken are massive; an estimated two thousand traps were set one particular summer day in 1998 when ten crab boats were working at once. While this number is exceptional, crabbers come and go constantly, all year round. The hundreds of bright floats marking their traps have become a regular feature of the seascape. The impact on the number and diversity of the crab population is inevitable; very seldom now do the big purple crabs, weighing well over a kilogram, show up in the traps. Because of the pressure of the crab fishery, some observers believe that the male crabs are breeding at a younger age, threatening the genetic strength of the population.

Looking across the harbour from the beach at Boat Basin, the pale horizon often seems alive with activity. Mirages appear and disappear. Oil supertankers in the distant sea lanes heading up to Alaska seem to float above the horizon. The cresting swells far out to sea, the silver break of waves across Hesquiat Bar, the sudden white spray of water at rocky points all give the impression, fleetingly, of phantom boats coming and going. This trick of light and deception of sight quickly pass, and once again both the horizon and the harbour are empty.

Not altogether empty, though, and certainly not in the early spring, for then the whales come in. They come to the shallow waters of the harbour to feed on the herring roe, scouring the sandy sea floor and filtering this rich food through their baleens. When they arrive, anyone watching from shore is instantly energized, alive to every sound, every sighting. When the whales are here, the harbour seems entirely different.

Their arrival is quiet. Suddenly a spout of water appears, then perhaps two or three spouts, then a huge back lifts and rolls in the water, then another appears nearby, then a fin is hoisted high, or half of a large body surges out of the water. Great grey whales with barnacle-encrusted backs, these leviathans come right in to Boat Basin, rising like dark islands in the water, sometimes only twenty metres from shore. The sounds of their blowing and spouting fill the air. Up to fifty of these whales have appeared in the harbour at once. They mill around for weeks, stopping off in this safe harbour for a feast on their annual migration up to their feeding grounds in Alaskan waters.

The whales were not always safe here. According to Hesquiat elder Alice Paul, who passed away in 1991, the presence of the whales inside the harbour is a new phenomenon. She never saw them here when she was a child. Then the whales kept their distance, for then they were the most highly desired, the most revered, the most valuable of prey. Father Brabant mentions them more than once in his diary. "They are considered the best and most wholesome food," he writes "and the oil is used with all kinds of dry fish." Brabant vividly describes the fever of activity in the village when a dead whale has been spotted in the water. When a whale came their way in such a lucky fashion, the Hesquiat people rejoiced.

You can see the excitement at sea, you can hear the shouting and singing as the monster of the deep is being towed toward the shore. . . . Meanwhile knives are prepared, and the chiefs and principal men who alone are entitled to a share of the big fish, secure a number of inferior men to give them a hand next day. . . . Long before daylight the whale is surrounded by half-naked Indians. They all know the share they have a right to, but no one seems satisfied with what belongs to him—there is no end of quarreling. . . . After half a day of fighting and general disturbance, the whale being cut up, the Indians all retire to their houses, happy at the prospect of enjoying the delicacies of whale blubber and whale oil for the next few months.

Brabant then goes on to speak of an old chief called Koninnah who had recently died at Hesquiat.

> *This man enjoyed the reputation of bringing dead whales, almost at will, to the shores of the Hesquiat. . . . For the Indians say that their chiefs do not forget their friends and subjects when they reach the other world. Hence, Koninnah, by his influence, sent them a dead whale as a token of good-will.*

Perhaps now it is the living whales which are tokens of goodwill from the spirit world. Perhaps they come as a reminder that an abundance of life still thrives in these coastal waters, despite the often extreme changes of recent years. Ever since the sea otter was rendered nearly extinct by the white man's obsessive lust for otter fur in the infamous, decades-long slaughter during the late eighteenth and early nineteenth centuries, one species after another on this coast has been put at risk. Many species have suffered grievously due to fishing and harvesting practices and the outlook for a number of others is questionable. With encouragement, or left to their own devices, populations do sometimes recover. Sea otters have been re-introduced on the West Coast and they now appear in the kelp beds in front of Estevan Point and in groups of up to fifty at Hesquiat Bar. With such positive signs, and with the whales sometimes filling the horizon, and with spawns of herring bringing a surge of life in their wake, hope remains alive on the coast for the future of at least some of the species which have been so gravely depleted.

From their high perches at the tops of the trees and wheeling overhead on the updrafts, the countless eagles in the harbour keenly observe everything that comes and goes. They are focused intently on the fish, the small mammals, the birds— any potential prey. Over the years they have even spied the occasional domestic cat out on the beach. If a cat survives here it is a canny beast. It learns to avoid the exposed beach, to slink darkly in the shadow of logs, to flatten itself close to the earth, to look upwards warily to the fierce predators overhead. Only the most clever of cats survives.

The eagles miss nothing, though some activities seem barely worthy of their attention. The human race is granted only wary and scornful regard. Yet should they deign to notice, the eagles are positioned to observe, indifferently and haughtily, all the strange and brave ventures that come and go on these beaches, all the bizarre undertakings, all the human follies.

Think of the continuously interesting spectacle provided by the academics. They arrive in Hesquiat Harbour in small enthusiastic groups, paying avid attention to their particular subjects, their chosen species of interest, strategically placing themselves—usually on or near the beach—to observe, record, take notes for whatever brief period they can. Owl experts, bat experts, clam experts, salmon stream experts; researchers seeking the endangered elk and the dwarf pink trillium and the elusive marbled murrelet —all of these have landed here on the beach, not to mention geologists and archaeologists and ethnologists, and they have all earnestly gone about their business.

From the buttermilk sky the eagles look down at this flurry of activity on the beach with their usual disdain and fly on, uncaring. As far as they are concerned, the marks left by humans here on the beach are negligible, usually washed away by he next forgiving tide. Yet each tide also brings in undeniable evidence of human activity; odd offerings which can be beautiful, incongruous or hideous.

The offerings are deposited at high-tide mark, pushed back sometimes by the pounding of logs and driftwood almost to the forest fringe: crab floats and plastic bottles, a child's tricycle, a sodden leather wallet. For a while in the early 1990s the coast was infested with Nike runners, floating in one by one from a container ship which dumped its load far out to sea. A few made their way into Boat Basin and arrived wet and clean and mismatched on the shore. More recently a load of ice hockey gloves and shin pads floated to shore. Wooden deadeyes have appeared once or twice, relics from early sailing schooners, and occasionally a perfect piece of fruit—grapefruit, orange, or apple—bobs to shore from a passing boat. Back in 1918, Father Moser awoke one morning at Hesquiat to the happy discovery that the beach was "covered with canned salmon, evidently there had been a wreck or a tow broken. This was a godsend to us." Exotic hardwoods drift in to these shores from Asia. Frank Rae-Arthur had a shed on the beach full of intriguing driftwood from far away, including bits of mahogany and ebony.

Lost in the tidal debris at Boat Basin, sometimes visible, sometimes covered with gravel and logs, is a heavy iron keel about fifteen feet long. Tossed up on the shore decades ago, this is from the government launch *Alberta* which, according to Father Moser, was wrecked inside Boat Basin in July of 1914. Remnants of old

On the beach at Boat Basin, mid 1970s

shipwrecks are more often discovered on the outer coast. A few miles north of Homais, a pile of rusting anchor chain is all that remains of the *C.S. Holmes* which foundered there in 1950. Inside Homais Cove a length of battered wood, perhaps a bit of a rudder, may be all that remains of the *Malleville*, wrecked there over a century ago.

Evidence from damaged fishnets far out at sea also comes ashore. The floats escaping from Japanese nets are the glass balls so prized by West Coast beachcombers. Sea-coloured and translucent, large and small, these glass balls usually come to shore on the outer coast, but sometimes they float into the harbour, landing in the tangle of driftwood high on the beach at Boat Basin. Academics and researchers, loggers and road builders, hikers and kayakers have all had their lucky finds here. Every tide, every storm brings in new oddities from the empty horizon, new reminders that this place, seemingly so far removed from the outside world, bears constant witness to the wayward impact of humanity.

CHAPTER 15

The Later Years

To HEAR PEOPLE speak of Ada Annie Lawson during her later years is to hear a legend unfold. Because she had lived so long on the coast, rarely leaving, because few people knew her well, because her background, her husbands, her achievements, her very character attracted rumour and speculation, she cast a strong spell. People who visited her fully expected to be intrigued and she rarely let them down, leaving most visitors with powerful and enduring impressions.

> *When you shook hands, she would always press your hand, feeling for callouses. If you had callouses you knew how to work—she had no time for people with soft hands. Her hands were big and rough and hard—she was a tiny old lady with hands like a logger.*

> *At first she wouldn't let us take a photograph—she just refused. But you could see she quite liked the idea really. She made us wait while she combed her hair and fixed it back with hair slides, and then she told us to take the picture from her good side.*

> *It was like a dream, like walking into another era. All that old stuff in the store had probably been there for fifty years, and the house was crammed with piles of junk, and a dead chicken was strung from the ceiling, ready to be plucked and there were some stinking pelts hanging near the stove, dripping oil.*

She could be completely charming one moment and totally hard the next—
wily and conniving, always scheming to make people help her. She was
incredibly selfish—I guess she had to be to survive. And she sure loved
that place.

In the late 1960s, when her last husband departed never to return, Ada Annie Lawson was nearly eighty years old, left to fend for herself with the help of her son Tommy. They were not on their own for long. In 1967 Robert Culver returned to Boat Basin. Twelve years had passed since he brought his children here and he had never forgotten Ada Annie. He knew she had married again and he was curious to know about events at Boat Basin. According to Cougar Annie, he asked an administrator at the pension office if George Lawson was still alive; the administrator then let Cougar Annie know of Culver's request. In his next pension cheque, Culver received a note saying that Mrs. Lawson would like to hear from him. He wrote immediately and soon found himself back at Boat Basin.

Cougar Annie in her garden, early 1970s.

"I don't think we were surprised when he went back, not at all," says Culver's daughter Nairne. "He had always liked Mrs. Lawson and he liked that kind of life. I wondered at the time if he was going back just to be helpful or if there was a romantic interest. I never asked him, but I do think that after my mother died he never found another soulmate till he met Mrs. Lawson."

For four years Robert Culver spent most of his time at Boat Basin, helping around the garden, taking evident pleasure in the work. He was an ingenious man and liked nothing more than tinkering with various gadgets and inventions. He was particularly proud of the motorized wheelbarrow he invented to help haul loads of feed up to Cougar Annie's garden from the beach. He also tried to fix up a set of removable wooden rails that would lead down across the beach and out to Frank Rae-Arthur's boat—or any other boat—moored in the shallow water in front of the boardwalk to the farm. The idea was to run the motorized wheelbarrow over these rails, or to winch a cart over the rails and up the beach, easing the ceaseless labour of unloading the boat and packing supplies up to the boardwalk.

Robert Culver was also handy around the garden. He mended fences, he handled goats and chickens and geese with ease and skill, he turned the soil and planted the various crops, and helped with the harvest. In his memoirs he recalls picking twenty-two different varieties of apples one autumn. He genuinely loved being helpful, particularly to assist the woman he admired so much. Visitors who met him recall a small, shy man, softly spoken and profoundly hard of hearing, who always wore a safari hat out in the garden.

When Robert Culver arrived in 1967, Tommy Rae-Arthur was able to take his first long break from Boat Basin in years. Writing to his mother from Victoria, just before Christmas of 1967, Tommy seems both delighted and utterly at a loss to be away from home. He left in October, seeking medical attention and a change of scene, but his mind remained at Boat Basin.

> *I sure miss seeing you, very sorry that I am not home to help you with the work but I am sure glad that Mr. Culver is helping you this winter and hope he will stay there all winter. Sure hope the goats are fine.... I just hope the cougar has not got any of the goats yet I sure miss seeing them and they must miss me putting them in every night. I sure wish that I could have finished fixing the roof of the goathouse.... I sure hope the dahlias and glads didn't get frozen and also hope that you got the vegetables put in the house before the frost ... I sure hope the roof of the back room is not leaking bad and I sure wish I could of put shakes on. Please let me know how the roof is holding out this winter.*

Even when safely away from Boat Basin, Tommy could not help but fret about the work that was endlessly awaiting his attention. The demands of the place were often too much for him, yet he always took pleasure in the goats and in his vegetable garden. This was a vast rambling patch right in front of the house, messily fenced with chicken wire and corrugated tin, lush with lettuce and beans and potatoes and carrots and turnips. Tommy knew everything there was to know about growing vegetables here: when to dig, when to lay manure, when to get the seaweed onto the beds. "Tommy would say to me, 'Turnips don't like seaweed,' he'd tell me that every year," Diane Ignace recalls. His production of turnips and carrots was legendary. "He gave me sacks full of them," says Peter Buckland. "He grew far more than they could use, and every year he'd plant just as many again."

While Robert Culver remained at Boat Basin, he shared Tommy's workload and he tried his best to improve the living conditions in Cougar Annie's increasingly shabby house. Writing from Penticton in the summer of 1969 when he was visiting his daughter, Culver happily reports that he has found a good used washing machine for twenty-five dollars and that he is having it shipped up to Boat Basin. "Don't know where we'll put it," he writes genially, "but we'll manage somehow. I'll fix it." Later in the same letter he adds "I think of you a lot and am lonesome for you but wish we could have a less rigorous life together than at present. I just love being someplace where there's a fridge and hot running water." He signs off, "All my love to you (our style), Robert."

Robert Culver, late 1960s.

But despite his love for Ada Annie, Robert Culver was not—could not possibly be—as attached to her place at Boat Basin as she was or as she may have wished him to be. In a letter written in 1971, Culver admits he has had enough. "Boat Basin is much too much for me," he declares sadly. In 1972, he decided to leave once again, this time for good, to live in Penticton. "The cold and the damp were really hard on him, I honestly think that's why he left," says his daughter Nairne. "I did feel sad for him when he left Boat Basin, but he didn't like being quite so isolated." Regular summer visits to Boat Basin then became part of Robert Culver's life, his last in 1975. After that, though he often talked of making another visit, he never saw Ada Annie Lawson again.

Robert Culver was devoted to Cougar Annie. According to some, he wanted to marry her, and certainly in his letters he is staunch in his insistence that she needs someone to help her and look after her. After he left he wrote frequently, sometimes more than once a week, loving and kindly letters often lamenting that they are not together: "I love you and how lonesome I am for you. True enough, but nothing I can do about it. That isolation is just too much for me." In 1974 he writes enthusiastically of the possibilities opened out by the new logging road, looking forward to the day it connects, as it surely will, to Gold River or Tofino so that "civilisation" will be within easy reach, without boat or plane.

As much as she may have enjoyed his attentions, Cougar Annie made no major changes to accommodate him. Her "ever loving Robert" writes rather sadly from his home in Penticton: "I'm as lonesome as ever for you and can't see any relief. You don't write and you don't tell me if you can see any change coming." And when he does receive news from her, it is not always to his liking: "I'm very glad to hear you got such a big crop of bulbs and in such good shape. How do you account for things apparently going so much better when I am not there? It almost makes me afraid to suggest that we should be together again!"

Culver clearly liked to be needed. In his letters he describes bustling around getting Cougar Annie her eyeglasses; he repeatedly advises her to go to Port Alberni to have her eyes tested properly; he arranges to have a stamp made with the new postal code for the Post Office; he makes little purchases for her and sends them by mail, every penny accounted for carefully. "I forgot to

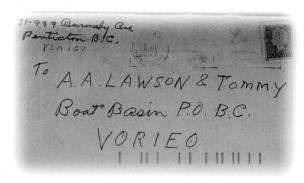

tell you in the last letter, after crediting the stamps you sent and charging for the vitamin E I sent you, you still have a credit balance of $2.46."

By 1980 the tone of Culver's letters has changed. They were both, by then, getting well on in years. Culver was eighty, Ada Annie was ninety-two. He writes affectionately from his home in Penticton, and signs himself "Your old friend," telling her of his various carpentry projects, about the weather, about his own fading eyesight, but no longer speaking of visiting Boat Basin himself. "I expect you are glad winter is about over, so you can get at your beloved plants again, but you do need someone there all the time to be your eyes for you," he writes. At the end of his letter he says, "Well, I really do wish I could be with you, helping you with your work and business, so if you do decide to live in a civilized place, let me know."

Letters from Robert Culver kept coming, right until the end of Cougar Annie's time at Boat Basin. Barry Lorton, who helped look after the garden during the winter of 1981, recalls being asked to read one of Culver's letters aloud to the old lady he called "Granny." "I felt a bit uncomfortable, it was really a love letter to her," he recalls. "Very affectionate, very private, really. But she couldn't read by then, so I read it out to her."

Chris Marshall and her husband Nils, who helped to care for "Granny" and the garden during the final years, remember the letters from Robert Culver as regular highlights. "We'd sometimes read them out to her, or someone else would. And we always knew when she'd had a letter from him," says Chris. "Then she'd be singing, and talking to her chickens, and she'd go and get out her mirror and do some 'tittivating,' that's what she used to call it." Robert Culver knew his letters had to be read by other people; one that survives has a note to Tommy Rae-Arthur attached. "Nothing private in here, Tommy, go right ahead and read it to your mother now."

Robert Culver died in 1983. His surviving letters are memorable and moving documents. That a woman in her nineties can attract such comments as, "I will close now, and lots of love to you my gentle darling," is a tribute both to the good and gentle man who wrote the letter and to the enduring charm of the strong old lady who was once the lovely young Ada Annie Jordan.

When Robert Culver left Boat Basin in 1972, Cougar Annie was eighty-four years old and had been at Boat Basin for nearly sixty years. She had no intention of going anywhere. With the help of her son Tommy who lived at Boat Basin in his own little cabin in the garden, and her son Frank who brought supplies up from Tofino in his fishing boat and often stayed for a few days, the place continued to tick over much as it always had. The garden kept right on working, with orders for dahlia bulbs and other plants continuing to come in response to Cougar Annie's advertisements. The post office, while not exactly humming with business, at least continued to survive thanks to the dahlia business and the ingenious bookkeeping. The business at the store, never great, dwindled slowly to nothingness. The latest receipt book for the store covers the 1970s, and it has precious few entries.

During the 1970s, Cougar Annie lost two of her sons. George died of a heart attack in 1973 at the age of sixty-two. In 1979, Frank drowned off Vargas Island when his boat struck a deadhead and sank. He was buried alongside George in the Tofino cemetery. Their mother attended neither funeral.

Frank's death deprived his mother of her most reliable supply line. Time beyond number, Frank had moored his fishboat at Boat Basin and unloaded heavy sacks of feed, two at a time, into his dinghy, rowed them to shore, and packed them up the boardwalk to the house. He did this work happily enough; after all, he wanted to be up in this area as much as possible. He loved Boat Basin. "This is the best place in the world, you know," he once said. "The very best in the world."

Peter Buckland knew Frank well, and agrees with him. From the time of his first visit to the Hesquiat area in the spring of 1969, Peter also concluded that this was the best place in the world. Year after year he made regular visits from his home in Vancouver, staying in Rae Basin at Bus Hansen's prospector's shack, tramping through the bush to inspect mining claims, exploring the beaches, getting to know the area. On Easter Sunday, 1969, Peter met Cougar Annie for the first time. He and Bus Hansen hiked up from Rae Basin through the bush, entered the front gate of the garden, went up to the house and rang the bell. "We just dropped in to say hello and to buy some eggs," remembers Peter. "And from then on I was hooked."

Following this visit, Peter saw Cougar Annie on nearly every trip he made to Boat Basin. He developed an immense respect and liking for her; to him she was always "Mrs. Lawson." He cheerfully became part of her supply line, hauling heavy loads of feed up to her house, helping in the garden, packing groceries, bringing care packages from her daughter Rose, once bringing in a new goat on the scheduled float plane that served this part of the West Coast for several years during the 1970s. He also accompanied Cougar Annie back home after she had been in hospital in Vancouver for a spell.

In her old age, Cougar Annie's once bright blue eyes filmed over with cataracts, and she lost all her teeth. Inevitably, she also lost her strength. Once able to kill a chicken by breaking its neck with a flick of her wrist, in later years this technique failed both Cougar Annie and the chickens, who would wobble about, necks askew, neither dead nor alive after she had tried and failed to kill them. She was still able to crush the skull of a mouse between thumb and forefinger if she found one in the grain bin, but seeing the mice became almost impossible.

When she consented at last to go to Vancouver to have her cataracts treated she was in for some surprises. Although she could see very little, she could see how brightly lit the city was. "It must have changed a lot," she commented to her grandson. She remembered a much different Vancouver, a place with few bright lights, when major thoroughfares like West Broadway were still gravel roads.

On a couple of other occasions, Cougar Annie had to go out to hospital in Tofino for medical attention, once because she fell and broke her knee. In the hospital, the excessive hygiene offended her. Being washed so regularly, she believed, would destroy the natural protective oils on her skin. To add insult to injury, at the hospital some kind soul decided to wash her dress and it fell apart. She was infuriated. "I've had that dress for fifty years," she declared. The new dress she was given as a replacement did not feel right, and she was unmollified.

In 1980, Tommy Rae-Arthur wrote to a friend that "The logging camp is still closed down and we hear it will stay closed for quite a long time, so its sure dead and lonely down their road and nothing but bears everywhere now." These intermittent closures of the camp increased the anxiety of friends and family when they considered Cougar Annie's isolation and extreme old age. Even though Tommy was with her most of the time, his health was uncertain and each year more and more outside help was required.

By 1980 she was ninety-two, almost completely blind, and the place posed many hazards. Various members of the family came and went as best they could, checking up on her and sending care parcels to help out, but no one felt easy about her continuing to live out there with so little support. Cougar Annie did not see matters in the same light. She remained untroubled by having to collect drinking water in barrels from the roof; she was not bothered by the lack of electricity, by having to use an outdoor toilet, by having to keep a wood fire going. "When she couldn't see any more, she used her hands to see if the fire was still alive. She would gently feel inside the stove and she'd know if more wood was needed. She never burned herself as far as I know," recalls Leo Mattson.

Cougar Annie still had no intention of leaving, none whatsoever, and she was prepared to scheme up whatever was needed in order to stay put. In 1981, after first suggesting the idea to him shortly after Frank's death, she persuaded Peter Buckland to buy her property on the understanding she could remain there at no cost as long as she wished, with extra help provided by Peter. They reached an agreement, and shortly afterwards Peter employed Chris Marshall and her husband Nils to look after Cougar Annie.

A number of other people came and went, helping Cougar Annie during her final years at Boat Basin. They all faced a very old lady with a very strong will. She wanted help, but she wanted it on her own terms. She was not about to listen to any new-fangled ideas about improving the place or trying new food or enhancing communications. When the old crank telephone had to be replaced with a new push-button plastic model, she roundly declared she would not use it. The telephone engineer obligingly tinkered with the equipment until he managed to install the new telephone inside the casing of the old wooden crank phone, so she would not have to press any of those fiddly buttons.

"She was not an easy person to help," Donna Sharpe recalls, looking back at the time she spent helping to care for Cougar Annie. "She wanted to control everything and worried about waste all the time. She would feel with her hands to make sure I'd used up all the onion skins."

Chris Marshall has similar memories of how Cougar Annie constantly kept checking on her. One of Chris's jobs was to spread human waste around the base of the fruit trees, for fertilizer. It looked and smelled terrible, but Cougar Annie insisted that this be done, a job Chris would happily have ignored. "But she knew exactly what was going on. She had a sixth sense about everything that was happening the garden," recalls Chris. "Once I'd been out digging up the American Beauty bulbs, and when I came in she knew I'd done it, and I hadn't said a word about it."

During the time Barry Lorton was at Boat Basin, although he was sometimes exasperated by the place and by the stubborn, unchanging ways of Cougar Annie, he learned a few valuable tricks from her. She introduced him to the culinary art of making impressive messes of stew that would last for days without refrigeration. He would do what she requested, perhaps adding some chicken to a stew that had started the day before as a concoction of tinned corned beef with onions, potato and carrot, or adding a new tin of meat or canned soup or a few vegetables. "It tasted better than it sounds. Day after day it would evolve into a new kind of stew," he says. "We did the same with the porridge, I learned about porridge out there. She just kept adding more to the same batch of porridge and we'd cook it up. We never washed out the pot."

Barry also learned how to pluck and can chickens. One memorable night a slaughter occurred in the chicken coop when a mink found its way in and killed eighteen chickens. "We loaded the dead bodies into a wheelbarrow and spent two days plucking and canning those skinny chickens," Barry recalls. "They were

Tending the chickens, early 1970s.

covered with fleas, too." What's more, Cougar Annie was determined to get the mink that had caused this havoc. The creature was so bloated with chicken blood it did not run away, but lay drunkenly inside the coop. Under Cougar Annie's instructions, Barry first had to shoot it, then she showed him how to skin it. "I can do it in six minutes," she declared. Half an hour later, Barry was still skinning the mink and cursing. Afterwards she showed him how to sew up the skin carefully so the Hudson's Bay Company fur buyers would not notice the bullet hole in the pelt. "You don't forget lessons like that," he comments.

The last time Hughie Clarke saw Cougar Annie she was still able to get about, nearly blind, feeling her way around the garden by going from fencepost to fencepost, all of which were topped with white plastic containers, enabling her to distinguish where she was going.

We were hollering for Tommy and she comes along the path from the goat shed with this little tin can with a wire on it and we asks her, "What're you doing, Mrs. Lawson?" "Oh, getting some milk for Tommy's breakfast," and she had about an inch of milk in the bottom of the tin can with a dead fly in it. She couldn't see much of anything then.

Cougar Annie became more or less housebound in her last couple of years at Boat Basin, yet she still insisted that her helpers should try to tend the increasingly overgrown garden. When Chris Marshall explained that she needed time with her young child, Cougar Annie's response was crisp. Chris must go off and work in the garden for a few hours, and as for the baby "Just tie him in the highchair beside me and if he cries I'll jiggle this rope for him to play with." Even with the dahlia business fading away, and the garden becoming uncontrollable, the *idea* of the garden was, for Cougar Annie, paramount.

"Towards the end the garden was in her head. It wasn't a reality any more," Donna Sharpe remarks. "She didn't go outside much, but she could go round the garden in her head. She knew where everything was, all the Latin names, when she planted what, and where it came from."

In all her waking hours, even in her sleep, the garden haunted Cougar Annie. More than once, her caregivers found her sleepwalking out of doors. Frail as she was, and blind, she could still make her way, unconsciously, instinctively, out into the night, out into the garden that had possessed her so completely, for so long.

Cougar Annie's days at Boat Basin were drawing to a close. The wishes of her family prevailed, and she eventually was taken out to end her days elsewhere. Accounts of her final departure from Boat Basin vary. She left in the autumn of 1983, out of her house, out through the front gate of the garden, and by truck along the logging road to Stewardson Inlet, where a float plane was waiting. "She walked out proud, her head up. She was sharp as a tack and knew exactly what was going on," says one friend. "She was strapped into a stretcher and straining to get free, swinging this little hammer around, hitting out at everyone, and crying," says another. "She didn't even know this was the end. She just thought she was going out for a checkup," says a third. Whatever the manner of the departure, once the door of the airplane closed on Cougar Annie, she had gone forever from her garden.

The animals were left behind. Peter Buckland rescued what he could, walking the three remaining goats down to the beach and carrying them, protesting, out to his boat. The rabbits escaped their hutches to end their limited days grazing freely in the forest. The roosters and chickens went in different directions—some to roost in the old prospector's cabin in Rae Basin, some in squawking sacksful down to Hughie Clarke at Ahousat. The geese had to fend for themselves; they did not last long on their own.

None of the people who cared for her like to speak of Cougar Annie's final days. These were punctuated by long spells of hospitalization and marked by inevitable deterioration. Some visitors who saw her in hospital believe she was not really there at all; in her head she had never left Boat Basin; she was back there sitting at her kitchen table, nodding to sleep over her dahlia bulbs, the sharp paring knife falling from her grasp onto the floor, the pot bubbling on the back of the stove while, outside, the garden was waiting for her.

Ada Annie Lawson, neé Jordan, died in hospital in Port Alberni on April 28, 1985, a few weeks before her ninety-seventh birthday. Later, her ashes were scattered by her family from an airplane flying low over her garden at Boat Basin.

The ashes fell into a garden reverting to wilderness. No one lived there. The vegetable patch was obscured by weeds, the dahlia beds had all but disappeared, salmonberries were taking over the pathways, blackberry brambles and broom were running rampant. The house stood abandoned and dank. Cougar Annie was dead, and the fate of her garden appeared to be sealed. Unless someone intervened, it would die with her.

CHAPTER 16

Back to the Garden

I N T H E Y E A R S immediately following Cougar Annie's death, her garden, abandoned to its own devices, staunchly refused to die. As the encroaching jungle
of salmonberries and broom, salal, brambles and young conifers advanced im-
placably on the garden, a remarkable number of trees and shrubs she had planted
managed to survive, along with countless perennials and bulbs. The entire garden entered a holding pattern, almost a trancelike state as, blurred and half-
choked by the overgrowth, these plants and trees struggled for light and space.
They were surviving, but only just.

The former lines and boundaries of the garden lost their meaning as the forest advanced. Rotten fenceposts and indistinct tangles of chicken wire showed
dimly through the growth of broom and young trees around the edge of the
clearing. Only vague outlines remained of garden beds. Gates appeared unexpectedly, their function long forgotten. Leading to no obvious destination, they
hung crookedly open, clinging by perhaps half of a rusty hinge to a post, the sup-
porting fence rails slowly decaying in the thick moss.

As the fences collapsed, animals long barred from entering were at last free to
roam as they wished. Bears were able to enjoy the fruit and the berries without
facing a gun or a trap; deer nibbled happily on the new growth in the perennial
beds; the Stellar's jays snacked on azalea buds and seedlings without interfer-
ence, while the ruffed grouse—formerly destined, like the jays, for the pot—
picked freely at the fresh blossom on the fruit trees.

In the forestlike thickets of invasive growth, many of Cougar Annie's flowering shrubs became spindly and weak. A weigela, completely engulfed by young hemlock trees, was visible only by a single straggly branch bravely blossoming above the conifers. Skinny branches of viburnum reached above an abundant grove of salmonberries; berberis struggled through dense patches of salal; deutzia and escallonia and pieris shrubs grew leggy and tall, their lower branches lost in a sea of broom, their upper branches fighting towards the light. Many of the trees Cougar Annie had cultivated disappeared from sight: a small grove of hazelnuts was lost in the jungle, a linden tree virtually smothered in the matted growth of lichens and mosses. Confused tangles of climbing roses became hopelessly entwined with blackberries. Great swathes of perennials vanished without a trace as their beds became choked with brambles, while daffodils and crocuses and many other bulbs stopped flowering and lay dormant, lost in the messy tangle rising over them.

Rhododendron overgrown with broom.

Few people came and went. Tommy Rae-Arthur left the place when his mother did; the caretakers who had looked after Cougar Annie in her final years were long gone. Occasionally a visitor would stray through the silent garden, perhaps a hiker or a fisherman or a logger or a road builder who knew something of this place or had heard of Cougar Annie and wanted to see what was left in her garden. Little appeared to be left, for it was difficult to see beyond the sense of abandonment, difficult to imagine the place back to life. Certainly to the casual visitor the garden seemed too far gone to hope that it might be reclaimed—except by the surrounding rainforest.

Yet an optimistic eye could see that the signs of continuing life in the garden contained promise. Bright splashes of leaf and flower kept surfacing, half-visible in the tangled growth. Imported shrubs and trees, lost in forgotten enclosures of the garden, continued to make a brave show against the dark forest background: an English chestnut, a horse chestnut, a black locust, a liriodendron, laburnums, hawthorns, flowering quince, forsythia, buddleia, decorative fruit trees and many varieties of berberis, spiraea, hebe, escallonia, viburnum and pieris. Some plants even seemed to thrive amid the chaos of overgrowth —or at least they continued to flower abundantly—particularly the rhododendrons and some azaleas. Waves of many different heathers still bloomed all year round, though partially obscured by grass and broom. Ivy flourished; gorse and heather and montbretia spread haphazardly through the open areas of the garden; holly and cotoneaster bushes, seeded by birds, popped up everywhere; honeysuckle thrived; and the old fruit trees continued to blossom, spring after spring.

Peter Buckland was well aware of what was happening in the garden. In earlier years he had explored it frequently, sometimes with Cougar Annie. Although he had owned the property since 1981, he lived and worked in Vancouver and was unable to give it his full attention. On his monthly visits, he usually cleared away

Peter Buckland.

a bit of overgrowth and kept the paths open as best he could, but he knew that tending this garden properly would be a full-time job. He was doggedly optimistic about the place, convinced the garden could be reclaimed. For several years he kept a distant eye on it and planned how he would release the garden from its captivity in the bush and give it a new lease on life. In 1987 he came to live permanently at Boat Basin. Once he had settled into his new house near the beach, he readied himself to tackle the garden. A daunting task lay ahead, for by then the place was a bedraggled mess.

The bones of the garden remained, however. The drainage ditches were still at least partially working, and the old pathways of the garden remained reasonably distinct. Having known the garden for almost twenty years by the time he came to live at Boat Basin, Peter was aware of its basic shape and style: he knew where the working garden and dahlia beds had been, where Willie Rae-Arthur's grave was, where Cougar Annie had her "pleasure garden" enclosures on the property. Yet despite this, the garden was profoundly mysterious to him. He had no detailed knowledge of what was planted here, no idea of what had survived, no notion of what would be revealed when he got to work. "All I knew was that I had to let it breathe again—then I could figure out what to do with it."

The scale of the undertaking ahead inspired Peter to develop the art of what he terms "chainsaw gardening." Wielding a noisy saw, he attacked towering, self-seeded plantations of broom, some with branches as thick as fenceposts. He sliced through salmonberry bushes so tall they dwarfed the huge rhododendrons nearby and so old and tough their limbs, matted with moss, were several inches thick. He laid waste to hundreds of young conifers, to large thickets of

Back garden near Willie's grave

salal, to vast patches of blackberries. The technique was straightforward: beat through the thickets of overgrowth, clear out the obvious garden invaders such as broom and salmonberry, spare any interesting-looking bushes or trees, and then wait to see what would happen. "I'd just wade in —it was chainsaw madness." A few of Cougar Annie's shrubs and trees were sacrificed in the process, for speed was the hallmark of this type of gardening, not finesse.

As the work progressed and as one small section of the garden after another was freed from the choking hold of the invading growth, a seemingly endless variety of Cougar Annie's own shrubs and plants emerged. No one was more surprised than Peter by the impressive and, to him, largely nameless array appearing throughout the five-acre clearing. "I was amazed at how much was there. Cougar Annie spent a lifetime planting it all, but I never realized the full scale and diversity of what she'd done."

Friends visiting the garden entered the fray. Armed with loppers and machetes, clippers and rakes they were instructed to hack away, to liberate azaleas and rhododendrons choked by young trees and bushes, to clear patches of blackberries, to lop till they dropped, to rake till they ached. And when the visitors left, Peter carried on alone, single-minded in his determination to free the garden from the pervasive growth threatening its existence. All year round, throughout the late 1980s and 1990s he worked in the garden nearly every day. He seems taken aback when questioned about how he kept going in such isolation. "This is normal now. Sometimes it's a bit tough—especially if it rains for two weeks solid in the winter—but working in isolation can give you a real rush." Call it dedication, call it obsession—whatever drove Peter to work like this in Cougar Annie's garden was a powerful force. "I've been captivated by this place and controlled by it," he says. "It's unique—no one could ever feel they're in control here, or that they own it. It's the other way around. The place owns you, and takes over your whole life."

The rewards have been great. Once freed from the stranglehold of the matted overgrowth, the garden revived. Above all it had needed light and air. Each season, newly cleared corners of the garden produced fresh surprises. Daffodils of many kinds, and narcissi, suddenly shone forth again and bloomed and spread. Spindly and determined shrubs—pernettya, mock orange, kolkwitzia, hydrangea, kerria, fuchsia—leafed out and blossomed. Rhododendrons that had been visible only as fleeting glimpses of colour through the thick bush, flourished openly. Entire beds of hostas and lilies resurrected themselves; sweeps of crocuses, star of Bethlehem, columbines, lily-of-the-valley, alstroemeria, scilla, ajuga and primroses appeared as if from nowhere, liberated from a dormant

Trail to rock garden.

state to flower for the first time in decades. Sometimes up to two or even three years after a patch was cleared, little would happen other than the soft growth of moss, but then a solitary and hesitant flower would appear. A single spray of Solomon's seal that showed up several years ago in an unpromising little corner is now a graceful expanse.

In the reclamation of Cougar Annie's garden, nothing new has been introduced—everything that now flourishes was already there, half-hidden from sight or dormant. The first to admit he knew little about gardening or botany when he began this work, Peter was unfamiliar with most of the shrubs and trees he was rescuing. "I didn't know the names of any of them," he says with a grin. "And I still don't know them all. Who cares, anyway? The point is to enjoy them." One of the greatest joys in the garden is to see how, every year, unknown plants surface. "I still have the 'plant of the year' surprise when I come across something new that I've never seen before, planted by Cougar Annie ages ago. A couple of years ago it was the enkianthus tree—it had been practically buried for years. And last year it was a little vine called epimedium and also those little yellow flowers over by the old goat shed—they just appeared. I haven't figured out yet what they are."

Importantly, at the same time as liberating Cougar Annie's garden, Peter has also created a setting where his own ideas and projects can flourish. He has transformed her place from a rambling working garden, intersected with only a few main paths, into a creative maze. One of his chief pleasures has been making

⑥ Sushi bar

⑧ Monet's walk

⑩ Goat shed

BOAT BASIN FARM

GARDEN CENTRE

⑧

⑨

⑩

⑫

To Trapline Trail

⑪ Greenhouse

⑨ Dahlia gardens

COUGAR ANNIE'S GARDEN

DAY LILY · MONTBRETIA · HOSTA · DAFFODIL · IRIS · AZALEA · RHODODENDRON · HEAT

SCALE

0 5 10 15 20 25 30 35 40 45 50 m

→ To Rae Lake

⑤ Wheelbarrow in rock garden

POST OFFICE BOAT BASIN

④ House & post office

✝ Willie's grave ⑦

Enkianthus ①

⑥

③ Memorial statue

To Wheeler Creek

⑤

④

③

N

② ROSE

...ale sculpture

① ↑
ENTRANCE

① Walkway and pergola

KEY (FOR FLOWERS SEE LEFT)

■ MOSS & GRASS

SALAL & BUSH

BORDER PLANTS

FRUIT TREES

VIEWING ROUTE

①↗ VIEWING POINTS

FENCELINE

P99

pathways, dissecting overgrown areas of the garden with curving walks, linking different sections together. How these pathways taper and curve and link together is always determined by the existing plants within the garden. Choosing hitherto hidden shrubs or trees as focal points, time and again Peter has hacked his way through the overgrowth with a chainsaw, creating a pathway designed to draw the eye toward the next vista beyond. Around every corner is another curve, another carefully framed view that lures the visitor into another half-hidden section of the garden.

Over two kilometres of interconnected trails now meander hypnotically around the garden. Visitors regularly find themselves lost, mesmerised into following the looping and wandering pathways from one area of the garden to another. From "Rhodo Row" to the "Monet Zone" to "The Hub" where seven pathways converge, all the trails are soft underfoot, carpeted with lush moss. Brilliant light-absorbing mosses grow freely throughout the garden, as do many native plants. Cleared mossy areas

often have an abundance of wildflowers in the spring, including the native lily of the valley, twinflower and bunchberry. Skunk cabbages thrive in the damp regions of the lower garden, surrounded by spiky sedges and the lush graceful fronds of ladyfern. Large clumps of swordfern and deerfern proliferate. Salal and evergreen huckleberry, now slashed back and under control, form curving walls and hedges. Cat-tail mosses, liverworts and licorice ferns cling to the branches of trees planted by Cougar Annie and the bark of many trees is white with lichen. The combination of indigenous and cultivated plants has become an outstanding feature of the garden. "Native plants flowed into this garden," says Peter, "They almost killed it, but now they make the whole scene work."

Peter has developed worlds within worlds within the world of Cougar Annie's garden. Where her vegetable patch once was, alongside the boardwalk, an intricate pattern of raised beds is featured in the "Memorial Garden." All of the beds angle and taper towards an enormous, splayed tree root, set in place like a bizarre garden sculpture. This great fir root flew into the garden, dangling from a helicopter all the way from Rae Lake where it had jutted from a long-submerged log for many years, perhaps for centuries. Determined to feature it in the garden,

Peter chainsawed it free and arranged for its flight. Also in the Memorial Garden is a massive arched cedar root that closely resembles a whale; this, too, was liberated from Rae Lake in the same fashion.

Leading away from the Memorial Garden is a recently constructed boardwalk of split cedar curving towards a large outcropping of rock, a natural setting for a rock garden. Hidden behind the rock, a dark pathway snakes towards an alley of rhododendrons planted decades ago, through a secluded area at the back

Fir tree root, Rae Lake.

of the garden, and on to the grave of Willie Rae-Arthur. Nearby, in all likelihood, are the now lost graves of all the others buried, according to their death certificates, "in their own grounds" at Boat Basin.

Discovering and enhancing the small secret enclosures within Cougar Annie's garden has been a particular delight to Peter. Tiny clearings, walled in now with mature shrubs and trees, appear in several odd and unexpected corners. In such spaces, Cougar Annie may have had a small garden bed, or she may have tethered her goats, or she may have experimented with new stock. Now, narrow pathways meander toward and through these areas, linking up with the other paths that weave through the more open stretches of the garden.

One of these hidden enclosures has recently become the "Japanese Garden." A short pathway of flat beach pebbles curls through a grove of young hemlock and leads to a heavy door of split cedar. When opened, this door reveals a blindly bright, massive slab of yellow cedar. Table height and sheltered by a shake roof, this slab is evidence of the imposing nature of the surrounding forest. Even people knowing the trees in this area well are taken aback by its size. Measuring twenty-five feet long, the slab is fifty-one inches wide at one end, tapering to forty-one inches at the other, and five inches thick. Peter milled this slab from a huge yellow cedar log on his portable sawmill. He calls it the "Sushi Bar" in recognition of the Japanese predilection for pale woods in their sushi restaurants. Two "Shinto gates" stand at the far end of the Japanese garden, deceptively simple structures made from two supports and one crosspiece, their dimensions exactly designed to complement the sushi bar and to give the impression of infinite distance leading into the deep forest beyond the garden.

Memorial Garden.

Sushi bar, Japanese Garden.

Peter's work in the garden consistently reflects how he enjoys playing with distance and dimension. Long fascinated by perspective design, he has made every structure, every pathway, even every raised bed to trick the eye of the viewer, to make distances seem either greater or lesser. At the entrance to the garden he has built a tapering boardwalk stretching from the logging road to Cougar Annie's house. Two hundred and fifty feet long, it measures four feet wide at the road, and reduces steadily to a width of two feet at the house. Above this walkway, a pergola spans the central section of the boardwalk for one hundred and fifty feet. Built from the "grey ghosts" of the nearby forest, small dead-standing cedars that have hardened and weathered over many years, the pergola looks as if it has been there for decades. Each dimension of the fourteen sections of the pergola reduces gradually in size as it progresses towards the house, giving the illusion of an endlessly long walkway as you enter the garden and as you leave, the trick of perspective is reversed, dramatically foreshortening the boardwalk.

A short distance from the garden, an extraordinary construc-

Entering the Japanese Garden.

tion rears up in the dark forest. In uncertain light, it seems like an enormous sculpture or a mythic beast, but it is merely the woodshed that services Peter's house. Shaped like an eagle fanning out its wings to dry, measuring fifty feet from wingtip to wingtip, the shed is semi-circular and made from long, lapped cedar shakes. This woodshed, like all of Peter's building projects, reflects a fascination for style and design that would have seemed indulgent luxury to a pioneer settler establishing a bush garden.

Cougar Annie probably would be mystified if she could see her garden now. She could never have conceived of such a time-consuming folly as opening out and maintaining a maze of pathways, simply for their beauty. She would never have encouraged a creative mixture of native and culti-vated plants. Nor would she have dreamed of spending her valuable time in de-signing and building a Japanese garden or an intricately designed pergola. For her, productivity was essential, aesthetics were secondary.

The building projects Peter undertakes at Boat Basin are made possible by two great benefits he enjoys. First is the availability of wood, particularly clear,

Shinto Gates

Eagle woodshed.

straight-grained cedar; second, the use of power tools, particularly chainsaws and a portable sawmill. In Cougar Annie's day—at least in the early years—every bit of wood for building purposes or for firewood was hand-sawed from logs felled by crosscut saw. Since the days of large-scale machine logging on the coast, the beaches are littered with an abundance of high-quality driftwood, logs which have escaped their barges or which have slid down clearcut slopes into the sea. Cougar Annie never had such an easy wood supply. Surrounded though they were by the abundant growth of the coastal rainforest, the Rae-Arthurs used wood sparingly, splitting their cedar shakes thinly, eking the most they could from every laboriously sawn log and shake block. Until her final days, Cougar Annie always used firewood as frugally as possible.

Because logs keep showing up on the shore, the driveway near Peter's house on the beach is often bright with freshly cut wood: red cedar that splits clean and straight along the grain; yellow cedar milled into boards; densely grained fir and rounds of alder that make excellent firewood; Pacific yew wood, hard and slow-growing, its cut ends shining strawberry red in the rain, ready for use in special building projects. For anyone who enjoys working with wood, here is a wealth of material and opportunity.

Whale in winter.

From the house on the beach three different pathways lead back up to the garden. The Rae-Arthurs' old raised walkway through the forest still stands but it is rotting and broken, now too dangerous to use. Veering off to one side, a new raised walkway made of split cedar swerves through the forest and leads to the boardwalk at the entry to the garden. The third way to the garden is indirect, a dark trail through the deepest forest. Anyone who has walked this trail knows it as the "Walk of the Ancients," for it passes by some of the oldest, largest trees on the face of the earth, red cedars up to a thousand years old. After about ten minutes of walking along this dim and silent path, it crosses the logging road and enters an entirely different habitat, a low-level coastal bog set in an open expanse of scrubby pine. Here a cedar shake boardwalk rests on the spongy mosses and protects the fragile plants underneath. It winds along the route of one of Cougar Annie's traplines, forks off and disappears into the forest in one direction and in the other direction it eventually enters the garden on the west side. Typical of so many of Peter's building projects, this boardwalk follows the natural contours of the land, it is deceptively simple, and it serves no immediately obvious purpose. "A lot of people think I'm completely nuts just for being here," he says. "No one seems to understand why."

Leaving the garden.

To take on a garden like Cougar Annie's, a person must be slightly crazed. Most gardens out in the bush tend to die with their founders, for who else would have the same dedication and drive, who else would be so committed to a parcel of land out in the middle of nowhere? The bush garden is a powerful symbol in the Canadian imagination, eloquently attested by Northrop Frye, Margaret Atwood and others. To establish such a garden was a guiding ambition in the lives of countless settlers hoping to create a private Eden far from the ways and the wiles of civilisation. This dream drove thousands of would-be farmers to tackle the impossible, to break their backs and their bank accounts and often their spirits as they pitted themselves against the wilderness. Few managed to do so gracefully, few stayed the course. It was too difficult. Those who did survive seem—with benefit of hindsight—to have been heroic or slightly mad or perhaps both.

No bush garden is ever achieved without human sacrifice. Plenty of this has occurred in Cougar Annie's garden, one way or another. Ada Annie Rae-Arthur was utterly determined to make a go of it at Boat Basin and the cost of her determination was huge, both to herself and to her family. This is not a gentle setting, not a place of ease. Hard work even now, it was more than hard work in the late 1910s and the 1920s as baby after baby arrived, as huge stumps failed to burn, as cougars ate the heads from prized goats that had been tethered out of sight for just a bit too long, as the food ran out and there was sometimes nothing but

Entering the garden.

porridge for the children. Experience in this garden was often bitter, the sacrifices great, the prospects dim.

The outlook now is different. For over a decade, Peter Buckland has devoted himself to Cougar Annie's garden, rediscovering it and redesigning it with stubborn persistence, and more often than not in complete solitude. The effort, the process of doing this work has kept him going, and has been, for him, an end in itself. But now the garden has been opened up and restored and reshaped, he recognizes that another era is dawning here, and that the significance of this property has increased considerably over the years. "In my time it's been a window to the past," he says. "But now it looks ahead."

The legacy of Cougar Annie will live on. Peter has been determined on this from the outset. He bought the property and restored the garden knowing that the place was not destined to be in his care forever, that his energy could carry it only so far and that new input would be essential to keep the garden alive. With this in mind, he has established the non-profit Boat Basin Foundation, and he is donating the property to the foundation. The aim of the foundation is to preserve and to maintain Cougar Annie's garden for future generations, and to encourage interest in botany.

This garden offers a unique setting from which to study the botanical diversity of the West Coast. Few private properties exist in Clayoquot Sound and Cougar Annie's is the only pioneer homestead that has endured in the region.

Most of the diverse ecosystems of Clayoquot Sound are readily accessible from Boat Basin, making it an ideal spot for botanical research and education. With the creation of the Boat Basin Foundation, this parcel of land will now be preserved for the future, protected from commercial development, and opened to fresh ideas and new energy.

The creation of the foundation comes at a significant juncture, when the land claims of First Nations people are under discussion and when the stewardship of the land all up and down the coast, and throughout British Columbia, is a matter of keen debate. The Hesquiat people are active participants in these discussions, for although they no longer live year-round in their traditional territories around the harbour, their connections here are profound and ancient.

In recent summers on quiet nights in Hesquiat Harbour, the sound of drumming can occasionally be heard. This comes usually from Iusuk, the reserve of land across the inner bay. Here is the site of the "Rediscovery" camps which bring young native people from many different backgrounds out to this area to rediscover their traditions and beliefs. The drums sound strong on the still air, night after night, as the young people listen to the elders speak and learn the ways of their people. The Rediscovery process may, in time, bring more people to this area and start to revitalize it. The potential of this initiative is great. So also is the potential of the Boat Basin Foundation. In different ways, each of these initiatives looks hopefully towards the future, while honouring the past.

When Ada Annie Rae-Arthur arrived at Boat Basin in 1915, she had no means of knowing what faced her. Confidently expecting development, she instead saw the gradual desertion of Hesquiat Harbour, the gradual decline of many ventures nearby, the slow death of many dreams on this coast. Her experience proves the unpredictability, the unknowability, of how history can unravel in any one location. Time has played—and continues to play—many strange tricks out here. Cougar Annie's garden has lived through decades of great social change on the West Coast; it has remained intact while the mountainsides nearby were devastated; it has survived her death to be transformed, and it now enters a new era.

Yet like every garden before, all the way back to Eden, this garden is balanced precariously between the past and the future. It could easily succumb to the chaos of overgrowth, to the indifference of time, to the destructions of humankind. But so far it survives. We can still find our way back into this garden. Perhaps in a hundred or two hundred years it will be forest again. Perhaps some developer will pave it and put up a parking lot. Or perhaps Cougar Annie's garden will go from strength to strength and, with obstinate beauty, continue to bloom in the wilderness.

Acknowledgements

Many people have helped me in writing this book. I could not have completed it on my own.

I would particularly like to thank Cougar Annie's daughters: Rose Nault, Isobel Large, Margaret Wilkinson and Helen Beecroft, and also her son Tommy Rae-Arthur.

For assistance with research, I am very grateful to Claudia Cole whose impressive knowledge of the B.C. Archives came to my rescue repeatedly. Thanks also to Jean Blackburn for doing interviews and research during the early stages of this book. Yvonne Hewett in London, England, braved many archives and libraries to dig up useful information, and she also  kindly read the manuscript for me. Elaine Maclean in Glasgow helped me to learn more about the Rae-Arthur background and Joan Coutu also went out of her way in Scotland for the sake of this book.

The staff of several different archives and libraries have been most helpful: the BC Provincial Archives; the Vancouver Public Library; the National Archives in Ottawa; Maybole Library in Ayrshire, Scotland; the Society of Genealogists in London, England; the Mitchell Library in Glasgow; the Port Alberni Museum. Particular thanks to Vera McIver, archivist of the Roman Catholic Archdiocese in Victoria, to Paula Hamilton, librarian at Mount Angel Abbey Library in Oregon, to Dan Savard of the Royal British Columbia Museum, and to Al Lompart at the Ministry of Environment, Lands and Parks in Victoria. Mrs. Kaye MacGregor of Cloncaird Castle in Scotland has also been most helpful.

Many people have shared their memories and local knowledge. I wish to thank Ed Arnet, Joe Balmer, Helen Beecroft, Ted Botfield, Peter Buckland, Nairne Carter, Art Clarke, Hughie Clarke, Stuart Culver, Don Culver, Ron Dalziel, Bob Foster, Ken Gibson, Walter Guppy, Dave and Diane Ignace, Jim Haggarty, Frank Harper, Dorothy Haywood-Farmer, Robert Hibberson, Ann Hill, Phil Hood, Alf Jensen, John Kingerlee, Isobel Large, Barry Lorton, Alex McGillivray, Ian Macleod, John Manning, Chris Marshall, Leo Mattson, Murray Meadows, Pat

Meadows, Theo Milne, Rose and Buster Nault, Harold Peters, David and Margaret Rae-Arthur, Donna Sharpe, Ruth Tom, John Trevor.

Thanks to Frank Harper for permission to quote from his play "Cougar Annie," to Ken Gibson for providing access to Mike Hamilton's unpublished memoirs, to Ray Deschesnes for permission to quote from Charles Morin's unpublished memoirs, to Ed and Dorothy Arnet for access to personal correspondence, to Stuart and Don Culver for permission to use their father's unpublished letters and memoirs, to Tommy Rae-Arthur for permission to quote from his letters, to Barry Lorton for providing notes of his conversations with Cougar Annie and to Richard Mackie for sharing his knowledge of cougar hunting.

For providing photographs, thanks to Don Benn, Peter Buckland, Don Culver, Annette Dehalt, Keith Fedoruk, Mary Fulton, Mark Hobson, Kaye MacGregor, John Manning, Murray Meadows, Rose Nault, Warren Wartig, Margaret Wilkinson. Thanks also to Mount Angel Abbey Library in Oregon for the use of several photographs from their collection.

To Takao Tanabe, many thanks for the painting of Hesquiat Harbour. Thanks also to Briony Penn for her maps.

To Gordon Elliott and to Sandra Gwyn, my continuing thanks for your support and kindness. And to my mother Anne and my daughter Emma, much love; may your gardens thrive.

Finally, to Peter Buckland, a special acknowledgment. Your dedication and determination, your energy and enthusiasm have made this book possible. From you I have learned what love of the land really means. Thank you.

Photo Credits

Apart from those listed below, the photographs in the book are by Peter Buckland.

Cougar Annie [inside front flap]. Photo by Mary Fulton.

viii   Cougar Annie with her gun. Photo by John Manning.

10   Old boardwalk through the forest. Photo by Keith Fedoruk.

21, 24, 25, *Margaret Coleman; Ada Annie in South Africa, about 1902; George*
27   *Jordan; Ada Annie, about 1907.* Photos courtesy of Margaret Wilkinson.

29   *Wedding Portrait, 1909.* Photo courtesy of Murray Meadows.

35   *William Rae-Arthur, Lord Provost of Glasgow.* Courtesy of the Mitchell Library, Glasgow.

39, 40   *Cloncaird Castle* and *Mrs. Isabella Wallace of Cloncaird Castle.* Courtesy of Mrs. Kaye MacGregor.

53, 55   *Willie Rae-Arthur at Boat Basin, about 1917* and *Allan Wheeler in front of his cabin.* Copyright Mount Angel Abbey, reproduced with permission, catalogued in the Royal B.C. Museum as MAA#2 and MAA#4.

57   *Anton Luckovich's house and store.* BC Archives H-0522, Accession File 98208-32 #76.

59   *Wheeler Creek.* Photo by Annette Dehalt.

67   *Land clearing at Hesquiat Village.* Copyright Mount Angel Abbey, reproduced with permission, catalogued in the Royal B.C. Museum as MAA #44.

75   Letter to Mrs. Arnet reproduced courtesy of Ed Arnet.

85   *The house, store and post office in 1979.* Photo by Mark Hobson.

87   House and vegetable garden. Photo by Keith Fedoruk.

92   *Princess Maquinna.* B.C. Archives I-26182.

Unless otherwise indicated, throughout the book all photographs of documents are by Mark Kaarremaa.

Notes On Sources

This book is based largely on primary sources: interviews, letters, unpublished memoirs, archival documents and private papers. Most of these are explained within the text. The following notes provide details about some of these primary sources; they also provide a selective list of the secondary sources I have used, and they show the origins of all quotations not already given within the text.

At the outset, a few sources deserve special mention. A particularly valuable source, used repeatedly in *Cougar Annie's Garden,* is the typescript of Father Charles Moser's memoirs, "Thirty Years a Missionary on the West Coast of Vancouver Island," compiled by Dorothy Abrahams (B.C. Archives Add MSS 2172/ 86-5.) Moser was, for much of his time on the coast, an enthusiastic observer of the changing social scene and his memoirs, despite their obvious limitations, are of great value. Another extremely valuable resource in the B.C Archives is the surviving correspondence between land pre-emptors and the British Columbia Lands Department; thankfully some of this correspondence has been preserved on microfilm—details of the files I have used appear below.

Charles Lillard's edition of Father Augustin Brabant's memoirs, *Mission to Nootka* (Gray's Publishing, Sidney, B.C., 1977) is another useful resource. George Nicholson's *Vancouver Island's West Coast, 1762–1962* (Morriss Printing Company, Victoria, 1965) provides a wealth of idiosyncratic detail about the coast. In the B.C. Archives, Augustin Brabant's "Miscellaneous Papers" (E/D/B72.4A) and the "Letters and Papers of Father Brabant" (Add MSS 2742) provide many insights, including Brabant's material concerning the *John Bright* affair. Charles Moser's *Reminiscences of the West Coast of Vancouver Island* (Acme Press, Victoria, 1926) is another source worth noting.

Cougar Annie's personal history has never been recorded in any detail, but I am not the first person to be drawn to write of it. Marnie Andersen's *Women of the West Coast: Then and Now* (Sand Dollar Press, Sidney, B.C., 1993) includes a chapter about Cougar Annie, and Frank Harper's unpublished play "Cougar Annie" (performed in 1996) was a creative tour de force.

Details of sources follow, chapter by chapter:

Chapter 2: Ada Annie

The details about Margaret Coleman and George Jordan and their families have been gathered from marriage and birth certificates, census entries, baptismal registrations. These were located at a number of different archives in England with the help of the Society of Geneaologists, the Family Records Centre and the East Sussex County Council. The Lambeth Palace Library, the Methodist Archive in Manchester and the Royal Engineers

Museum assisted with other enquiries, in this and the following chapter, as did the Hastings Library and the Colindale Newspaper Library.

Chapter 3: Willie

Details of William Rae-Arthur's civic career have been taken from several sources, including *The Lord Provosts of Glasgow from 1833–1902* (Gowans and Gray, Glasgow, 1902,) George MacGregor's *The History of Glasgow* (Thomas D. Morrison, Glasgow, 1881,) and contemporary newspapers, including the *Illustrated London News*. The scrapbook of the

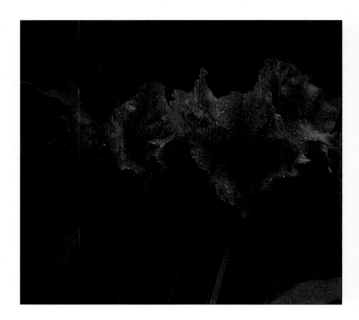

Mitchell Library, Glasgow, proved invaluable, along with the assistance of The Grand Lodge of Scotland, the General Records Office in Scotland, and the Maybole Library in Ayrshire.

In this chapter and elsewhere, Gordon Gibson's autobiography *Bull of the Woods* (written with Carol Renison, Douglas and McIntyre, Vancouver, 1980) has been a useful source.

For information about Willie Rae-Arthur's correspondence with the Lands Department, see below.

Chapter 4: A Parcel of Land

Willie Rae-Arthur's correspondence with the Lands Department concerning the pre-emption of Lot 1599 is preserved, at least in part, in B.C. Archives file 114917/12 (CG1608/487) GR 1440, reel B3139. Some of the correspondence concerning his attempt to pre-empt Lot 1598 can be found in file 057633, reel B3569. Allan Wheeler's correspondence about his pre-emption is in file 113162, reel B3139. The Land Classification reports quoted in this chapter are also in these files. The ledger of pre-emptions in the Port Alberni district is located in the B.C. Archives (GR112 Vol. 232.)

Correspondence about Anton Luckovich's pre-emption is also at the B.C. Archives (GR 1440, file 7929/97, reel B2711). Comments about Luckovich's role at Estevan Lighthouse are found in correspondence in the Estevan Site File at the Coast Guard in Victoria. The *Province* article mentioning Luckovich was published on December 1, 1894.

Details of land status, land pre-emptions and land purchases have been gathered from the Land Title Office in Victoria, the office of the Surveyor General, and through the Ministry of Environment, Lands and Parks. Al Lompart at the Ministry of Environment, Lands and Parks helped me find my way through the often bewildering maze of information.

Mike Hamilton's unpublished memoirs were brought to my attention by Ken Gibson, who kindly provided a photocopy.

Father Brabant's comments about agriculture appear in the *American College Bulletin*, July(?) 1893, an article filed in the archives of the Archdiocese of Victoria.

Dorothy Abraham's reaction to her arrival on Vargas is recorded in her autobiography *Lone Cone* (Victoria, 1945.) Mrs. Abrahams is also featured in Bob Bossin's book *Settling Clayoquot* (Sound Heritage Series, Number 33, Sound and Moving Image Division, Provincial Archives, Province of British Columbia, 1981.)

I am grateful to Richard Mackie for drawing my attention to Eustace Smith's comments about farming on Vancouver Island. These were quoted by David Day in his article "Eustace Smith: The Last Authority," *Raincoast Chronicles 6-10* (Harbour Publishing 1983.)

Chapter 5: The Early Years

The *Vancouver Sun* article published in 1974 was written by Shirley Culpin and appeared on February 14, 1974. The article by Alex MacGillivray appeared on October 19, 1957 in the *Vancouver Sun*.

Bob Bossin quotes Bill Sharp in *Settling Clayoquot*, and relates other similar stories about clearing land. He also tells the story of Fred Tibbs, including quotations from Tibbs' letters.

The Lands Classification Reports appear in the B.C. Archive files named above.

Chapter 6: The Working Garden

The timber cruise report quoted in this chapter was written by K.C. McCannel, *Cruise Report, West Coast V.I. 1926*, B.C. Forest Service, Victoria, B.C.

Chapter 7: Boat Basin Post Office

Official records about the post office at Boat Basin are located in the National Archives of Canada in Ottawa (Record Group 3, Records of the Post Office, Series D.3, Divisional Inspectors' Reports, Vol. 3490 and Record Group 3, Accession 88-89/282, Box 422, file "Boat Basin, B.C.") I have drawn repeatedly on documents from these files in writing this chapter.

Father Brabant's comment about infrequency of mail in his early years is made in the *American College Bulletin*, 1893.

Chapter 8: Staying Put

Information about Estevan Point Lighthouse during the war comes from the historical archives of the Canadian Coast Guard, and from the Estevan Site File at the Coast Guard headquarters in Victoria. One of several useful secondary sources about the lighthouse is Donald Graham's *Keepers of the Light* (Harbour Publishing, Madiera Park, 1985.)

The letter quoted from Father Joseph Schindler comes from the archives of the Archdiocese of Victoria.

Chapter 9: Animal Tales

For information about cougars, Del Hall's *Island Gold: A History of Cougar Hunting on Vancouver Island* (Cougar Press, Victoria, 1990) is helpful. References to the Hesquiat cattle appear frequently in documents in the Estevan Site File at the Coast Guard. The cattle are mentioned also in *The Province*, December 1, 1894, and in *Farm and Home*, December 27, 1928.

Chapter 10: Around the Harbour

This chapter draws on and refers to many secondary sources. Amongst these are: James Colton Haggarty's unpublished PhD thesis "The Archaeology of Hesquiat Harbour: The Archaeological Utility of an Ethnographically Defined Social Unit" (Washington State University, 1982;) Randy Bouchard and Dorothy Kennedy's *Clayoquot Sound Indian Land Use* (prepared for MacMillan-Bloedel, Fletcher Challenge, and the B.C. Ministry of Forests; B.C. Indian Language Project, Victoria, B.C. November 1990;) Jerome S. Cybulski's *An Earlier Population of Hesquiat Harbour, British Columbia* (Cultural Recovery Paper No.1, British Columbia Provincial Museum, 1978;) Nancy Turner and Barbara Efrat's *Ethnobotany of the Hesquiat Indians of Vancouver Island* (Cultural Recovery Paper No. 2, British Columbia Provincial Museum, 1982.)

Philip Drucker's *The Northern and Central Nootkan Tribes* (Bureau of Ethnology, Bulletin 44, Washington D.C., Smithsonian Institution, 1951) and *Indians of the Northwest Coast* (Natural History Press, Garden City, N.Y., 1955) are important sources. Derek Pethick's *First Approaches to the Northwest Coast* (J.J. Douglas Ltd., North Vancouver, 1976) and George Nicholson's *Vancouver Island's West Coast* are also useful.

The correspondence and comments of O'Reilly of the Indian Reserve Commission are available in the "Minutes of Decisions", held in the B.C. Archives and in the Crown Lands Branch in Victoria.

Many documents exist concerning the *John Bright* affair. Court records are at the B.C. Archives (C/AA/30.3P/3 B.C. Supreme Court Vancouver Island. Court of Assize. Feb 18 1867 to June 10 1870. See also GR 2030, Vol. One.) For Father Brabant's writings about the affair and his correspondence with Higgins, see Brabant's *Miscellaneous Papers* (E/D/B72.4A) in the B.C. Archives.

Articles and letters about the affair appeared in the *Colonist* in Victoria with great frequency from mid-March until mid-August 1869 (of most interest: March 13, 15, 18; April 23, 24, 30; May 9, 28, 29; June 23, 24; July 6, 8, 31.) The affair again received attention in the paper on February 24 and August 10, 1871. Articles in the press in later years include: "Two Tales of the Sea: A Great Crime and its Punishment," *Victoria Semi-Weekly Colonist,* March 25, 1904; "Veteran Pilot Hero of Indian Massacre of Early West Coast," *The Daily Colonist*, May 9, 1924; "The Bark John Bright Lost With All Aboard," *The Daily Colonist,* March 19, 1934, "Shipwrecked Sailors got Short Shrift in Early Days on Coast," *The Daily Colonist,* April 1, 1939; "The West Coast Massacre," by W. J. Christensen, *The Daily Colonist,* October 15, 1950; "Christiansen's Persistence Uncovered Hesquiat Murders," *The Daily Colonist,* December 15, 1974.

Information about sealing on the West Coast comes from many sources including Lewis and Dryden's *Marine History of the Pacific Northwest*, edited by E.W. Wright (Antiquarian Press, New York, 1961, reprinted with corrections, originally published 1895,) Briton Cooper Busch's *The War Against the Seals* (McGill-Queen's University Press, 1985) and the "Origin of Pelagic Sealing in B.C. and its Progress" (B.C. Archives I/BS/SP8.)

Chapter 11: The Mission

This chapter draws on many documents concerning Father Brabant and Father Moser, from the B.C. Archives (file numbers listed above) and from their own memoirs. I also have made use of a number of documents and letters housed in the archives of the Archdiocese of Victoria; these include the letters of Father Fred Miller. Brabant's diary of the Hesquiat language, along with a document called "A Few Remarks about the Language of the Hesquiats" are at the B.C. Archives (reel 623a) and the original is in the archives of the Archdiocese of Victoria.

Paula Hamilton of Mount Angel Abbey Library in Oregon provided me with Andreas Eckerstorfer's unpublished thesis entitled "'To do Some Good Among the Indians' Mount Angel Benedictines as Missionaries on the West Coast of Vancouver Island: A Forgotten Chapter of the Abbey's History," March 1994 (Mount Angel Abbey Library).

The unpublished memoirs of Charles Morin, entitled "The Story of a Courageous Man," were made available to me by Ray Deschesnes.

Chapter 12: Land Lines

Surveyors' notes have been extremely helpful in this chapter, also the annual *Report of the Minister of Mines*. Mike Hamilton's unpublished memoirs have been useful, also W.J. Bowerman's "Early History of the Government Wireless Service on the British Columbia Coast" (B.C. Archives Add MSS 2393) and the typescript diary of Francis Gerrard, who worked for the Dominion Telegraph. (B.C. Archives Add MSS 46.) Ron Dalziel's memoirs, *It was Quite a Performance* (Classic Memoirs, Victoria, 1997) have also been most helpful. Information about the plank road between Estevan and Hesquiat emerges repeatedly in the Estevan Site File at the Coast Guard in Victoria, including many comments about the unfortunate horse.

Chapter 13: Above the Garden

In this chapter I am indebted to the memoirs of Ron Dalziel *It Was Quite a Performance*, to Gordon Gibson's *Bull of the Woods,* and I am grateful to have had access to copies of correspondence concerning the aborted "Ecoreserve #61."

Chapter 14: Down by the Sea

For information about dogfish, K.S. Ketchen's *The Spiny Dogfish in the Northeast Pacific and a History of its Utilization* (Department of Fisheries and Oceans, Special Publication of Fisheries and Aquatic Sciences 88, 1986) has been helpful.

COUGAR ANNIE'S GARDEN

Cougar Annie's Garden offers an intriguing perspective on West Coast history.
A must for anyone who knows, or who wants to know, the coast.
A perfect gift. This book is a limited edition,
available by direct order only.

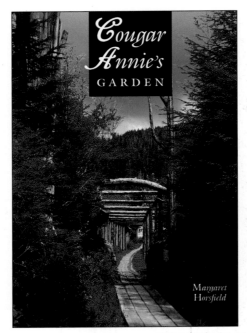

ISBN 0-9697008-1-4

$40.00 CDN plus GST / $28.00 U.S.
add $5.00 postage + handling per order

To order call
1-888-858-5455
or fax
1-250-753-9468
or write
Salal Books
P.O. Box 1021, Station A
Nanaimo, B.C.
Canada V9R 5Z2